W9-CBZ-744

The Bedford Bibliography for Teachers of Basic Writing

Third Edition

Gregory R. Glau
Northern Arizona University

Chitralekha Duttagupta
Utah Valley University

for the Conference on Basic Writing

Bedford/St. Martin's   Boston   ◆   New York

writing and a document, an artifact, that contributes to educators' understanding of the field of basic writing — its past, present, and future.

The conscientious efforts of the roughly 200 teachers who annotated nearly 400 entries made *The Bedford Bibliography for Teachers of Basic Writing* possible. We list their names here as contributing editors and hope that one day we can thank each one of them personally for contributing in this significant way to the ongoing conversations in our field:

Heather Abreu, Eastern Michigan University
Sonja L. Andrus, Collin College
Anne Aronson, Metropolitan State University
Fred Arroyo, Saint Louis University
Kathleen A. Baca, Doña Ana Branch Community College
Kim Ballard, Western Michigan University
Anis Bawarshi, University of Washington
Jennifer Bay, Purdue University
Tony Becker, Northern Arizona University
Susan Naomi Bernstein, LaGuardia Community College
Leann Bertoncini, College of Wooster
Subrata Bhowmik, Arizona State University
Barbara Blackburn, Jefferson Community College Southwest
Joyce Bogdan, University of Connecticut
Kurt Bouman, Indiana University of Pennsylvania
Annette Bradford, Virginia International University
Rick Branscomb, Salem State College
Kaitlin A. Briggs, University of Southern Maine
Lindal Buchanan, University of Louisiana at Lafayette
Jonathan Bush, Western Michigan University
Elizabeth A. Butts, Delaware County Community College
Lew Caccia Jr., Kent State University
Jeff Cain, Sacred Heart University
Vicky Campo, Arizona State University
Nick Carbone, Marlboro Graduate Center
Robin M. Carstensen, Texas A&M University–Corpus Christi
Shannon Carter, Texas A&M University–Commerce
Judy Casey, University of Arizona
Pisarn (Bee) Chamcharatsri, Indiana University of Pennsylvania
Anita Chaudhuri, Arizona State University
Janice Chernekoff, Kutztown University

Dennis Ciesielski, University of Wisconsin at Platteville
Shelley Circle, Modesto Junior College
AnDrea Cleaves, Bowling Green State University
Jennifer L. Clifton, Arizona State University
Terence Collins, University of Minnesota–General College
Colleen Connolly, University of South Florida
Jeffrey Conrad, University of Delaware
Steven J. Corbett, University of Washington
Susan Corbin, El Camino College
Virginia Crank, University of Wisconsin at LaCrosse
MaryAnn Krajnick Crawford, Central Michigan University
Virginia Crisco, University of Nebraska at Lincoln
Mary Kay Crouch, California State University at Fullerton
Angela M. Dadak, American University
Andréa D. Davis, California State University at San Bernardino
Shelley DeBlasis, Illinois State University
Teagan Decker, University of Washington
Bill DeGenaro, The University of Michigan Dearborn
Susan H. Delagrange, The Ohio State University
Kevin Eric De Pew, Purdue University
Phillip A. Douglas, Purdue University
Dylan Dryer, University of Maine at Orono
Suellynn Duffey, Georgia Southern University
Patricia A. Eliason, University of Minnesota–General College
Todd English, The Ohio State University
Heidi Estrem, Eastern Michigan University
Matt Ferrence, Clarion University of Pennsylvania
Evelyn M. Finklea, St. Petersburg College
Lauren Fitzgerald, Yeshiva University
Sallyanne H. Fitzgerald, Napa Valley College
Chris Fosen, California State University at Chico
Robin Gallagher, University of Central Arkansas
Bre Garrett, Miami University
Amy Getty, Tillamook Bay Community College
Kenneth Gillam, Missouri State University
Kimberlee Gillis-Bridges, University of Washington
Barbara Gleason, City College of New York
Sara Glennon, Landmark College

Marian Woyciehowicz Gonsior, Madonna University

Babs Gordon, Arizona State University

Judy Diane Grace, Arizona State University

Laura Gray-Rosendale, Northern Arizona University

Kathi R. Griffin, Millsaps College

Laurie Grobman, Pennsylvania State University, Berks–Lehigh Valley College

Kay Halasek, The Ohio State University

Christina Harralson, California State University at Fresno

Susanmarie Harrington, Indiana University–Purdue University Indianapolis

Sophia Harrison, University of Delaware

D. Alexis Hart, Virginia Military Institute

Katherine Heenan, Arizona State University

Christine W. Heilman, College of Mount St. Joseph

Marie Hendry, University of Louisiana at Lafayette

Thomas Henry, Northern Arizona University

Nels P. Highberg, University of Illinois at Chicago

Matthew Hill, Michigan Technological University

Deborah Hodgkins, University of Maine at Presque Isle

Joanna Howard, Montgomery College–Rockville

Li-Shih Huang, University of Victoria

Rebecca Ingalls, Drexel University

Wendi Jewell, University of Oklahoma

Kerrie L. Karsey, Miami University

Jason King, Texas Christian University

Judith Mara Kish, University of Findlay

Marisa A. Klages, LaGuardia Community College

Marcia Kmetz, University of Nevada at Reno

Rick Kmetz, University of Nevada at Reno

Kathryn E. Lane, University of Louisiana at Lafayette

Bob Lazaroff, City University of New York Graduate Center

Rachel Lewis, University of Arizona

Barbara Little Liu, Eastern Connecticut State University

Susan Loudermilk, Texas A&M University–Corpus Christi

Meredith Love, Francis Marion University

Brad Lucas, Texas Christian University

Annette M. Magid, Erie Community College

Loren Loving Marquez, Salisbury University

Paul Kei Matsuda, Arizona State University

Mark McBeth, John Jay College of Criminal Justice

Crystal McCage, Central Oregon Community College

Bruce McComiskey, University of Alabama at Birmingham

Ben McCorkle, The Ohio State University

Margaret McLaughlin, Georgia Southern University

Gerry McNenny, Chabot College

Ildiko Melis, University of Arizona

David Menchaca, University of Arizona

Holly Middleton, New Mexico Highlands University

Susan Kay Miller, Mesa Community College

Marsha Millikin, Texas A&M University–Commerce

Rebecca Mlynarczyk, Kingsborough Community College
    & the Graduate Center, City University of New York

Ryan Moeller, Utah State University

Clyde Moneyhun, University of Delaware

Michael R. Moore, Michigan Technological University

Katia Vieira Morais, University of Arizona

Katona Mulholland, Blue River Community College

Miguel Muñoz, UNED, Spain

Robin Murie, University of Minnesota

David Nentwick, College of Coastal Georgia

Lee Nickoson-Massey, Elon University

Janice M. Norton, Arizona State University

Kimme Nuckles, Baker College

Mary Lou Odom, Kennesaw State University

Liana J. Odrcic, University of Wisconsin–Milwaukee

Peggy O'Neill, Loyola College

Sara Pace, Lamar University

Thomas Peele, Boise State University

Dawn Penich-Thacker, Arizona State University

Val Perry, Lewis University

Linda Elizabeth Peterson, Central Michigan College

Daisy Pignetti, University of South Florida

Elena Poltavtchenko, Northern Arizona University

Jingjing Qin, Northern Arizona University

David A. Reinheimer, Southeast Missouri State University

James Reynolds, University of South Florida
Marcia Ribble, University of Cincinnati
Chris Richardson, Rogers State University
Duane Roen, Arizona State University
Annette C. Rosati, Clarion University of Pennsylvania
Debbie Rowe, Rensselaer Polytechnic Institute
Carol Rutz, Carleton College
Cynthia Ryan, University of Alabama at Birmingham
Christina Saidy, Purdue University
Lori Salem, Temple University
Maureen Salzer, University of Wisconsin–Superior
Susan J. San Jule, University of Arizona
Michael J. Sasso, The Ohio State University
Ellen Schendel, Grand Valley State University
Joanna Schmertz, University of Houston–Downtown
Bonnie Selting, University of Central Arkansas
Randall Seltz, Western Michigan University
Sarah J. Shin, University of Maryland–Baltimore County
Ira Shor, City University of New York Graduate Center
Marti Singer, Georgia State University
Ryan Skinnell, Arizona State University
Trudy Smoke, Hunter College
Nancy M. Staub, Lamar University
Sharon Strand, Black Hills State University
Donna Strickland, University of Missouri–Columbia
Michael J. Strickland, Elon University
Gail Stygall, University of Washington
James Sullivan, Fashion Institute of Technology
Martha Swearingen, University of the District of Columbia
William Sweigart, Indiana University Southeast
Sharon Talley, Texas A&M University–Corpus Christi
John Paul Tassoni, Miami University
Linda Tetzlaff, Normandale Community College
William H. Thelin, University of Akron
Sharon Thomas, Michigan State University
Brenda Tuberville, University of Texas–Tyler
Karen S. Uehling, Boise State University
Cynthia M. VanSickle, Wayne State University

Cynthia Walker, Faulkner University

Samantha Ward, Texas A&M University – Corpus Christi

Sara Webb-Sunderhaus, The Ohio State University

Kristen Dayle Welch, Longwood University

Theresa M. Welford, Georgia Southern University

Kathleen A. Welsch, Clarion University of Pennsylvania

Danielle Zawodny Wetzel, Carnegie Mellon University

Edward M. White, University of Arizona

Gwen Whitehead, Lamar State College – Orange

Mark Wiley, California State University at Long Beach

Kent F. Williams, University of Rio Grande

Rosemarie Winslow, The Catholic University of America

Nur Yigitoglu, Georgia State University

We owe special thanks to Karen S. Uehling, former Conference on Basic Writing cochair, for kindly allowing us to include her revised and updated history of the CBW, as well as to the Center for Research on Developmental Education and Urban Literacy (now part of the New College of Education and Human Development at the University of Minnesota) for its permission to reprint this adapted history. At Bedford/St. Martin's, we wish to thank Karen Henry and Kate Mayhew, who have been wonderful to work with on this project, and Nick Carbone, who was always ready with helpful advice. We also wish to thank Joan Feinberg and Denise Wydra for their continued support of the *Bibliography*.

Introduction

Teachers of basic writing know that much is at stake when they talk about students, classes, or programs. In this climate of restructuring, budget cuts, standardized testing, state-mandated assessments, and performance-based definitions of literacy, no conversation about writing—especially basic writing—is ever neutral or conducted in a vacuum. With each conversation, teachers and students alike become increasingly engaged in a larger debate about language and literacy and contribute to the narratives that continue to shape the field of basic writing.

This third edition of the *Bibliography* continues to serve as a resource for those participating in conversations about basic writing and students in basic writing classes. But this edition of the *Bibliography* is also an artifact, a body of scholarship that provides the basic writing community with an opportunity to reflect on its history and the narratives about basic writing that have emerged over the past decades. By exploring basic writing's past and present, we hope to better understand the questions and issues that will shape the field in the years to come.

In every era, campaigns have been waged to exclude from the academy those values, ideologies, and abilities that are perceived to be threatening by those in power. Matthew Arnold led a movement to preserve the humanities in nineteenth-century England, Cambridge University intellectuals created a literary canon in the early 1900s, and teachers and parents raised concerns about "why Johnny can't write" in American schools in the 1960s. Indeed, such campaigns often have sought a "return" to an idealized, mythical time when all citizens knew the same things and shared the same values, ideologies, abilities, and, presumably, culture.

However, none of these campaigns has ever been or could ever be wholly successful because the mythical past never existed. Individuals and groups understand education differently, and some will fight what Michel de Certeau called a "war of position" within (and sometimes against) the seemingly staggering opposition of the dominant authority. The Conference on Basic Writing (CBW), which celebrated its silver anniversary in 2005, is one such group fighting for position, and the research produced by basic writing researchers chronicled in this bibliography attests to the positioning that has taken place in the midst of and sometimes in response to discussions and debates about basic writing and literacy.

For those looking for a citation, a resource, or an article, the third edition of this volume is certainly enormously useful, but it is also useful as a collective summary of the conversations about basic writing that have taken place and the narratives that have been constructed over the last thirty years. In addition, Karen S. Uehling's "The Conference on Basic Writing, 1980–2005" (8) provides historical context to these conversations and

1

narratives, tracing how the CBW has grown and adapted to changes in the field. In this sense, the third edition of the *Bibliography* captures the threads that these conversations have followed, and perhaps it can give basic writing teachers insight into the field's next thirty years.

While compiling these three editions of *The Bedford Bibliography for Teachers of Basic Writing*, we reflected frequently on some of the field's most compelling issues: questions about what basic writing is, who basic writers are, how teachers should work with students in basic writing courses, and what the future of basic writing holds.

Who Are Basic Writers?

Beginning with Mina Shaughnessy's *Errors and Expectations* [117], basic writing researchers have sought to answer several questions about basic writers: Do students who are labeled as basic writers share characteristics or qualities? Do scores on placement measures indicate whether students are prepared for college writing? Along with Shaughnessy's foundational text, many of the other articles and books included in the *Bibliography* address these questions as well.

Like *Errors and Expectations*, some works seek to define the characteristics associated with basic writers. More recently, however, some authors of early works have reconsidered these definitions, even questioning whether they are harmful to students. Peter Adams's article "Basic Writing Reconsidered" [318], for example, explores whether the *basic writer* label becomes a controlling feature in students' work. Thomas Hilgers's "Basic Writing Curricula and Good Assessment Practices" [328] echoes this sentiment, arguing that students often are defined as basic writers because of the work that they do on problematic assessment measures. Laura Gray-Rosendale's "Back to the Future: Contextuality and the Construction of the Basic Writer's Identity in *JBW*, 1999–2005" [60] continues the tradition of examining who basic writers are by how we in the field construct their identities.

Other works—like "Remediation as Social Construct" (Hull et al. [69]), "Defining Basic Writing in Context" (Troyka [46]), "Redefining the Legacy of Mina Shaughnessy" (Lu [98]), and "Literacies and Deficits Revisited" (Scott [104])—suggest that definitions of basic writers often stem from deficit models that ultimately marginalize students' literacies in the face of academic discourse.

What Do (Students Called) Basic Writers Do?

Researchers who focus on what basic writers do generally are trying to define who basic writers are, and the research included in this bibliography addresses this line of inquiry in several ways. Early cognitivist basic writing researchers investigated the writing processes of basic writers. This orientation can be located in early studies like *Errors and Expectations* (Shaughnessy [117]), for example, and in works like "A Look at Basic Writers in the Process of Composing" (Perl [137]). It is also reflected in some later pieces, like "Using a 'Write-Speak-Write' Approach for Basic Writers" (de Beaugrande and Olson [125]), that examine the effectiveness of particular approaches to basic writing.

In the late 1970s and early 1980s, some researchers shifted their focus away from the writing process and began considering the relationships between students' discourse communities and the academic discourse community, as it was then conceptualized. Studies like "Inventing the University" (Bartholomae [2]) examined students' texts rather than students' processes to identify the ways in which students diverged from the discourse conventions of academic writing. From "Clothing the Emperor" (Purves [103]) to "Dark Shadows" (Haswell [327]), a broad range of work included here reflects this approach to studying what basic writers do.

In work based on ethnographic methodologies, like "'This Wooden Shack Place'" (Hull and Rose [127]), *Writing in an Alien World* (Mutnick [74]), and *Rethinking Basic Writing* (Gray-Rosendale [63]), researchers delve into students' culture by spending time with and listening to students placed in basic writing classes. A few articles, like "Demythologizing the 'Basic Writer'" (Gray-Rosendale and Leonard [156]), also incorporate the voices of the students whose work serves as the subject of the research.

What Is Basic Writing?

Researchers who have sought to understand who basic writers are and what they do have also tried to form a definition of basic writing that different audiences can accept—and their efforts have grown more urgent as basic writing students, courses, and programs face increasing challenges from inside and outside the academy. The works included in this bibliography represent several perspectives on basic writing. Some works are ambivalent and argue that the institution of basic writing is unjust but serves an important function for the university and its students. Works like *Lives on the Boundary* (Rose [115]), which incorporates portraits of both somnambulant and lively basic writing classes, and "The Tidy House" (Bartholomae [3]), which argues that basic writing classes are important but exist in part to segregate students and employ writing teachers, reflect this position.

Other works, most notably "Our Apartheid" (Shor [42]), argue that the institution of basic writing should be dismantled because it perpetuates the unequal class system that currently exists in American culture. A number of articles, like "A Response to Ira Shor's 'Our Apartheid'" (Collins [8]; Greenberg [15]) and "Finding Basic Writing's Place" (Sheridan-Rabideau and Brossell [39]), counter this position, arguing that basic writing courses benefit students and the academy alike by ensuring the inclusion of a broader range of students.

How Can Basic Writing Teachers Help Students Work on Writing?

The question of how teachers can help basic writers work on writing has long dominated basic writing research, and teacher-researchers have examined specific approaches and strategies for teaching basic writing. For instance, a number of articles discuss successful strategies for working on aspects of the writing process with basic writers. Works like "Writing as a Mode of Learning" (Emig [147]) and *The Journal Book for Teachers of At-Risk College Writers* (Gardner and Fulwiler [148]) focus on invention. Pieces as diverse as "Rethinking the 'Sociality' of Error" (Horner [159]) and "Connections between Reading and Successful Revision" (Moran [165]) cover revision. *Grammar and the Teaching of Writing* (Noguchi [180]), "The Effect of Error Correction on Learners' Ability to Write Correctly" (Truscott [181]), "When Is a Verb? Using Functional Grammar to Teach Writing" (Fearn, Leif, and Farnan [171]), and "Explaining Grammatical Concepts" (Harris and Rowan [173]) center on editing, style, and grammar.

Other researchers have looked at additional aspects of writing, such as reading and texts, that are crucial for basic writing classes and students. Works like "Reading and Writing" (Deming [94]) and "Uses of Background Experience in a Preparatory Reading and Writing Class: An Analysis of Native and Non-native Speakers of English" (Becket [255]) focus on issues related to work with developmental readers. "Critical Literacy and Basic Writing Textbooks" (Bruch and Reynolds [90]), "Writing to Learn: The Nickel and Dimed Project" (Bernstein and Johnson [161]), "BWe 2007: Practice, Professional Development, and Favorite Books" (Bernstein [107]), and "Are You Using?" (Jones [163]) explore issues related to the use of textbooks and other texts in the basic writing classroom.

In addition to examining these specific strategies for practice in basic writing classes, researchers have also investigated how best to work with student populations, particularly second- and foreign-language students. This third edition of the *Bibliography* includes a greatly expanded section on special student populations. Books like *Understanding ESL Writers* (Leki [285]), *Second Language Writing Research: Perspectives on the*

Process of Knowledge Construction (Matsuda and Silva [299]), *Teaching ESL Composition* (Ferris and Hedgcock [268]), *On Second-Language Writing* (Silva and Matsuda [312]), and *Generation 1.5 Meets College Composition* (Harklau, Losey, and Siegal [276]) include essays that address questions of practice and power as they relate to second-language writing classes.

A number of scholars feel that basic writing classroom strategies are problematic and have challenged some of the research focusing on these strategies. "Reinventing the University" (Hindman [20]), "Warning: Basic Writers at Risk—The Case of Javier" (Reagan [241]), "Failure: The Student's or the Assessment's?" (Harley and Cannon [326]), and *Basic Writing as a Political Act* (Adler-Kassner and Harrington [1]) challenge existing approaches to basic writing instruction. The view that some of these approaches help students to learn the discourse conventions of the academy—but not to understand or challenge them—resonates in these works.

What Alternative Models Have Been Used in Basic Writing Programs?

One outgrowth of the debate over the function of and possible approaches to basic writing courses is that some researchers have examined questions related to program design. The articles on that subject in this bibliography share some common characteristics: they explain the rationale for an "alternative" approach to basic writing programs, describe the model used and the work done in the programs, and describe the effects of the alternative design. Some of these models are summarized in "A Basic Introduction to Basic Writing Program Structures" (Lalicker [360]), which outlines alternative models used in shaping basic writing programs. "*Stretch* at Ten" (Glau [353]) provides ten years of data on that pioneering program at Arizona State University. "Repositioning Remediation" (Grego and Thompson [356]) describes and analyzes the "writing studio" model used at the University of South Carolina (a model that has now been adopted or modified at many other institutions; see, for example, "Re-modeling Basic Writing" (Rigolino and Freel [370]). "From the Margins to the Mainstream" (Soliday [378]) focuses on a mainstreaming project at the City University of New York. "What's It Worth and What's It For?" (Rodby [371]) and "Basic Work and Material Acts" (Rodby and Fox [372]) discuss the institutional challenges created when the noncredit basic writing course at California State University, Chico, was dismantled and replaced with a curriculum that mainstreamed students and supported them in their work. Similarly, "Basic Writing in One California Community College" (Fitzgerald [350]) describes how Chabot College integrated transitional strategies throughout its curriculum.

What Is the Current State of Basic Writing?

As basic writing has been established as a subfield of composition, some researchers have analyzed how basic writing scholarship has shaped the discipline. Some of their works—like "Conflict and Struggle" (Lu [235]), "Negotiating the Contact Zone" (Harris [200]), and "Basic Writing and the Issue of Correctness, Or, What to Do with 'Mixed' Forms of Academic Discourse" (Bizzell [5])—have explored the ways that powerful ideas have shaped teaching and research in the field. Other works, like "Iconic Discourse" (Gunner [17]), question the ways in which research has constructed teachers and students and how those constructions affect the basic writing classroom. Still others, like "The Dilemma That Still Counts" (Harrington and Adler-Kassner [18]) and "Writing on the Margins" (Bartholomae [52]), analyze how work in the field has defined basic writers and basic writing.

In addition to examining how the discipline has constructed a narrative of its own development, researchers have also looked at how the scholarship has shaped approaches to teaching and research. "Rethinking Basic Writing" (Gray-Rosendale [63]), for instance, suggests that fixating on defining who basic writers are has come at the expense of studying what basic writers can do. "Discoursing Basic Writing" (Horner [21]) argues that basic writing's historical association with Marxian philosophies has been neglected, marginalizing questions of the social, cultural, and institutional "realities" faced by basic writing instructors and their students.

What Is the Best Case for Basic Writing, and Who Should Make It?

If—as some researchers and theorists argue—basic writing teachers have not always made the best case for basic writing and basic writers, as is argued in some of the analyses of basic writing research described earlier, what should that case be, and how should we make it? Increasingly, basic writing teachers and students have realized that they must voice their own positions on basic writing in public venues.

Research like *Defending Access* (Fox [110]) and "The Strategic Value of Basic Writing" (Mutnick [31]) makes the case that access to higher education for students called basic writers ensures diversity at colleges and universities. Additionally, basic writing instructors and administrators must forge alliances among themselves, students, and external constituencies to ensure the programs' survival.

Other work, like "Going around in Circles" (DeGenaro and White [10]), approaches this question slightly differently, arguing that basic writing researchers frequently miss opportunities to produce a "convincing generalization" that might present a united front among basic writing teacher-researchers in discussions of writers and writing.

How Are Writing, Language, and Culture Interrelated?

All of the previous questions asked in this introduction are linked to this larger one, which suffuses many of the pieces annotated in this bibliography. Some of the works here also directly address issues of language and culture.

For instance, "Assessing Our Assessments" (Bruna et al. [324]) discusses students' desire to master standard English as a key to accessing power in the broader culture. "Basic Writing, Cost Effectiveness, and Ideology" (Gilyard [11]) argues that basic writing is double-edged: the term *basic writing* is problematic, but the courses in basic writing ensure university access for students who would not have been accepted without them.

At the same time, however, research in basic writing must consider students' cultural and ideological contexts and not examine writing divorced from those contexts. Articles like "Conflict and Power in the Reader-Responses of Adult Basic Writers" (Coles and Wall [227]) and "Basic Writing and the Process Paradigm" (Collins [124]) employ this approach.

A number of the works included in this bibliography also study specific aspects of the larger question of social context. "Class Talk" (Tate, McMillan, and Woodworth [249]), "Group Work and Autonomy: Empowering the Working-Class Student" (Hidalgo [201]), "Bourgeois Realism or Working-Class Kitsch? The Aesthetics of Class in Composition" (Ryden [243]), and "When Working Class Students 'Do' the Academy" (Marinara [236]) focus on issues of class. "Basic Writing Class of '93 Five Years Later" (Agnew and McLaughlin [221]) and "Some Effects of Culture-Referenced Topics on the Writing Performance of African American Students" (Norment [239]) focus on race. "Giving Voice to Women in the Basic Writing and Language Minority Classroom" (Cochran [226]) focuses on gender.

All these questions have contributed to the history and development of basic writing as a subfield of composition and continue to shape it as it emerges as a distinct discipline. The research represented here reflects the work that the editors and contributors find important. We hope that the third edition of this bibliography will continue to serve as a useful resource for those interested in the field of basic writing.

The Conference on Basic Writing

The Conference on Basic Writing (CBW) is a special-interest group of the Conference on College Composition and Communication. Over its thirty years of existence, CBW has developed into a vibrant community of teachers and scholars. For this third edition of the *Bibliography*, we wanted to provide as much of the historical record as possible, so we have again included Karen Uehling's thoughtful retrospective on our group.

The Conference on Basic Writing, 1980–2005[1]

In 2005, the Conference on Basic Writing celebrated its silver anniversary as an organization. As we celebrated our first quarter century, we took the time to look back at the critical issues and defining moments of the past and forward to the future.

Twenty-Five Years of Community

The Conference on Basic Writing is an inclusive organization composed of a spectrum of basic writing faculty—those new to the field as well as tenured professors who serve as writing administrators on their campuses. CBW members teach at diverse institutions: community colleges, private rural colleges, research universities, and urban state universities from all regions of the country. Jeanne Gunner, CBW chair from 1995 to 1997, describes the variety of people within CBW and the organization's democratic nature:

> They may be interested because they have taught BW [basic writing] classes for years and have made BW the center of their professional lives, or because they are about to begin to teach them and are seeking information and support from experienced BW teachers. They may be famous researchers we all read and whose ideas inform our classes, or graduate students who will be the next generation of famous names. They may be BW instructors with ideas . . . to share on pedagogic and curricular innovations, or those who defend traditional approaches. They may teach graduate students or freshmen, at community colleges or research institutions. What they have in common are professional and personal concerns related to the field of basic writing. ("From the Chair" 1–2)

Perhaps the key motive for developing a professional basic writing organization over the years has been the genuine concern that basic writing instructors feel for their students and their desire to work collaboratively with them. Students are placed into classes labeled "basic writing" by a variety of measures and have varying degrees of control over this

---

[1]Adapted with permission from Uehling, "Conference on Basic Writing."

placement. At one pole of the placement spectrum are institutions that place students (without consultation) based on their performances on standardized tests like the COMPASS test of grammar or the ACT or SAT, which claim to measure students' reading comprehension and acuity with logic and vocabulary. At the other pole are institutions that use directed self-placement, a strategy originally developed at Grand Valley State University (Royer and Gilles, "Basic Writing and Directed Self-Placement" and *Directed Self-Placement*). Here, students receive information about writing and reading on the campus, details about the writing courses offered, and a list of questions about their own writing and reading practices. Students then choose the courses they feel are best for them. In the middle of the placement spectrum are institutions that use other placement methods, from timed writing exams to portfolio placement systems, although the number of institutions using portfolio placement is dwindling due to cost.

The students who take basic writing courses, for whatever reason, are especially vulnerable within higher education because they are often the first to be excluded or considered for exclusion when budget cuts or demands for "excellence" are issued (Fox, *Defending Access* and "Standards and Access"; McNenny, "Writing Instruction" 1–6; Rose 5–8). Sometimes basic writing students are viewed as misusing taxpayers' money to pay for a "second chance" at education when those tax dollars could be better spent on students who are already doing well.

However they are placed, students in basic writing classes represent a diverse and shifting population—first-generation college students, people of color or speakers of more than one language or dialect, refugees or immigrants, reentry students (such as displaced homemakers, older learners who are retraining, or former members of the military), people who experienced erratic or interrupted high school educations or who dropped out of high school and later earned a general equivalency diploma, people with learning or other disabilities, very young parents, and people who work long hours. Sometimes characterized as "at risk" or "underprepared," some basic writing students have experienced especially difficult lives. Some have waited many years, craving an education, and are grateful for any help and instruction. Others of traditional age are equally committed because they want to escape their parents' lives of monotonous, low-paying jobs and make the most of their sports or other scholarships. Some are traditional-age college students who have had less than positive experiences with writing and reading. Others took the basic writing placement tests on days when their attention was focused on other matters. Whatever their situations, they contribute to the rich diversity within our educational institutions.

Perhaps because basic writing students are sometimes viewed as marginal within the university, the faculty appointed to teach these students

Emergence as the Conference on Basic Writing, 1988–1992

By 1987, CBWS was in a state of institutional limbo, and early chairs were concerned that the organization might fall apart. However, in 1988, CBWS was reborn and renamed as the Conference on Basic Writing under the guidance of Peter Dow Adams and Carolyn Kirkpatrick, who served as chair and associate chair, respectively, from 1988 to 1991. The decision to drop the word *skills* from the organization's name was influenced by the 1986 publication of David Bartholomae and Anthony Petrosky's ground-breaking *Facts, Artifacts, and Counterfacts*, which made a persuasive case for full-length discourse in beginning writing instruction, immersion reading, and the teaching of basic writing as a rich, seminar-type course.[2] Indeed, the first issue of the revived newsletter contained an enthusiastic review by Adams of *Facts, Artifacts, and Counterfacts* ("Review").

Bartholomae and Petrosky's influence is also apparent in the 1988 CBW reorganizational special-interest group meeting. This particularly memorable SIG, held in St. Louis, is described by Suellyn Duffey, who served as CBW chair from 1992 to 1994:

> We had come from all over North America and from different types of schools: a community college in New Orleans, a Big Ten public university, Chicago and St. Louis, Nevada and Kentucky. . . . Nicholas Coles, Marilyn DeMario, and Mariolina Salvatori, contributing authors to David Bartholomae and Anthony Petrosky's *Facts, Artifacts, and Counterfacts*, and all teachers of the basic reading and writing course described in the book, were behind the table at the front of the room. . . . The time was right for renewing the Conference on Basic Writing. (4)

Adams and Kirkpatrick capitalized on this spirit of camaraderie to continue developing the organization. In an appeal for volunteer members for the Executive Committee in 1991, Adams and Kirkpatrick wrote: "Keep in mind that most CBW members (including the officers) don't know each other except through this organization; it's here that we are meeting new friends in the profession" ("From the Chairs" 2). By spring 1989, membership had grown to 325 members, and bylaws had been proposed (Adams and Kirkpatrick, "The State of CBW" 2). From 1988 to 1992, chairs Adams and Kirkpatrick (and later Duffey) edited the *Conference on Basic Writing Newsletter* and published nine issues.[3] Responding to

---

[2]Although the founders of CBW believed strongly in working with whole texts and were never especially skill-and-drill oriented, they felt it appropriate to drop *skills* from the organization's name because of the word's negative connotations.

[3]The newsletter continued publication, sometimes intermittently, until 1998. Twenty-two issues were published. Editors and contributors for the 1993 to 1998 issues included Suellyn Duffey, Jeanne Gunner, Kay Puttock, Gerri McNenny, and Sallyanne Fitzgerald. In 1995, CBW entered the electronic age with the development of the CBW e-mail list and Web site. In 1999, the newsletter became *BWe: Basic Writing e-Journal* at <http://orgs.tamu-commerce.edu/BWe>. Both the newsletter and *BWe* are indexed through CompPile at <http://comppile.org>.

the interests of CBW's membership, the editors made articles, book reviews, and columns permanent features of this more "scholarly" newsletter.

Along with the increasing visibility of basic writing scholarship, CBW's revival contributed to a renewed sense of community among basic writing professionals. The revitalized commitment to basic writing was evident in special-interest group meetings at the Conference on College Composition and Communication as well. In 1989, the SIG in Seattle featured presentations by the contributing editors of A *Sourcebook for Basic Writing Teachers*: Theresa Enos, David Bartholomae, Andrea Lunsford, and Lynn Quitman Troyka. At the Chicago CCCC in 1990, CBW sponsored a panel titled "Black Students, Standard English, and Basic Writing" that drew more than 180 attendees (Adams and Kirkpatrick, "SIG Scoreboard" 2). Panelists included Miriam Chaplin, Eugene Hammond, Lisa Delpit, and Geneva Smitherman, respondent. An increased sense of professionalism in the organization was also reflected in the SIG. At the 1991 meeting in Boston, *Journal of Basic Writing* editors Bill Bernhardt and Peter Miller presented the biannual Shaughnessy Writing Award for the best *JBW* article to Kathleen Dixon for her essay "Intellectual Development and the Place of Narrative in 'Basic' and Freshman Composition."

The Fourth National Basic Writing Conference: Mainstreaming and Marginalization, 1992

The Fourth National Basic Writing Conference, held in College Park, Maryland, in 1992, was a turning point for the organization and for basic writing teacher-researchers. The Conference on Basic Writing organized this conference, which grew from one to three days. Carolyn Kirkpatrick stepped down as associate chair of CBW to cochair the National Basic Writing Conference with Eugene Hammond, CBW member and earlier board member. Titled "Critical Issues in Basic Writing: 1992," the conference marked the emergence of two critical issues that have continued to stimulate discussions in the field: (1) Should basic writing students be placed in separate courses or be mainstreamed into freshman composition courses, and (2) how do we keep from marginalizing basic writing students?

At the Maryland conference, discussions of these questions emerged in presentations about defining and assessing literacy, the politics of error, the place of grammar, connections between basic writing and English as a second language, the design of basic writing programs, and adaptations of Bartholomae and Petrosky's *Facts, Artifacts, and Counterfacts* approach (Uehling, "Report"). One notable example was David Bartholomae's keynote address, "The Tidy House: Basic Writing in the American Curriculum," in which he argued that students entering the curriculum should not be negatively labeled by being placed in a basic writing class and should instead be mainstreamed. At the 1992 conference (and in the subsequent special issue of the *Journal of Basic Writing* published in spring 1993),[4] issues that had long been at the core of CBW—how to work with students in basic writing classes and who was doing that work—converged with new questions related to instruction, most notably whether the enterprise of basic writing was the most just and ethical way to work with students or whether alternatives should be sought. These issues moved to the forefront of discussions within the organization and the field.

A Foundational Shift: Grappling with Mainstreaming, the Mid- to Late 1990s

The mid- to late 1990s were marked by vigorous debates on mainstreaming, which were initiated at the 1992 conference. These arguments raged in meetings and in the halls at the Conference on College Composition and Communication. The 1995 special-interest group in Washington, D.C., was a defining moment for the Conference on Basic Writing. As Gunner recalls, "The politics of mainstreaming proved a uniting topic, even as different points of view made for intense exchanges" ("From the Chair" 2). The importance of continuing these conversations and keeping in touch generally led to some new initiatives, including the creation of the CBW e-mail list and Web site in 1995 and the proposal for a pre-CCCC all-day workshop in lieu of a national conference. Participants in the 1996 workshop, called "Exploring the Boundaries of Basic Writing," at CCCC in Milwaukee heard, among others, presentations by Tom Fox, Judith Rodby, Charles Schuster, and Ira Shor in which each challenged the advantages and disadvantages of mainstreaming as it was perceived at that time. Shor's remarks were later developed in "Our Apartheid," published in the *Journal of Basic Writing* in 1997. In response, Karen Greenberg and Terence Collins published separate, vigorous rebuttals.

In 1996, in reaction to this debate, Gerri McNenny, CBW cochair from 1997 to 1999, proposed that CBW support a collection of essays on basic writing and mainstreaming. CBW distributed a flyer soliciting manuscripts, and McNenny, with the assistance of Fitzgerald, saw the volume through to publication as *Mainstreaming Basic Writers: Politics and Pedagogies of Access.*

---

[4]See Bartholomae; Adams, "Basic Writing Reconsidered"; Berger; Fox, "Standards and Access"; Greenberg, "The Politics of Basic Writing"; Gunner, "The Status of Basic Writing Teachers"; Jones; and Scott. In addition, a particularly interesting conference panel called "Rereading Shaughnessy" focused on Mina Shaughnessy; two of these presentations were also published in the fall 1993 issue of *JBW* (Gay; Laurence).

Subsequent workshops continued to address questions related to mainstreaming and marginalization,[5] but presenters also began to focus more on innovative classroom strategies designed to help students challenge definitions of literacy and status in the classroom. The annual pre-CCCC one-day workshop has developed into one of the highlights of the CCCC for basic writing professionals. Bill Lalicker, 2002 to 2005 cochair, remarks that workshops need to be both "theory-stimulating and practice energizing in ways that make a difference in BW classrooms all year" because workshops must "serve people at community colleges, regional schools, all kinds of universities" (e-mail). Tom Reynolds, 2002 to 2005 cochair, also comments on those varied local situations: "The workshop, and the SIG group always remind me of how conditions in one state, one city, one school, differ so greatly from another" (e-mail).

The 1995 special-interest group meeting in Washington, D.C., also led to the formation of the CBW-L, the Conference on Basic Writing e-mail list, which provides a forum for online exchanges about mainstreaming and other issues relevant to the work of basic writing instructors and students in basic writing classes. "An ongoing discussion of the theory and practice of basic writing," the CBW-L allows subscribers to engage in professional conversations that are fast, frequent, and far ranging. The CBW Web site was also a response to the 1995 special-interest group discussions on mainstreaming and the resulting need for greater communication. Like the e-mail list, the special-interest group meetings, and the preconference workshops, the Web site is another way that basic writing teacher-researchers can build community and access resources useful for their work. The site contains links to information on CBW membership, the CBW e-mail list, online resources, basic writing programs, a reading list, the *Journal of Basic Writing*, the CBW archive, and the CBW Award for Innovation.[6] The Web site also has a link to *BWe: Basic Writing e-Journal*, a free, peer-reviewed online journal that began publication in summer 1999 and is designed to expand conversations about basic writing.

CBW Defines the Field of Basic Writing with Its Bibliography, 1999–2005

The years 1999 to 2005 again brought new direction to the Conference on Basic Writing as it faced state budget cuts, "outsourcing" of basic writing,

---

[5]The 1997 CBW workshop, for example, was titled "Race, Class, and Culture in the Basic Writing Classroom," and the presentations from this workshop, as well as pieces by the cochairs, were published in a special issue of the *Journal of Basic Writing* (see Gunner and McNenny; Maher; Royster and Taylor; Shor; Soliday and Gleason; Tate, McMillan, and Woodworth; and Villanueva).

[6]The CBW Web site can be accessed at <http://orgs.tamu-commerce.edu/CBW>.

and high-stakes testing. In response to these challenges, CBW continued to make the work of basic writing teacher-researchers more public and to advocate for teachers and students in basic writing classes.

Perhaps CBW's most notable achievement to date is the publication of three editions of *The Bedford Bibliography for Teachers of Basic Writing*. The first two editions were edited by Linda Adler-Kassner and Gregory R. Glau, CBW cochairs from 1999 to 2002; this third edition is edited by Gregory R. Glau and Chitralekha Duttagupta. The *Bibliography* abstracts books, articles, and periodicals; more than two hundred teachers from around the country annotated more than four hundred entries for this third edition. As Mike Rose notes, "In the academy . . . your life [is] the record of all you [have] to say about the particular booklists you [have] made your own" (70). The same can be said of CBW as an organization and the field of basic writing: our life is the record of all we have to say about the particular booklists we have made our own.

With the support of Bedford/St. Martin's, the *Bibliography* remains a free publication; it is also available online at <bedfordstmartins.com/basicbib>. The fees the editors would normally receive from the *Bibliography* are used to fund the CBW Fellowship, which supports travel to the annual Conference on Basic Writing workshop and to the Conference on College Composition and Communication meeting. CBW Fellowship applications are judged on their benefit to the instructor's professional interests, their benefit to students, and the applicant's clear dissemination plan.

An important aspect of the CBW community has always been an emphasis on informal collegiality. This tradition continues, especially at conferences, with a primary focus on the special-interest group meeting as a place to gather. Glau observes, "I've been especially pleased at the special-interest group meetings over the past couple of years—more and more people (we often are overflowing our room!) with lots of good ideas and suggestions and comments" (e-mail).

Honoring those who have made contributions to the field and celebrating their successes have sometimes been features of SIG meetings. This idea was revived in 2004 with the institution of the annual CBW Award for Innovation. According to the CBW Web site, this award "recognizes writing programs for innovations that improve educational processes for basic writers through creative approaches" (Glau, *Conference on Basic Writing*). The winning schools are presented with a plaque and invited to give a brief presentation about their innovative program to SIG members. Lalicker identifies the CBW Award for Innovation and the CBW Fellowship as "the newest high points and those with the most transformative potential for the future" (e-mail).

CBW-L, the Conference on Basic Writing online discussion list, continues as an electronic forum. Topics of discussion include reading in the basic writing classroom, basic writing and learning disabilities, and teaching the process of writing.

Over the last thirty years, the Conference on Basic Writing has established a professional community that is interested equally in practice and theory. Lalicker characterizes the equal focus on research and teaching as an "exemplary dialectic" and adds that "the emphasis on both of these values is something that attracted me to the organization. . . . The invitation to newcomers operates productively to bring new ideas and practical energy to counter the natural institutionalization of theory" (e-mail). The CBW community was developed through a network created by the early newsletters, its online successors CBW-L and *BWe*, the Web site, books, the early national conferences and current annual workshops, and the continuing special-interest group meetings. Through informal conversations, information sharing, formal presentations, debates, and scholarship—in person, in print, and in electronic media—the organization has developed into a thriving community of diverse educators who work together to create a rich, professional practice.

The Next Thirty Years, 2010 and Beyond

As the Conference on Basic Writing looks forward to its next thirty years, the students will always be there. But how can basic writing educators meet their needs? Some issues we may need to address include reduced funding for education, high-stakes testing, widely varying local conditions, working conditions for basic writing faculty, the community college voice, and global literacy.

As state budgets tighten, we may need to work to reduce or eliminate extra fees for basic writing instruction, particularly because basic writing students often are the ones who can least afford them. Another challenge is motivation: basic writing is often a noncredit course, and our students are frequently controlled by mandated tests for initial placement or for prerequisites for higher-level classes, which essentially lock them out of a serious education.

One response to these external demands is to link them back to our local situations and particular students. Reynolds conveys the importance of local conditions and programmatic assessment: "The CBW group has been valuable to me, as a program administrator and a scholar, for its constant attention to the differences among BW programs. . . . If there's a unifying factor in these discussions, it seems to be that everyone is under pressure to show results, usually through state-mandated testing of one sort or another. A high point of my time as cochair has been to see people sharing knowledge of these pressures and, in so doing, making it a national concern" (e-mail). Reynolds identifies program accountability as "one of the major issues facing the field": "Although we are getting better at documenting what it means for an individual writer to advance one's writing 'skills' through our classes, a more difficult challenge is to show that an approach, identifiably 'BW,' can be applied and measured (quantitatively) to show progress" (e-mail).

McNenny agrees: "As cautionary tales, the dismantling of various basic writing programs signals a need for a more public, proactive role for writing program administrators and instructors, to present a convincing and comprehensive picture of the gains that students achieve through writing programs, and the intellectual work involved for both students and faculty" ("Writing Instruction" 5). Lalicker suggests that we create a picture of ourselves based on broadly defined goals "in terms not just of discrete student 'skills' but in terms of students' inclusion in the academy and students' power in the larger culture. . . . We need to define program goals and outcomes in ways that are congruent with real student needs (as students see them, not just as we dictate them)," and we need to argue for "ways of assessment that can recognize these qualitative outcomes" (e-mail).

Perhaps as another response to external mandates, the Conference on Basic Writing might become a clearinghouse for information on high-stakes assessment, state mandates, local conditions, and programmatic assessments. The CBW Web site offers a venue for posting this information. There has already been some excellent work done in this area by CBW members such as Terence Collins ("Basic Writing Programs") and Greg Glau (*Arizona State University's Stretch Program*).

We also must address the conditions under which basic writing faculty work. Reynolds notes how "BW classes are still handed off as 'last resort' teaching assignments. . . . Most BW courses are not part of a formal BW program but rather some other 'remedial' effort at colleges" (e-mail). Lalicker mentions how "too many outstanding BW teachers [are] . . . seen as pieceworkers, contingent faculty in the pink-collar ghetto" (e-mail). Reynolds suggests that a challenge for CBW is "to improve working conditions and make the job of teaching BW an attractive one," perhaps by "seeing the job as a wider project, one that embraces literacy issues more generally" (e-mail). Lalicker agrees: "In too many of our institutional relationships, BW is seen as a separate room, a kind of subacademic support center" instead of "an academic field" that draws "creatively on the knowledge bases" of several subdisciplines: "mainstream composition, reading and literacy, ESL, and advanced rhetoric" (e-mail).

A related working-condition issue is employment contracts for adjunct faculty teachers. No one can survive on wages that are paid by the course and do not include benefits. "Freeway flyers" who are worried about paying their utility bills, buying food for their children, finding a parking space, and making it to class at the next institution cannot be expected to make a serious commitment to students and teaching. Improving working conditions is part of what Lalicker calls "the continuing struggle to encourage the several levels of academia (the department, the institution, the national professional establishment) to see BW instructors as serious professional practitioners" (e-mail). Being taken seriously means being funded and offering "well-theorized and practical programs," and as Lalicker concludes, "only those with a first-class institutional voice proportionate to their educational role can influence budgets, program goals, syllabi, and teaching methods. . . . Politics are pedagogy" (e-mail).

In some states that follow a business model, basic writing instruction has been "downsized" and "outsourced," moved from four- or six-year colleges to community colleges or from colleges to private providers. Another challenge for the future of the Conference on Basic Writing is to allow more space within the community for community college and private provider voices. Although three of CBW's chairs have been from community colleges (Adams, Kirkpatrick, and Fitzgerald), community college teacher representation in CBW has not been broad. In the first volume of this bibliography, only nine of the 119 contributors were from community colleges (although some contributors were working in the community college arm of four- or six-year institutions). McNenny notes that "much of the mainstreaming debate has indeed excluded the voices of two-year college decision makers" (Preface vi). Fitzgerald adds, "Where do our community college students and faculty fit in the discussion? . . . Why do my colleagues in the Conference on Basic Writing have to be reminded that basic writing is a universal term that can be applied to many contexts, not just the universities where they teach?" ("The Context Determines Our Choice" 222).

Within the organization, the Conference on Basic Writing must also continue to include instructors from many types of institutions, from two-year colleges to Ph.D.-granting institutions. We serve every basic writing student. Conversations between teacher-researchers and researcher-teachers across geographic boundaries, between private and public environments, across open admissions and selective admissions lines, and among differing levels of academic institutions strengthen our practice.

Another challenge is global literacy and online teaching. As Reynolds notes, "We will have to start to address more global literacy issues. Our students are already in competition with students overseas now for employment, and literacy issues here are literacy issues there. Education offered through accredited online colleges has started to include lower-division courses, including composition. I expect that we need to start thinking more carefully about how to bring our theoretical and practical concerns to current global literacy practices" (e-mail).

In his final column as the chair of the Conference on Basic Writing, Adams articulated the importance of CBW's work:

> The teaching of basic writing is important—as important as anything being done in higher education. Often we are the last chance at college-level education for students who have plenty of ability but who have not been served well previously or who have not taken advantage of the opportunities offered. . . .

Further, we are one of the few areas in the academy where differences between students are reduced rather than exaggerated. . . .

Because the teaching of basic writing is so important, the work of this organization is similarly important. . . . CBW's most important role is to insure CCCC continues to provide a place where teachers of basic writing feel that their needs are being addressed and to insure that the considerable intelligence of the combined membership of CCCC continues to address the thorny problems involved in teaching basic writers. ("From the Chairs" 2–3)

As Charles Guilford, founder of the Conference on Basic Writing, said before he retired in 2004, "There are many, many students who continue to need quality teaching." The future of those students rests in the hands of those teachers and scholars who are committed to students and serious about providing them with access to quality education.

Works Cited[7]

Adams, Peter. "Basic Writing Reconsidered." *Journal of Basic Writing* 12.1 (1993): 22–36. Print.

————. "From the Chairs: From the Old Chair." *CBW Newsletter* 11.2 (1992): 2–3. Print.

————. "Review of *Facts, Artifacts, and Counterfacts.*" *CBW Newsletter* 7.1 (1988): 1–3. Print.

Adams, Peter, and Carolyn Kirkpatrick. "From the Chairs." *CBW Newsletter* 10.2 (1991): 2. Print.

————. "From the Chairs: SIG Scoreboard." *CBW Newsletter* 9.2 (1990): 2. Print.

————. "From the Chairs: The State of CBW." *CBW Newsletter* 8.2 (1989): 2. Print.

Bartholomae, David. "The Tidy House: Basic Writing in the American Curriculum." *Journal of Basic Writing* 12.1 (1993): 4–21. Print.

Bartholomae, David, and Anthony Petrosky. *Facts, Artifacts, and Counterfacts: Theory and Method for a Reading and Writing Course.* Portsmouth: Heinemann, 1986. Print.

Berger, Mary Jo. "Funding and Support of Basic Writing Programs: Why Don't We Have Any?" *Journal of Basic Writing* 12.1 (1993): 81–89. Print.

Collins, Terence G. "Basic Writing Programs and Access Allies: Finding and Maintaining Your Support Network." *CBW Newsletter* 13.3 (1998): 1–6. Print.

————. "A Response to Ira Shor's 'Our Apartheid: Writing Instruction and Inequality.'" *Journal of Basic Writing* 16.2 (1997): 95–100. Print.

[7]The CBW Web site, the *CBW Newsletter*, and issues of *BWe: Basic Writing e-Journal* can now be accessed at <http://orgs.tamu-commerce.edu/CBW/>.

Dixon, Kathleen G. "Intellectual Development and the Place of Narrative in 'Basic' and Freshman Composition." *Journal of Basic Writing* 8.1 (1989): 3–20. Print.

Duffey, Suellyn. "A Drama: The Tinkling of Glasses, the Sound of a New CBW." *CBW Newsletter* 8.1 (1988): 4. Print.

English Department at Arizona State University, n.d., Web. 16 Feb. 2004.

Enos, Theresa, ed. *A Sourcebook for Basic Writing Teachers*. New York: Random, 1987. Print.

Fitzgerald, Sallyanne. "Basic Writing Conference Scheduled for St. Louis in September." *CBW Newsletter* 8.2 (1989): 1–3. Print.

———. "The Context Determines Our Choice: Curriculum, Students, and Faculty." *Mainstreaming Basic Writers: Politics and Pedagogies of Access*. Ed. Gerri McNenny. Mahwah: Erlbaum, 2001. 215–23. Print.

Fox, Tom. *Defending Access: A Critique of Standards in Higher Education*. Portsmouth: Boynton, 1999. Print.

———. "Standards and Access." *Journal of Basic Writing* 12.1 (1993): 37–45. Print.

Gay, Pamela. "Rereading Shaughnessy from a Postcolonial Perspective." *Journal of Basic Writing* 12.2 (1993): 29–40. Print.

Glau, Gregory R. Home page. *Conference on Basic Writing (CBW)*. 23 Jan. 2004. Web. 10 Aug. 2009.

———. Message to the author. 16 Apr. 2001. E-mail.

Greenberg, Karen L. "The Politics of Basic Writing." *Journal of Basic Writing* 12.1 (1993): 64–71. Print.

———. "A Response to Ira Shor's 'Our Apartheid: Writing Instruction and Inequality.'" Journal of Basic Writing 16.2 (1997): 90–94. Print.

Guilford, Charles. *Introducing CBWS*. 1980. Print.

Guilford, Charles, and Karen Uehling. "A Word from the Founders of CBW." *CBW Newsletter* 7.1 (1988): 4. Print.

Gunner, Jeanne. "From the Chair." CBW Newsletter (1996): 1–2. Print.

———. "The Status of Basic Writing Teachers: Do We Need a 'Maryland Resolution'?" *Journal of Basic Writing* 12.1 (1993): 57–63. Print.

Gunner, Jeanne, and Gerri McNenny. "Retrospection as Prologue." *Journal of Basic Writing* 16.1 (1997): 3–12. Print.

Jones, William. "Basic Writing: Pushing against Racism." *Journal of Basic Writing* 12.1 (1993): 72–80. Print.

Lalicker, William. Message to the author. 11 Feb. 2004. E-mail.

Laurence, Patricia. "The Vanishing Site of Mina Shaughnessy's *Errors and Expectations*." *Journal of Basic Writing* 12.2 (1993): 18–28. Print.

Maher, Jane. "Writing the Life of Mina P. Shaughnessy." *Journal of Basic Writing* 16.1 (1997): 51–63. Print.

McNenny, Gerri, ed. *Mainstreaming Basic Writers: Politics and Pedagogies of Access*. Mahwah: Erlbaum, 2001. Print.

————. Preface. *Mainstreaming Basic Writers: Politics and Pedagogies of Access*. Ed. Gerri McNenny. Mahwah: Erlbaum, 2001. xi–xvii. Print.

————. "Writing Instruction and the Post-Remedial University: Setting the Scene for the Mainstreaming Debate in Basic Writing." *Mainstreaming Basic Writers: Politics and Pedagogies of Access*. Ed. Gerri McNenny. Mahwah: Erlbaum, 2001. 1–15. Print.

Reynolds, Tom. Message to the author. 5 Feb. 2004. E-mail.

Rose, Mike. *Lives on the Boundary: The Struggles and Achievements of America's Underprepared*. New York: Free, 1989. Print.

Royer, Daniel J., and Roger Gilles. "Basic Writing and Directed Self-Placement." *BWe: Basic Writing e-Journal* 2.2 (2000): n. pag. Web. 10 Aug. 2009.

————, eds. *Directed Self-Placement: Principles and Practices*. Cresskill: Hampton, 2003. Print.

Royster, Jacqueline Jones, and Rebecca Greenberg Taylor. "Constructing Teacher Identity in the Basic Writing Classroom." *Journal of Basic Writing* 16.1 (1997): 27–50. Print.

Scott, Jerrie Cobb. "Literacies and Deficits Revisited." *Journal of Basic Writing* 12.1 (1993): 46–56. Print.

Shor, Ira. "Our Apartheid: Writing Instruction and Inequality." *Journal of Basic Writing* 16.1 (1997): 91–104. Print.

Soliday, Mary, and Barbara Gleason. "From Remediation to Enrichment: Evaluating a Mainstreaming Project." *Journal of Basic Writing* 16.1 (1997): 64–78. Print.

Tate, Gary, John McMillan, and Elizabeth Woodworth. "Class Talk." *Journal of Basic Writing* 16.1 (1997): 13–26. Print.

Uehling, Karen S. "The Conference on Basic Writing: 1980–2001." *Histories of Developmental Education*. Ed. Dana Britt Lundell and Jeanne L. Higbee. Minneapolis: Center for Research on Developmental Education and Urban Literacy, 2002. 47–57. Print.

————. "Report on the Fourth National Basic Writing Conference." *CBW Newsletter* 12.1 (Winter 1993): 1–4. Print.

Villanueva, Victor. "Theory in the Basic Writing Classroom? A Practice." *Journal of Basic Writing* 16.1 (1997): 79–90. Print.

History and Theory: Basic Writing and Basic Writers

Basic Writing: Definitions and Conversations

1 Adler-Kassner, Linda, and Susanmarie Harrington. *Basic Writing as a Political Act: Public Conversations about Writing and Literacy.* Cresskill: Hampton, 2002. Print.

Basic writing instruction often perpetuates an autonomous model of literacy that separates writing and reading from the contexts in which they are situated. This model fails to help students familiarize themselves with the culture of the "academic community." To make this case, the authors analyzed basic writing research, interviewed basic writing students, and studied the portrayal of "remedial" writing in mainstream media. The authors find that basic writers and basic writing are portrayed as violating a narrative in which mastering autonomous literacy strategies is a key element. Basic writing programs are portrayed as successful when they place students within the narrative. The authors suggest new curricular strategies for basic writing classes and new terms for conversations about basic writing, arguing that these will help writers and others to develop connections between writing and culture and will make basic writing a political act.

2 Bartholomae, David. "Inventing the University." *When a Writer Can't Write: Studies in Writer's Block and Other Composing-Process Problems.* Ed. Mike Rose. New York: Guilford, 1985. 134–65. Print.

Basic writing students should be immersed in academic discourse so that they can begin to appropriate it for their own ends. Bartholomae contends that basic writing studies should not center simply on error. Instead, we must better understand how basic writers' lack of understanding about constructions of authority and the rules of academic discourse put them at a disadvantage in an arena that values such knowledge. As a result, Bartholomae argues that the basic writer "has to invent the university by assembling and mimicking its language" (135), often long before the skills of writing in an academic setting are learned. Drawing from scholars such as Linda Flower, John Hayes, and Patricia Bizzell, Bartholomae supports his own conclusions while investigating potential reasons for the choices made in student discourse.

3 Bartholomae, David. "The Tidy House: Basic Writing in the American Curriculum." *Journal of Basic Writing* 12.1 (1993): 4–21. Print.

Borrowing from historian Carolyn Steedman, Bartholomae argues that basic writing courses segregate students and replicate social divisions. "In the name of sympathy and empowerment," he writes, "we have once again produced the 'other' who is the incomplete version of ourselves, confirming existing patterns of power and authority, reproducing the hierarchies we had meant to question and overthrow . . . in the 1970s" (18). He also argues that these classes are ultimately necessary because they provide an entry point for students. However, Bartholomae offers several curricular possibilities for basic writing classes in which students are segregated: looking for students' abilities to provide unusual texts as a placement mechanism, eliminating tracking, and creating classes that become "contact zones" in which writers examine and engage differences between one another and the academy. Echoing Mary Louise Pratt, Bartholomae proposes a "curricular program designed not to hide differences . . . but to highlight them, to make them not only the subject of the writing curriculum but the source of its goals and values (at least one of the versions of writing one can learn at the university)" (13).

4   Bernstein, Susan Naomi. "Social Justice Initiative for Basic Writing." *BWe: Basic Writing e-Journal* 7.1 (2008): n. pag. Web. 11 Aug. 2009.

Bernstein discusses the continued marginal status of basic writing students, teachers, and courses. She argues that basic writing should not be defined as "remedial," but as educational enrichment, and that basic writing students should be seen as authentic members of their colleges and universities. She also proposes a formal resolution for the Conference on Basic Writing to argue for improved funding for basic writing programs; to remove any "remedial" label and to conceptualize basic writing classes as college level; to educate students about and to provide adequate resources for basic writing students as well as for better articulation with K–12 teachers and administrators; and to link basic writing to social justice concerns for historically disenfranchised communities.

5   Bizzell, Patricia. "Basic Writing and the Issue of Correctness, Or, What to Do with 'Mixed' Forms of Academic Discourse." *Journal of Basic Writing* 19.1 (2000): 4–12. Print.

By reflecting on how hybrid, or mixed, discourses have appeared in academic work and how these discourses might affect basic writing pedagogy, Bizzell seeks to extend and refine arguments raised in her earlier article, "Hybrid Academic Discourses." In this follow-up article, she argues that the increased use of mixed forms means that students no longer need initiation into traditional academic discourse but may need time and assistance to try out various forms combining the academic and nonacademic. Bizzell acknowledges two main points that were not emphasized clearly enough in her earlier article. First, because of cultural fusion in the United States, students come to college with "already mixed linguistic and discursive resources" (9). Second, these mixed, comfortable forms are "being used by everyone," as "they allow their practitioners to do intellectual work in ways they could not if confined to traditional academic discourse" (10).

6   Bizzell, Patricia. "Cognition, Convention, and Certainty: What We Need to Know about Writing." *PRE/TEXT* 3.3 (1982): 213–43. Print.

Compositionists form two theoretical camps: those who are outer-directed, thereby focused on the social processes that influence language learning and thinking, and those who are inner-directed, hence interested in universal writing processes and individual capacities. As inner-directed theorists, Linda Flower and John Hayes support a linear, cognitive model of writing that separates thought, or "planning," from writing, or "translating," yet Flower and Hayes fail to account for individual knowledge and contextual influences. Outer-directed theorists remain skeptical of all models that claim an understanding of inner processes. Accordingly, outer-directed theorists stress the role of community, ethics, politics, and social interaction in the development of thinking and language. A synthesis of theories from both camps will offer a fuller understanding of writing.

7   Bloom, Lynn Z. "A Name with a View." *Journal of Basic Writing* 14.1 (1995): 7–14. Print.

Bloom focuses on the issue of renaming the *Journal of Basic Writing* in view of its changing perspective and content. Naming and renaming are significant actions because of the connotations and expectations related to a name. When the journal began publishing in 1974, its goal was to change the connotation of *remedial*, which suggests deficiency, to a more positive descriptor, *basic*. The topics covered over the next ten years focused mainly on methods of teaching basic writers, but even in the first years, some articles dealt with issues that applied to other composition students. After the 1980s, articles routinely covered a greater range of topics and writing populations. Bloom thinks that the diversity covered currently in the journal suggests a revision of the name to better situate basic writing studies in the field of composition today and to attract more diverse contributors. Over time, *basic writer* has taken on the connotations that *remedial writer* had in the past.

8   Collins, Terence G. "A Response to Ira Shor's 'Our Apartheid: Writing Instruction and Inequality.'" *Journal of Basic Writing* 16.2 (1997): 95–100. Print.

Collins contends that Ira Shor is "emphatically wrong" (95) in his assertions about basic writing. Shor presents an "artificially homogenized landscape" (95) of basic writing when, in fact, institutions of higher education deal with the needs of these underprepared writers in diverse ways, some successful and authentic, some not. Furthermore, Shor was in error when he stated that the University of Minnesota General College's basic writing program was a "cash cow" (95) for the university, paying part-time instructors to teach full-tuition students. Rather, General College's basic writing program operates with four full-time, tenured or tenure-track faculty who are among the best paid in the college. The program has an excellent track record as an integral part of the "eventual success" (97) of General College students. With his "mis-statements" (96) about General College's basic writing program and his correlation of basic writing with "cynical apartheid" (99) agendas on the part of institutions of higher education, Shor paints basic writing instruction as destructive and exploitative and misses the opportunity to discuss the pedagogy in more realistic terms.

See: Ira Shor, "Our Apartheid" [42].

See: Karen L. Greenberg, "A Response to Ira Shor's 'Our Apartheid'" [15].

9   DeGenaro, William. "Why Basic Writing Professionals on Regional Campuses Need to Know Their Histories." *Open Words: Access and English Studies* 1.1 (2006): 54–68. Print.

Much basic writing scholarship is framed within a "literacy-as-generative model," which often focuses on the development of the individual rather than the historical and material conditions that shape literacy education at a given moment and location. In response to what he identifies as an apolitical and ahistorical realm of basic writing (57), DeGenaro calls for a comprehensive history of basic writing situated within local histories and institutional narratives. Works such as Ira Shor's "Our Apartheid: Writing Instruction and Inequality" (1997) and, more recently, Mary Soliday's *The Politics of Remediation: Institutional and Student Needs in Higher Education* (2002) model the political possibilities that historical methodologies can uncover, and it is through Soliday that DeGenaro transitions from the larger historical terrain into his own situated history at a regional campus designing and implementing a new basic writing course.

See: Ira Shor, "Our Apartheid" [42].

See: Mary Soliday, *The Politics of Remediation* [105].

10   DeGenaro, William, and Edward M. White. "Going around in Circles: Methodological Issues in Basic Writing Research." *Journal of Basic Writing* 19.1 (2000): 22–35. Print.

Basic writing studies has not reached professional consensus on such fundamental issues as the mainstreaming of developmental writers and the "universal requirement." While most writers in the field work to democratize educational practices, few share similar research methodologies or even agree about what counts as valid evidence. A critical perspective on methodology reveals the ways in which some texts blend philosophical, practitioner, and historical work but does not allow other voices or perspectives into the scholarly conversation. As a result of this lack of dialectic, researchers frequently reiterate basic positions and overlook opposing claims instead of debating and testing findings to produce convincing generalizations. At a time when those in charge of basic writing programs frequently need to present a unified front to outside groups, such as administrators and policy makers, more methodological awareness could help them to build consensus and establish common ideological goals.

11   Gilyard, Keith. "Basic Writing, Cost Effectiveness, and Ideology." *Journal of Basic Writing* 19.1 (2000): 36–42. Print.

Looking back on the history of basic writing at the City University of New York and his own experiences as a student, teacher, and scholar, Gilyard asserts that the future of basic writing should involve critiquing "cost effectiveness" arguments in favor of basic writing and framing arguments for students' abilities to voice and gain facility with language. He also challenges the easy use of the term *basic writing* for its inherent racism, sexism, and classism, while recognizing that it has institutional and personal value for many students and teachers. For Gilyard, basic writing scholarship that ignores students' own social, political, and cultural ideologies often results in privileged pedagogies that center on the formal considerations of students' writing alone. Citing the critical nature of scholarly work like Deborah Mutnick's, Gilyard favors basic writing scholarship that involves continued careful critique of its ideological, political, cultural, and social practices and interests.

12   Gleason, Barbara. "Reasoning the Need: Graduate Education and Basic Writing." *Journal of Basic Writing* 25.2 (2006): 49–75. Print.

In this essay, which appeared in the twenty-fifth anniversary edition of the *Journal of Basic Writing*, Gleason uses her 2005 speech from the Conference on College Composition and Communication as a jumping-off point for discussing the future of basic writing. She carefully examines just how well today's graduate students schooled in rhetoric, composition, and English studies are being prepared to actually teach the growing numbers of nontraditional basic writing students appearing in community colleges and adult literacy programs. Gleason looks closely at various graduate courses in basic writing theory and practice taught across the country from 2000 to 2005, lists key scholarly texts recommended to graduate students interested in basic writing research, charts important theoretical and practical developments in the discipline (such as the publication of the *Bedford Bibliography*), and discusses the Two-Year College Association's commitment to better serving basic writing students. In the end, Gleason creates a compelling argument for why we must create more and better graduate courses that prepare future teachers to teach basic writers.

13 Greenberg, Karen L. "The Politics of Basic Writing." *Journal of Basic Writing* 12.1 (1993): 64–71. Print.

Greenberg responds to David Bartholomae's contention at the Fourth Annual Conference on Basic Writing that basic writing programs generally do more harm than good to students. She points out that many writing instructors fall into the trap that Bartholomae describes. Refusing to include themselves in the design and implementation of assessment procedures in basic writing, these writing teachers relinquish responsibility for their program to administrators, legislators, and others who know little about basic writing. Greenberg then draws on her own experiences at the City University of New York. She shares some of the political challenges basic writing programs face and discusses strategies for meeting those challenges. She also suggests ways to improve basic writing instruction and assessment that will empower basic writing students. Greenberg notes that if basic writing courses are eliminated, our colleges and universities will once again become bastions of elitism.

See: David Bartholomae, "The Tidy House" [3].

14 Greenberg, Karen L. "Research on Basic Writers: Theoretical and Methodological Issues." *A Sourcebook for Basic Writing Teachers*. Ed. Theresa Enos. New York: Random, 1987. 187–207. Print.

Greenberg addresses the importance of research methods and priorities in basic writing. After summarizing Janet Emig's formative research in composition, Greenberg recommends that the best research on writing and writers will have "an explicit, comprehensive theoretical foundation based on past and current research in applied linguistics, in cognitive-developmental psychology, in discourse analysis, and in literary theory" (191). Greenberg then describes more than a dozen such studies of basic writers and writing, concluding that they depict developing writers as struggling with writing tasks, rules, and errors due to three interrelated problems: "(1) distorted notions about writing and the composing process, (2) intense writing apprehension in certain contexts, and (3) a tendency to block while writing specific academic tasks" (202). These findings, Greenberg contends, have implications for teaching and for future research in basic writing.

15   Greenberg, Karen L. "A Response to Ira Shor's 'Our Apartheid: Writing Instruction and Inequality.'" *Journal of Basic Writing* 16.2 (1997): 90–94. Print.

Greenberg offers a strong counterpoint to Shor's contention that basic writing courses should be eliminated in favor of courses based on cultural ideologies and empowerment. Basic writing courses are not "grammar graveyards" or "ghettos" (91) populated only by "Blacks" and "children of poor and working families" (90). They are safe places for a diverse population of underprepared college writers who can use these opportunities for individualized attention to better achieve their own potential in higher education. Greenberg accuses Shor of being an outsider to basic writing issues, of making decontextualized overgeneralizations about basic writing programs, and of treating basic writers stereotypically. Greenberg counters by depicting an effective basic writing classroom that is fully integrated into the English course sequence, displays progressive teaching strategies (such as workshopping, collaboration, and writing process), and provides a safe environment for students to develop necessary writing and critical thinking abilities. Greenberg argues that Shor's approach would lead to the exclusion of underprepared students and support "reactionary" efforts to restrict such students' access to higher education (94).

See: Ira Shor, "Our Apartheid" [42].

See: Terence G. Collins, "A Response to Ira Shor's 'Our Apartheid'" [8].

16   Gunner, Jeanne. "Afterthoughts on Motive." *Journal of Basic Writing* 16.1 (1997): 3–6. Print.

Gunner examines the professional and personal motives behind her creation of the 1997 workshop "Race, Class, and Culture in the Basic Writing Classroom." The Conference on College Composition and Communication workshop was sponsored by the Conference on

Basic Writing and was a forum for the discussion of professional issues like mainstreaming and analysis of class, identity, and cultural awareness in the basic writing classroom. The invited speakers, including Victor Villanueva, Gary Tate, Jacqueline Jones Royster, and Ira Shor, offered both professional and institutional gravitas to the workshop and to the topic's importance in the profession. Gunner's personal motives emerged from her realization that basic writing concerns were not addressed as an independent field but took place "in other professional arenas" (4). Responding to a paper presented by Charles Schuster in that session, Gunner recognized the need to bridge basic writing and "mainstream" composition. Gunner also admits to being motivated by a "concern for status" (5), in that she identified with and raged against the outsider status, loss of agency, and powerlessness that basic writers experience.

17   Gunner, Jeanne. "Iconic Discourse: The Troubling Legacy of Mina Shaughnessy." *Journal of Basic Writing* 17.2 (1998): 25–42. Print.

Gunner outlines the debate between scholars and teachers of basic writing, identifying two primary types of discourse. Iconic discourse relies on the legacy of Mina Shaughnessy and her work as an iconic teacher-figure. Critical discourse challenges basic writing conventions. Researchers like Min-Zhan Lu and Ira Shor question Shaughnessy's work and other accepted practices in the field and threaten to diminish the iconic status of Shaughnessy. Gunner maintains that these conflicting discourses can explain the attention and widespread resistance to such critiques of Shaughnessy.

18   Harrington, Susanmarie, and Linda Adler-Kassner. "'The Dilemma That Still Counts': Basic Writing at a Political Crossroads." *Journal of Basic Writing* 17.2 (1998): 1–24. Print.

Harrington and Adler-Kassner summarize current debates in the field of basic writing at a "pivotal moment" (3) in its history. To answer the call issued by an increasingly wide range of audiences to define basic writing and basic writers, they explore how these terms have been defined in basic writing scholarship. Their review of twenty years' worth of literature shows that basic writing serves "compelling educational and political functions" (4). It also suggests that basic writing scholarship has taken two perspectives: cognition-based work, which "focus[es] on the writers themselves and what happens in the act of composing" (9), and culture-based work, which "focuses less on individuals than on a sense of institutional or social culture" (12). Ultimately, the authors outline three areas for further investigation: why writers make the decisions they do about their writing, how students define themselves and their work, and how basic writing programs are constructed and administered.

19   Hindman, Jane E. "Inventing Academic Discourse: Teaching (and Learning) Marginal Poise and Fugitive Truth." *Journal of Basic Writing* 18.2 (1999): 23–43. Print.

Despite compositionists' commitment, they have failed to create a transformative pedagogy—primarily because, as teacher-scholars, they do not disrupt the university's hegemonic discourses. Critical pedagogy illuminates but does not disrupt processes of discursive power and authority because compositionists at the center of those discursive processes self-authorize academic discourse. Even more important, critical pedagogy has not changed perceptions of academic discourse or changed the way we evaluate student writing. In response, Hindman offers a curricular approach to basic writing. It puts evaluative processes at the center of instruction by involving students in mock sessions for grading freshman placement exams. This curricular approach has numerous pedagogical advantages, including destabilizing the power relations between student and teacher, improving student writing, and illustrating how academic discourse standards are socially constructed.

20   Hindman, Jane E. "Reinventing the University: Finding the Place for Basic Writers." *Journal of Basic Writing* 12.2 (1993): 55–76. Print.

Although David Bartholomae and Anthony Petrosky's *Facts, Artifacts, and Counterfacts* [186] "acknowledges that for basic writers the problem of writing in the university is the problem of appropriating power and authority" (62), only a curriculum that interrogates the professional politics of English, including placement practices, would enable students to gain access to the discursive power that drives academic authority. Problematizing the notion of marginality, Hindman argues that students must learn the intellectual gesture of setting their discourse against the apparently commonplace or naïve, thus enabling them to adopt the margins as a conscious position from which to critique mainstream writing practice. For instructors to facilitate the reawakened agency of basic writers, we must be willing to read against the grain of our own professional discourse.

21   Horner, Bruce. "Discoursing Basic Writing." *College Composition and Communication* 47.2 (1996): 199–222. Print.

In this alternative history of basic writing, Horner reads a number of texts that are often neglected in basic writing scholarship (including City University of New York memos and internal documents and Mina Shaughnessy's unpublished or lesser known writings) as well as well-known texts (including *Errors and Expectations* [117] and the *Journal of Basic Writing*). He argues that these texts were critical in basic writing's formation as a discourse during the 1970s. Through close readings informed by Marxist and poststructuralist theory,

Horner criticizes the ways in which this discourse has marginalized the concrete material, political, institutional, and sociohistorical realities facing basic writing teachers and students. Horner also investigates this discourse's convergence with an ongoing public discourse on education that problematically denies the academy's involvement in material, political, social, and historical worlds. Finally, Horner calls for more histories of basic writing that recover and expose the material, historical, and political contexts of basic writing, teaching, and theorizing.

22   Horner, Bruce, and Min-Zhan Lu. *Representing the "Other": Basic Writers and the Teaching of Writing*. Urbana: National Council of Teachers of English, 1999. Print.

In its descriptive representation of student needs and problems, the "new" discourse of basic writing that emerged during the 1960s and 1970s positioned basic writing outside the social, political, and historical contexts of its production and reception. Rather than trace what might be considered a canon of basic writing texts, the eight cultural materialist readings that Horner and Lu present in this book analyze the discourse of basic writing as a discourse of renegotiation shaped and reshaped by the context of its production and reception.

23   Hunter, Paul. "'Waiting for Aristotle': A Moment in the History of the Basic Writing Movement." *College English* 54.8 (1992): 914–27. Print.

Hunter provides a rhetorical analysis of "Toward a Literate Democracy," the 1980 *Journal of Basic Writing* issue published in memory of Mina Shaughnessy. Hunter applies the characteristics of the *epitaphios logos* (funeral oration) to the essays gathered in this memorial volume: the *enkomion* (praise), *parainesis* (lament), and *paramythia* (consolation). At the same time, he describes the political purpose of the funeral oration in Athenian society and raises questions concerning the political dimension of the current addresses. Noting that none of the five speakers included from the First Shaughnessy Memorial Conference had any experience teaching basic writing, Hunter considers the focus of each of the speakers' addresses and attempts to assess Shaughnessy as outside the historical context in which she worked, which served to "enshrine [her] within the tribe of a conservative academic elite" (925).

24   Laurence, Patricia, et al. "Symposium on Basic Writing, Conflict and Struggle, and the Legacy of Mina Shaughnessy." *College English* 55.8 (1993): 879–903. Print.

These six presentations explore and critique the foundations and philosophies of basic writing. Four of the contributors to this symposium are responding to critiques by Min-Zhan Lu and Paul Hunter in the December 1992 issue of *College English* of the work of basic writing pioneers Kenneth Bruffee, Thomas Farrell, and, especially, Mina Shaughnessy. Lu had argued for a pedagogy of conflict to help basic writers reposition themselves, and both Lu and Hunter had pointed to the influence of these pioneers and their followers as the conservative element resisting such pedagogy. Patricia Laurence and Barbara Gleason present the case for historicizing the discussion—for evaluating both the philosophy of the pioneers and the criticism of Lu and Hunter from the contexts in which each worked or works. Peter Rondinone, a former open-admission student at the City University of New York and now a college English professor, takes Lu to task for missing the point about conflict in the lives of many basic writing students, while Thomas Farrell includes personal experiences with Shaughnessy. The symposium concludes with responses by both Hunter and Lu, with Lu's being the more in-depth response to each of the preceding critiques.

25   Lerner, Neal. "Rejecting the Remedial Brand: The Rise and Fall of the Dartmouth Writing Clinic." *College Composition and Communication* 59.1 (2007): 13–35. Print.

Lerner argues that many universities, both public and private, are under increasing pressure to supplement shrinking government funding by securing private donations. To encourage alumni contributions, schools have to attract the highest achieving students, which they do by increasing their selectiveness and by adopting brands such as *flagship, excellence,* and *signature.* Lerner says, however, that adopting brands of excellence necessitates driving out or covering over any "remedial" brand of educational access, such as those that dominated the twentieth century. Lerner reads the history of Dartmouth's writing clinic in the context of the disappearance of remedial brands. He argues that Dartmouth's brand was re-envisioned in the 1950s to highlight the excellence of its students, and with the new brand, it was accepted that Dartmouth should expect the most of its students. The Dartmouth writing clinic, however, was branded from its inception in 1930 as "remedial," a place where students who needed extra help could go or to which they could be remanded. Ultimately, Dartmouth's institutional brand was in competition with the "remedial" brand of the writing clinic, which led to the eventual dismantling of the clinic as unhelpful and unnecessary. Lerner ends by calling for writing programs to present themselves in rhetorically savvy ways in order to avoid the fate of the Dartmouth writing clinic and to be afforded the opportunity to continue to serve the needs of developing writers.

26 Lu, Min-Zhan, and Bruce Horner. "Expectations, Interpretations and Contributions of Basic Writing." *Journal of Basic Writing* 19.1 (2000): 43–52. Print.

In its history of student-centered research and its commitment to students who have been traditionally marginalized and devalued by higher education, basic writing has been at the forefront of diversity and student-centered learning. Because students in basic writing exist in the borderlands between discourse communities, they are, presumably, the diverse students that the university's promotional materials seem to pursue. Thus Lu and Horner suggest that basic writers can teach faculty about the challenges diverse students face and the kinds of pedagogies that work for them. The authors also argue that basic writing must recognize and draw on basic writers' political agency, as students and faculty together fight against the nationwide assaults on basic writing programs.

27 Maher, Jane. "Writing the Life of Mina P. Shaughnessy." *Journal of Basic Writing* 16.1 (1997): 51–63. Print.

In this article, Maher introduces her biography, *Mina P. Shaughnessy: Her Life and Work*. Maher describes how her own education, ideals, and career have intersected with that of her subject. Similar working-class backgrounds, attendance (Maher) and teaching (Shaughnessy) at City University of New York colleges, and careers devoted to the education of basic writing students bring biographer and subject together. Maher tells the story of the biographical process—her interest in and respect for Shaughnessy's work, the initial impulse to write the story of Shaughnessy's life, the quest for information, and the difficulties of telling a life story. Readers are introduced to Mina Shaughnessy's life and, in its unfolding, discover what motivated her to advocate for open admissions and what made it possible for her to write the landmark work, *Errors and Expectations* [117]. The overview of Shaughnessy's life from her family history to her death provides a mini biography, while Maher's personal perspectives show the relationship of biographer to subject.

28 McBeth, Mark. "Arrested Development: Revising Remediation at John Jay College of Criminal Justice." *Journal of Basic Writing* 25.2 (2006): 76–93. Print.

Since the open admissions era of Mina Shaughnessy, "remedial courses" have shaped the identity of the City University of New York (CUNY); these sub-freshman courses have been revised depending on institutional missions, curricular initiatives, university policies, and political climates. Mark McBeth briefly reviews the history of remediation at CUNY and then describes an intensive developmental writing course implemented at John Jay College of Criminal Justice, explaining its strategies, rationales, successes, and remaining challenges. By synthesizing the perspectives of Lev Vygotsky and Mary Louise Pratt, this article demonstrates how this basic writing course combined these theories to offer students "a contact zone of proximal development." While responding to the constraints of a university policy where a gatekeeping exam (over)determines students' educational possibilities, this course curriculum resists teaching *to* the test and, instead, strives to teach *with* it. While helping students to fulfill a mandatory, high-stakes requirement, this instructional approach offers students the exposure to composing and critical thinking that productively launches their college careers.

29 McNenny, Gerri, ed. *Mainstreaming Basic Writers: Politics and Pedagogies of Access.* Mahwah: Erlbaum, 2001. Print.

This collection of essays presents many of the positions taken in response to recent challenges posed to basic writing instruction on four-year college campuses. At the same time, it offers alternative configurations for writing instruction that attempt to do justice to both students' needs and administrative constraints. Contributors include Edward M. White, Ira Shor, Mary Soliday, Trudy Smoke, Barbara Gleason, Terence G. Collins, Kim Lynch, Eleanor Agnew, Margaret McLaughlin, Marti Singer, Rosemary Winslow, Monica Mische, Mark Wiley, Gerri McNenny, and Sallyanne Fitzgerald.

30 Mutnick, Deborah. "On the Academic Margins: Basic Writing Pedagogy." *A Guide to Composition Pedagogies.* Ed. Gary Tate, Amy Rupiper, and Kurt Schick. New York: Oxford UP, 2001. 183–202. Print.

Mutnick outlines a detailed history of basic writing, beginning in the late 1960s with Mina Shaughnessy. She argues that Shaughnessy's major contributions were her ability to shift the focus of research from the students to the "teachers, administrators, and society" (185) and her understanding that the logical errors produced by students held the key to their attempts to arrive at conventional forms. Mutnick's history moves on to other theories of error that followed those of Shaughnessy and then to a discussion of process and cognitive theories and rhetorical theories. Mutnick also warns that we must prepare ourselves to counter political decisions now being made in higher education.

31 Mutnick, Deborah. "The Strategic Value of Basic Writing: An Analysis of the Current Moment." *Journal of Basic Writing* 19.1 (2000): 69–83. Print.

Like the political assaults on other opportunities for equal access to higher education—efforts to reverse affirmative action and to end open admissions—eradicating basic writing will re-segregate higher education. Thus well-meaning compositionists who fear that basic writing has reinscribed the injustices it sought to remedy should reconsider their efforts to eliminate basic writing. In documenting the success of basic writing programs, experiments with new models of instruction, and partnerships between high schools and universities, Mutnick argues that everyone in our discipline who cares about social justice should find ways to make basic writing more effective and just for traditionally underprepared and marginalized groups.

32 Ray, Brian. "A New World: Redefining the Legacy of Min-Zhan Lu." *Journal of Basic Writing* 27.2 (2008): 106–27. Print.

In this article Ray discusses exchanges between a number of scholars during the 1990s centering on Min-Zhan Lu's controversial essay "Conflict and Struggle: The Enemies or Preconditions of Basic Writing?" In some ways, "Conflict and Struggle" blazed a trail for later work in "hybrid" or "mixed" forms of academic writing while at the same time igniting debate over Mina Shaughnessy's legacy. Rather than take sides, Ray considers what perspectives and considerations were left out of this years-long standoff and attempts to reconcile this issue in basic writing theory through relevant but less-discussed work in linguistics. The concept of linguistic charity, an area of growing interest in composition studies, offers a particularly refreshing new direction for discussion regarding the ambiguous and often controversial role of Standard English in our pedagogies.

See: Min-Zhan Lu, "Conflict and Struggle" [235].

33 Ribble, Marcia. "Redefining Basic Writing: An Image Shift from Error to Rhizome." *BWe: Basic Writing e-Journal* 3.1 (2001): n. pag. Web. 11 Aug. 2009.

Ribble advocates a shift in our thinking about basic writing and writers: from error as the defining characteristic to the metaphor of a rhizome as a connected, ecological system. Ribble shows the way a student's paper simultaneously exhibits good writing, creativity in expressing ideas and feelings, and multiple errors in spelling, punctuation, and grammar. Drawing on Gilles Deleuze and Felix Guattari, Ribble discusses four rhizomic principles: connectivity relates to our desire to communicate with others; heterogeneity represents linguistic variety; multiplicity represents the complexity of writing and writers; and a signifying rupture addresses the fragmentation that change creates. Errors therefore are a necessary part of the life-long process of learning and writing. The rhizome metaphor is especially relevant to technological communication: "only a metaphor as complex as the rhizome can handle the multitasking our students are born into" (par. 33). We would do well, Ribble suggests, to re-think our conceptions of basic writing in similar ways.

34   Ritter, Kelly. "Before Mina Shaughnessy: Basic Writing at Yale, 1920–1960." *College Composition and Communication* 60.1 (2008): 12–45. Print.

Ritter's article is an insightful piece using archival materials to point out and describe the "Awkward Squad" at Yale. It includes a historical perspective of basic composition courses. She compares and contrasts the use of basic studies in composition as a means to hold standards high, to include the elite at Ivy League schools, and to exclude others. During that time a course to remediate basic writers was not officially on the course list. It had a derogatory name, and being a part of this unprepared group of students had a negative connotation. As Ritter brings the reader up to date with the changes in the academic world, in the makeup of college students and their preparation for the higher education experience, she argues for "a re-definition of *basic* in composition studies." (12). She cites many references and statistics to give readers insight into this topic.

35   Rose, Mike. "The Language of Exclusion: Writing Instruction at the University." *College English* 47.4 (1985): 341–59. Print.

Rose argues that "institutional language about writing instruction in American higher education" effectively "keeps writing instruction at the periphery of the curriculum" (341). This language and its attendant metaphors are based on behaviorist models and misunderstandings about writing and do not take students' abilities and needs into account. Rose discusses in detail the effects of behaviorism and quantification on thinking about writing: they emphasize correctness, mechanistic paradigms, and pseudoscientific reasoning rather than the social context of error. Defining writing as a "skill" rather than as a means of inquiry has political and educational implications. The terminology associated with remediation originated in law and medicine, and its application to writing instruction is critiqued in the context of this medical metaphor. The language of literacy and illiteracy is inadequate to represent the realities of basic writing instruction. Also, according to the "myth of transience" (355), the problems associated with basic writing and writers could be cured and thereby eliminated if certain criteria could be met.

Remediation as a metaphor must be abandoned. Rose concludes that "wide-ranging change will occur only if the academy redefines writing for itself, changes the terms of the argument, sees instruction in writing as one of its central concerns" (359).

36   Rose, Mike. *Possible Lives*. New York: Penguin, 1995. Print.

With this study, Rose seeks to inspire more careful critique of schools because "our national discussion about public schools is despairing and dismissive, and it is shutting down our civic imagination" (1). Rose observed classrooms across the country, concluding that good classrooms are safe classrooms where teachers respect students and manage to share authority with them. Teaching like this involves the interplay of multiple "knowledges," some of which are brought to the classroom by teachers, and some by students. Even in the "at-risk" environments Rose describes, there is great possibility for public education to construct active and critical citizens, but only if schools recognize the "possible lives" that fill the halls each day.

37   Royster, Jacqueline Jones, and Rebecca Greenberg Taylor. "Constructing Teacher Identity in the Basic Writing Classroom." *Journal of Basic Writing* 16.1 (1997): 27–50. Print.

Royster and Taylor challenge us to examine the place of teachers in the classroom, calling for a shift in the gaze that has been turned— nearly throughout the whole of basic writing scholarship—toward students. How are teachers, they ask, located in the basic writing classroom? This reading is decidedly against the grain of basic writing scholarship, for Royster and Taylor interrogate teacher identity and its absence as a focus of research in basic writing. They remark that they had "become impatient with the discussion of identity, most especially in basic writing classrooms, as the *students'* problem, rather than also as the *teacher's* problem" (28). Their call for additional research on teacher identity as an informing element of classrooms speaks to the tendency in composition studies at large to deny the power of teacher authority. The essay stands as a call for new and vigorous inquiry into the location of teachers in the college writing classroom, the ways students see teachers, and the implications of those constructs for the basic writing classroom.

38   Salas, Spencer. "Roberta; or, the Ambiguities: Tough Love and High-Stakes Assessment at a Two-Year College in North Georgia." *Journal of Basic Writing* 27.2 (2008): 5–28. Print.

This ethnographic narrative employs a neo-Vygotskian perspective (Holland et al.) to examine how, in the setting of a remedial English as a second language (ESL) program at a public two-year college in

North Georgia, the subject position of an ESL basic writing instructor was mediated by her understandings of and engagement with the multiple and interactive contexts of her professional activity. Despite a wide variety of tensions that complicated the instructor's understandings of who she was professionally, she was able to position herself in ways that allowed her to make sense of her professional choices. However, her construction of gatekeeping as advocacy brought with it an emotional toll at the end of each semester when some students passed and some students failed— shaking the sense of her tough-love pedagogical stance. Representations of basic writing professionals are critiqued to argue for the need for more nuanced research for and with basic writing faculty in the activist college composition literature.

39   Sheridan-Rabideau, Mary P., and Gordon Brossell. "Finding Basic Writing's Place." *Journal of Basic Writing* 14.1 (1995): 21–26. Print.
Sheridan-Rabideau and Brossell defend the effectiveness of basic writing courses on college campuses. They argue that colleges and universities are obligated to provide the support that enables students to succeed, particularly support for students who are underprepared. Inexperience leads basic writers to demonstrate a range of writing problems. Therefore, basic writing classes should not be a mix of more and less proficient writers, should have fewer students, should meet for more hours than regular composition courses, and should be taught by well-trained faculty who provide extensive feedback on students' writing. Basic writing classes should provide a safe, supportive environment where underprepared students can gain the confidence and skills that can help them achieve academic success.

40   Shor, Ira. "Errors and Economics: Inequality Breeds Remediation." *Mainstreaming Basic Writers*. Ed. Gerri McNenny. Mahwah: Erlbaum, 2001. 29–54. Print.
Shor begins this essay with an analysis of the work of Mina Shaughnessy, Adrienne Rich, and Leonard Greenbaum, all teachers of writing at the City College of New York during the open admissions period, who believed that the emphasis on "correctness" in language instruction could "debase" (Shaughnessy) and disempower students. Shor then connects their positions to John Kenneth Galbraith's proposal that economics drives education policy. An analysis of the economic context of first-year writing instruction, according to Shor, can help explain its political contradictions, complaints, and choices, such as its focus on error and correctness. This focus, he argues, reflects the values of an elite culture and reproduces the inequalities necessary for that culture to remain elite. The kind of

long-term instruction in the "correct" use of language embedded in K–16 writing instruction shapes students' and teachers' views of the world. To change those views, Shor proposes a critical writing curriculum that would replace the one currently in place and a democratic labor policy that would replace the exploitation of cheap labor in the staffing of courses.

See: Mina P. Shaughnessy, *Errors and Expectations* [117].

41   Shor, Ira. "Inequality (Still) Rules: Reply to Collins and Greenberg." *Journal of Basic Writing* 17.1 (1998): 104–08. Print.

This response to criticism by Karen Greenberg [15] and Terence Collins [8] repeats Shor's basic points from his original article: teachers of basic writing are an exploited labor force; claims for the success of basic writing programs are equivocal; minority and working-class students are overrepresented in basic writing classes; and most basic writing curricula perpetuate a pedagogy of disembodied language arts and impede a pedagogy of critical engagement with everyday life.

42   Shor, Ira. "Our Apartheid: Writing Instruction and Inequality." *Journal of Basic Writing* 16.1 (1997): 91–104. Print.

Shor argues that basic writing as a field is in a state of permanent crisis. While composition functions as a linguistic gatekeeper in the university, basic writing acts as a gate below the gate. As part of the undemocratic tracking system in mass education, basic writing successfully impedes the academic progress of nonelite students. In effect, Shor suggests that basic writing supports a top-down, business-oriented agenda that is designed to keep the status quo by moving nonelite students into vocational jobs and disciplined lives. As a basement course that is often taught by marginalized, overworked adjuncts, basic writing fosters depressed wages and few health benefits. Democratic education demands an end to educational apartheid through the dismantling of basic writing.

See: Terence G. Collins, "A Response to Ira Shor's 'Our Apartheid'" [8].

See: Karen L. Greenberg, "A Response to Ira Shor's 'Our Apartheid'" [15].

43   Stygall, Gail. "Unraveling at Both Ends: Anti-Undergraduate Education, Anti-Affirmative Action, and Basic Writing at Research Schools." *Journal of Basic Writing* 18.2 (1999): 4–22. Print.

Basic writing programs at West Coast research universities face a double bind: the privileging of research and graduate education in comparison to all lower-division undergraduate writing courses (especially basic writing courses) and the passing of anti–affirmative action ballot initiatives. The University of Washington is a case in point. The "unraveling" of its basic writing program is demonstrated through critical discourse analysis of three texts: the university's "master plan" for the next twenty years; a Seattle newspaper's take on the Educational Opportunity Program, which houses basic writing, and Initiative-2000, which bans "preferential" treatment in education; and the conclusions of the Washington 2000 Commission, a gubernatorial commission formed to determine the future of higher education in Washington State.

44 Summerfield, Judith, et al. "The City University of New York and the Shaughnessy Legacy: Today's Scholars Talk Back." *Journal of Basic Writing* 26.2 (2007): 5–29. Print.

Based on a thirtieth-anniversary roundtable discussion on the Shaughnessy legacy for the CUNY system, this article offers short contributions on topics ranging from a neglected text, *Beat Not the Poor Desk*, that was a direct challenge to the Shaughnessy project in *Errors and Expectations*, to the continuing necessity for educators to consider their own "deficiencies" as often as they consider those of the students; from the links that unite doctoral ways of researching with meaningful teaching to the ways Shaughnessy's attentiveness to systematic kinds of errors has enriched second language instruction. The focus is on Shaughnessy's legacy of understanding, of valuing students typically devalued by the academy, and of "access politics," or the ways students learn the language of the academy in order to gain entrance to the kinds of education previously denied them.

45 Trimmer, Joseph F. "Basic Skills, Basic Writing, Basic Research." *Journal of Basic Writing* 6.1 (1987): 3–9. Print.

Survey responses from 900 two- and four-year colleges and universities reveal that a majority have some form of basic writing program and that most are housed in English departments. Teaching assistants or part-time faculty teach the bulk of basic writing courses, with only a few receiving systematic teaching orientation. Building on Robert Connors's study of the remedial textbook market, Trimmer interviewed representatives from twenty publishing houses, who revealed that editors find the remedial textbook market "difficult and disheartening" (6) because schools are caught in political predicaments that force them to adopt workbooks or sentence-grammar texts. Editors have read extensively on basic writing research but have witnessed good textbook proposals become publishing disasters. Perhaps basic writing research has no impact because remedial English teachers are too overworked to read research, or perhaps the research simply is not known, not understood, or not believed because it challenges tradition.

See: Robert J. Connors, "Basic Writing Textbooks" [190].

46   Troyka, Lynn Quitman. "Defining Basic Writing in Context." *A Sourcebook for Basic Writing Teachers*. Ed. Theresa Enos. New York: Random, 1987. 2–15. Print.

Although *basic writing* is a much more positive term than the medical *remedial* and the condescending *developmental*, readers are cautioned not to generalize about what basic writers do or who they are. *Remedial, developmental,* and *basic* oversimplify the diverse students who are often labeled as *underprepared*. Troyka defines basic writing in historical relation to remedial writing and developmental writing as well as through a national survey of basic writing essays she completed to better shape future basic writing scholarship and teaching. She offers two crucial conclusions. First, basic writers are not simply writers; hence any definition of basic writing must take into account how "basic writers need to immerse themselves in language in all its forms" (13). Thus teachers and researchers need to consider the centrality of reading to writing. Second, teachers must define basic writers in context, which means teachers must "describe with examples our student populations when we write about basic writers" (13). This important essay demonstrates why the diversity of our students and the context of their specific writing situations cannot be generalized through the term *basic writing*.

47   Troyka, Lynn Quitman. "How We Have Failed the Basic Writing Enterprise." *Journal of Basic Writing* 19.1 (2000): 113–23. Print.

Written as a letter to the editors of the *Journal of Basic Writing*, this essay contends that basic writing scholars and practitioners have failed the "BW enterprise" (114). First, basic writing scholarship and practice have not dealt effectively with public relations issues. Troyka contends that to be more successful, basic writing needs to be more visible and articulate within the popular media. Second, Troyka argues that basic writing has suffered from the lack of real assessment outcomes. Since scholars have tended to avoid longitudinal studies, there has been little tangible evidence for the validity of the efforts. Third, Troyka contends that in an effort to value students' voices and political, social, and cultural differences, we have simultaneously ignored the potential values of grammar instruction. She urges us to find new and innovative ways to teach grammar rather than ignore it. Finally, Troyka proffers that basic writing has limited the kinds of scholarly inquiries that are considered valuable, necessarily marginalizing certain kinds of research while privileging others. In closing, however, she suggests that successes can be found in basic writing teaching, an important site for theorizing. For Troyka, this is a location where she feels innovative work continues to be accomplished, a place that, if studied closely, might help us rectify other problems.

48   Wiener, Harvey S. "The Attack on Basic Writing—and After." *Journal of Basic Writing* 17.1 (1998): 96–103. Print.

Basic writing is under attack on many fronts, and such attacks are at least partly caused by ineffective marketing. That is, too many people see basic writing as remedial without understanding what it is, what it is intended to do, or where it fits in the academy. Wiener suggests that such attacks on funding and the outsourcing of basic writing classes and students will go on but that we must continue to work to counter these attacks.

Basic Writers: Who We Teach

49   Adler-Kassner, Linda. "Just Writing, Basically: Basic Writers on Basic Writing." *Journal of Basic Writing* 18.2 (1999): 69–90. Print.

At the University of Michigan–Dearborn, Adler-Kassner and her colleague Randy Woodland interviewed sixteen randomly chosen students about basic writers and basic writing. Adler-Kassner identifies three issues that emerged from the students' responses. First, employing coursework designed to erase the stigma of being labeled a basic writer is a difficult endeavor because most students do not fully understand what that label means. In addition, students in the study tended to equate writing and reading with English courses only and found their composition coursework to be irrelevant to their purpose for attending college. Finally, instead of blaming grammatical conventions for their status as basic writers, these students spoke of an inability to transfer the thoughts in their heads onto paper successfully. Adler-Kassner states that we must address these issues when designing our basic writing courses and that we must first explain to students what this *basic writer* label means. After understanding the label, the students need to work to contest it. This may be accomplished through inquiry-based research during the class.

50   Adler-Kassner, Linda. "Review: Structure and Possibility: New Scholarship about Students-Called-Basic-Writers." *College English* 63.2 (2000): 229–43. Print.

Adler-Kassner discusses five important books that either explore basic writing and basic writers directly (Susan Gardner and Toby

Fulwiler's *Journal Book for Teachers of At-Risk College Writers* [148], Laura Gray-Rosendale's *Rethinking Basic Writing* [63], and Michelle Hall Kells and Valerie Balester's *Attending to the Margins*) or provide historical and social arguments relevant to theorizing and questioning the concept of basic writing (Bradford T. Stull's *Amid the Fall, Dreaming of Eden* and Paulo Freire's *Pedagogy of Freedom*). Adler-Kassner notes that research about basic writing students has changed from dwelling on what is wrong with basic writers to questioning the academic and social structures that perpetuate the "idea" of a basic writer. She finds that most of these books adopt the latter stance.

51   Bartholomae, David. "The Study of Error." *College Composition and Communication* 31.3 (1980): 253–69. Print.

Bartholomae extends Mina Shaughnessy's hope that teachers, especially basic writing teachers, will examine how they view errors in student writing. For example, he suggests that teachers who cannot understand student prose do not read the prose as complex texts and thus do not find the logic at work in many errors. Bartholomae demonstrates this point by showing the logic behind some student writing, drawing especially from the work of "John," who caught and corrected many of his errors while reading his paper aloud. Bartholomae ultimately offers a glimpse as to the effectiveness of error analysis and what it should accomplish: "It begins with the double perspective of text and reconstructed text and seeks to explain the difference between the two" (265). Overall, basic writing teachers need to separate performance from competence and focus on how to help students create strategies to accomplish each.

52   Bartholomae, David. "Writing on the Margins: The Concept of Literacy in Higher Education." *A Sourcebook for Basic Writing Teachers.* Ed. Theresa Enos. New York: Random, 1987. 66–83. Print.

Marginal writers differ from mainstream writers in the number and kinds of their grammatical errors and also in their methods of organizing, producing, and using texts. The precise nature of the fluency that separates marginal from mainstream academic literacy is explored in this examination of "borderline" texts. Beginning with Mina Shaughnessy's error analysis of basic writers' approximations of conventional sentences, Bartholomae argues that basic writers' use of language follows similar "styles of being wrong" (68). Academic literacy can be measured by the extent to which writers can appropriate the historical and social conventions of an already existing university discourse. Using historical and recent examples, the author analyzes writers' attempts to appropriate the language of the academy and suggests that basic writers should be assigned academic projects that will position them within its accepted discourses. Advanced literacy extends beyond the ability to use academic conventions successfully to a consciousness of speaking through appropriated forms and the capacity to push against them.

53 Bay, Libby. "Twists, Turns, and Returns: Returning Adult Students." *Teaching Developmental Writing: Background Readings*. Ed. Susan Naomi Bernstein. Boston: Bedford, 2001. 167–75. Print.

Bay reports on a research project that she conducted involving students over the age of twenty-four at Rockland Community College in Suffern, New York. Based on responses to questionnaires and one-on-one interviews, Bay concludes that adult students need help dealing with the unique issues they face when returning to school and that faculty and the school itself need help understanding and addressing adult students' needs. She recommends granting credit for adult students' life experiences and requiring a separate orientation to help adult students deal with time management and other issues that they face.

54 Bernstein, Susan Naomi. "A Limestone Way of Learning." *Chronicle of Higher Education* 10 Oct. 2003: n. pag. Web. 19 Nov. 2008.

Bernstein uses her personal experience in an introductory geology class to argue for the continued importance of basic writing classes at the university level—classes whose place in the college curriculum is being questioned both from within the university and from without. She also uses this experience to suggest how instructors might approach teaching a basic writing class. She explains that her early difficulty with nonverbal learning, in high school science and math classes, might have held her education back significantly had she not been born to a middle-class, suburban family. The benefit of expressive, creative assignments allowed her to capitalize on her writing ability, which either hid or compensated for her other learning difficulties. Bernstein thus argues that the challenge writing presents for students in basic writing classes encourages them to grow, personally and intellectually, just as her geology class challenged her and gave her a lifelong appreciation of the field. Likewise, the challenge for teachers of basic writers is to assume that they are eager and motivated learners and to support a holistic model of learning. Rather than define basic writers by the skills they lack, teachers must look to their strengths and to what they have overcome to reach their current position. Bernstein concludes that the benefits students can gain by being challenged through writing classes extend past the writing classroom to strengthen and enrich their world, both inside and outside the university.

55   Bizzell, Patricia. "Literacy in Culture and Cognition." *A Sourcebook for Basic Writing Teachers.* Ed. Theresa Enos. New York: Random, 1987. 125–37. Print.

Bizzell suggests that literacy scholarship is commonly divided into two main schools of thought: those who embrace the "Great Cognitive Divide" theory, which posits that the acquisition of literacy is a stage in human cognitive development, and those who question this theory and focus instead on literacy as social practice. This latter group demonstrates that literacy ought not be treated monolithically but rather examined within social and cultural contexts. In applying literacy research to the question of whether American college students are literate, Bizzell argues for a definition of academic literacy that takes into account its social context and its specific social purposes. While debate continues about literacy of any kind, functional literacy—"literacy that confers a reasonable degree of education and economic success and political participation" (135)—enables critical reflection on the different relations between social groups and on the educational, economic, and political differences that separate them.

56   Bizzell, Patricia. "What Happens When Basic Writers Come to College?" *College Composition and Communication* 37.3 (1986): 294–301. Print.

Three theories, none satisfactory in itself, answer the question posed by the article's title. Basic writers experience a clash between their home dialects and the language of college; basic writers experience a clash between the discourse forms and genres of their worlds prior to college and the discourse forms and genres of formal college writing; and basic writers experience problems arising from their lack of cognitive development (as measured by the developmental schemes of Jean Piaget or William Perry). These three reductive theories can be synthesized into a comprehensive view by means of the notion of discourse community. What basic writers experience is a profound clash of world views. While the discourse communities from which basic writers emerge have not been studied in sufficient depth, it seems certain that the world view favored by the academy will challenge that of basic writers new to college. The academy requires a skeptical, questioning frame of mind (what Perry calls a world with "no Absolutes") and a rational choice of beliefs (what Perry calls "Commitments"), rather than unquestioning faith.

57   DiPardo, Anne. "Whispers of Coming and Going: Lessons from Fannie." *Teaching Developmental Writing: Background Readings.* 3rd ed. Ed. Susan Naomi Bernstein. Boston: Bedford, 2007. 440–57. Print.

DiPardo's case study of Fannie, a struggling Native American student in a basic writing tutorial program, illustrates the ways in which multicultural writers and linguistic minority students—and often their teachers and tutors as well—must occupy multiple roles as they work together to navigate the terrain of academic literacy. Echoing previous calls by Shaughnessy, Hull, and Rose that entreat teachers both to listen to and learn from their students, the lessons of Fannie and her writing tutor, Morgan, emphasize the importance of relationship building when working with basic writers. To this end, DiPardo argues that teachers and tutors must be adequately prepared to engage in a process of true collaborative learning: "More than specific instructional strategies, Morgan needed the conceptual grounding that would allow her to understand that authentically collaborative learning is predicated upon fine-grained insight into individual students" (456). Finally, DiPardo notes that reflective practice, including the willingness to interrogate one's approaches and actions critically and consistently, is a key part of such collaborative learning both for the student and the teacher, who must model these strategies in his or her relationship with the basic writer.

58   Eves-Bowden, Anmarie. "What Basic Writers Think about Writing." *Journal of Basic Writing* 20.2 (2001): 71–87. Print.

Eves-Bowden chronicles her study of seven basic writers at a California college, examining how they perceive of themselves as writers, how they view their writing processes, and how their writing processes "might limit [their] ability to succeed on a typical college writing assignment" (71). Eves-Bowden discovered that these writers did have a writing process but that it was neither complex nor structured in any way. Most of the students admitted that they had no idea of what to say about an assigned topic, of how to generate any ideas, or of what revision entailed. As a result of her study, Eves-Bowden integrated Linda Flower and John Hayes's "cognitive process model" because "of its easy-to-follow diagram and simple explanations of each recursive step" (76). This particular approach provided her students with a structure from which they could "explore their beliefs, expectations, and perspectives" (81).

59   Fox, Tom. "Basic Writing as Cultural Conflict." *Journal of Education* 172.1 (1990): 65–83. Print.

Fox foregrounds the relationship between basic writing theories and the pedagogies that continue to marginalize students new to universities, including speakers of nonstandard English and, frequently, African Americans. Unfolding the pedagogical ideologies perpetuated by even the most well-meaning teachers, Fox illuminates inequities between the students' use of literacy to negotiate social identities and the institutions' authoritative positioning. He suggests that although recent explorations into discourse communities reveal differences and offer more helpful explanations, resultant pedagogies continue to be ineffective in dislodging the ideologies in which basic writing programs have been grounded. John Ogbu's theory of oppositional culture is offered as a more comprehensive ideological framework that "emphasizes the issues of historically based discrimination and the association of literacy as an instrument of domination" (74). As evidence of a need for a new consciousness in the classroom and political activism within the institution, Fox includes an essay, complete with "errors," written by a student in a basic writing course. He then describes how, in spite of the surface errors, the essay "is a successful piece of academic work" (80) in its use of literacy to "explore and discover connections and conflicts" (80) among the social contexts the student inhabits.

60   Gray-Rosendale, Laura. "Back to the Future: Contextuality and the Construction of the Basic Writer's Identity in *JBW*, 1999–2005." *Journal of Basic Writing* 25.2 (2006): 5–27. Print.

In a continuation of her previous historical review of the *JBW*'s collective construct of basic writing students' identities, Gray-Rosendale asserts in this recent review that three major shifts now dominate the *JBW*'s scholarly landscape of basic writing students' identity construction. The most important shift in this construction repositions much of the scholarly activity as deconstructing locally contingent and place-specific influences, a move that places identity formation "as *in situ*—or context dependent" (8). The second shift suggests that basic writing students have been cast as reformers of theory, academic discourse, and history. The author synthesizes a growing number of scholars who argue that this construction of identity reveals a growing need to reflect on our own scholarship, and especially those representations of implied and explicit powers held by students to reform institutions and themselves. The third shift in scholarship seems to distract attention away from the construction of students' identities and instead moves toward the formalized study of students' personal habits and practices and asks what these practices reveal about the personal, institutional, and political conditions of the basic writing student and how we might use these studies to enrich basic writing scholarship.

61   Gray-Rosendale, Laura. "Inessential Writings: Shaughnessy's Legacy in a Socially Constructed Landscape." *Journal of Basic Writing* 17.2 (1998): 43–75. Print.

Min-Zhan Lu's 1992 article "Conflict and Struggle: The Enemies or Preconditions of Basic Writing?" [235] inspired a flurry of feminist, Marxist, and poststructuralist reexaminations of Mina Shaughnessy's work. These critiqued Shaughnessy on three counts: for forwarding an "essentialist" conception of language that separates thought from expression and views discourse as a transparent vessel for meaning; for promoting basic writers' accommodation to mainstream linguistic standards and thereby minimizing the political dimensions of language use; and for overlooking materialist considerations such as the economic, social, and institutional issues surrounding basic writers and the teaching of basic writing. Gray-Rosendale systematically explores each of these charges through close readings of critics' and Shaughnessy's texts and ultimately concludes that "Shaughnessy's works render ambiguous if not outright defy many such negative characterizations" (46).

62 Gray-Rosendale, Laura. "Investigating Our Discursive History: *JBW* and the Construction of the 'Basic Writer's' Identity." *Journal of Basic Writing* 18.2 (1999): 108–35. Print.

Focusing on research that has appeared in the *Journal of Basic Writing*, Gray-Rosendale reviews the history of basic writing and describes how this history has influenced the construction of basic writers' identities. She discusses how trends such as the growth, initiation, and conflict metaphors have influenced the way that the scholarship defined basic writers. Lastly, Gray-Rosendale discusses the current state of the basic writer's identity in basic writing scholarship and points toward the future of basic writers in our research.

63 Gray-Rosendale, Laura. *Rethinking Basic Writing: Exploring Identity, Politics, and Community in Interaction.* Mahwah: Erlbaum, 2000. Print.

Gray-Rosendale introduces her study by asking, "Who is the Basic Writer?" Quickly declaring that this question is not useful, she asks, "What can and does the Basic Writer do?" (5). In addressing this generative question, Gray-Rosendale explores students' agency in an array of literacy tasks. She begins by using poststructural, ethnographic, and conversational theories for her analysis of a summer "bridge" course at Syracuse University designed for students considered "at risk by the higher administration" for failure in first-year composition (1). She then focuses on the interactions of the four students in one peer group in the class, analyzing their conversations about drafts of papers and showing how these students helped each other to make informed and remarkably diverse choices as they composed. After demonstrating some motivations for students' writing, she offers suggestions for teachers, administrators, and legislators.

64   Gray-Rosendale, Laura. "Revising the Political in Basic Writing Scholarship." *Journal of Basic Writing* 15.2 (1996): 24–49. Print.

Gray-Rosendale suggests that focusing on a definition of basic writers interferes with developing a complete, sound pedagogy. She argues that basic writers' definitions of themselves do not match those of basic writing faculty or higher-education administration, that their reflections of self have been largely ignored, and that their constructions of identity must be placed in the forefront. Her analysis of a conversation among four Syracuse University students during a reader review of a politically charged writing assignment demonstrates the complexities of these constructions. Gray-Rosendale recommends that studies of in-class interactions be done to determine how the students "construct new identities" (47). Such extended examination of student interactions is the next step for basic writing as a discipline.

65   Gray-Rosendale, Laura, Loyola K. Bird, and Judith F. Bullock. "Rethinking the Basic Writing Frontier: Native American Students' Challenge to Our Histories." *Journal of Basic Writing* 22.1 (2003): 71–106. Print.

The three authors draw on their own experiences—as an administrator of a program serving many Native American basic writers (Gray-Rosendale), as a Jicarilla Apache Indian formerly classified as a basic writer and currently a graduate student in English (Bird), and as a tutor of Native American basic writers in a boarding high school (Bullock)—to challenge assumptions made about Native American writers and metaphors used in basic writing scholarship. The authors contend that many Native Americans face difficulties with college writing because researchers have ignored them in basic writing research and because the "myth of frontierism" (74) informs both basic writing studies and American ideology. Metaphors like "frontier," "pioneer," and "insider/outsider" (75), frequently used in basic writing, are based on a pioneer mentality in which the civilized university culture tames and assimilates the uncivilized Native Americans. The absence of a sustained critique of these metaphors and of the ways they are used to frame understandings of writers has led to an essentialist view of Native American students of English as foreign language students largely unfamiliar with the culture of the academy. The authors urge teachers, administrators, and scholars to elicit stories from their Native American students by meeting on "Indian land" as "settlers" rather than "pioneers" (83).

66   Gruber, Sibylle. "On the Other Side of the Electronic Circuit: A Virtual Remapping of Border Crossings." *Journal of Basic Writing* 18.1 (1999): 55–75. Print.

Gruber questions the simplistic categorizing of students into majority and minority in this case study of an African American student's participation in a basic writing class's online discussions. Depending on the context of the discussion, the student occupies multiple subject positions—an ethnic minority, a majority male, and a minority homosexual—while recognizing the connection between being a gay black man in a white, patriarchal, homophobic society. Gruber argues that teachers must avoid homogenizing nontraditional students and must recognize the multiple and complicated subjectivities reflected in their language use in online communities.

67   Harrington, Susanmarie. "The Representation of Basic Writers in Basic Writing Scholarship, or Who Is Quentin Pierce?" *Journal of Basic Writing* 18.2 (1999): 91–107. Print.

Harrington examines the research published in volumes 1–17 of the *Journal of Basic Writing* by reviewing trends in research topics. She reveals the tendency in the research to focus on teacher expectations rather than on student needs. The article argues that the research could be enriched by considering students and their voices when conducting and writing research.

68   Haswell, Richard H. *Gaining Ground in College Writing: Tales of Development and Interpretation.* Dallas: Southern Methodist UP, 1991. Print.

Students arrive in writing classes in the midst of complex lives, bringing a great deal of knowledge with them. The changes they undergo as maturing, growing, changing organisms reflect influences throughout their personal, physical, and psychic histories, and the more developmental metaphors teachers employ to understand changes in students and themselves, the better teachers can describe and celebrate the ground students gain. Overlooking change in dimensions separate from writing, he argues, may mean missing evidence of students' gains. What appears to be regression to an earlier skill level may be daring experimentation that needs to be brought under control. What appears to be confidence in a given genre may be a retreat into a rhetorical safety zone. To study student writing, Haswell employs tales of development and interpretation from sources that range from Jean Piaget to William Wordsworth and from Erik Erikson to Hans-Georg Gadamer. Haswell demonstrates repeatedly that skill acquisition occurs as a result of competing tensions: as students experiment with new syntactical forms, they temporarily lose control of forms that had functioned reliably. Growth is a destabilizing activity, and the new always disrupts the status quo.

69 Hull, Glynda, et al. "Remediation as Social Construct: Perspectives from an Analysis of Classroom Discourse." *College Composition and Communication* 42.3 (1991): 299–329. Print.

Explanations for the low achievement of some students have pointed to deficits within the student (via the student's character, intellect, environment, or culture). Thus instructors working with remedial writers will easily enter a cycle in which they (1) ascribe a student's nonmainstream behaviors to a cognitive or social deficit, (2) construct their interaction with the student in response to that perceived deficit, and (3) limit the kinds of interactions and activities students are allowed in the classroom. Such limitations subsequently serve to eliminate discourse and activities that would disprove the deficit label or move the student and teacher beyond it. Evidence of this cycle is offered through analysis of classroom interactions between June, a well-trained writing instructor, and Maria, a student whose style of conversational turn taking does not match that valued by June. This case, in which June constructs Maria as a remedial, scattered thinker—despite the cogency of much of Maria's commentary and her history of achievement in academic and literary pursuits—shows that teachers must pay closer attention to the complex dynamics surrounding classroom talk to avoid making misleading judgments about students' abilities and deficits.

70 Kutz, Eleanor, Suzy Q. Groden, and Vivian Zamel. *The Discovery of Competence: Teaching and Learning with Diverse Student Writers.* Portsmouth: Heinemann, 1993. Print.

Over a ten-year period, the authors collaborated on a research project that engaged their urban basic writing students, whose primary language was not English, in the work of an academic community. In this book, the authors focus on how language is acquired; how teachers can facilitate students' development of this acquisition; how culture is represented through language; how thinking, speaking, and writing develop; how active inquiry facilitates these understandings; and how curricula can provide the necessary context for this learning to occur. Through their research, the authors recognized that students learn the structure of writing and language through active engagement and practice with written language in a collaborative environment in which they are expected to build on their knowledge and reflect on their learning processes.

71 Liese, Daniela. "Review Essay on Marilyn Sternglass's *Time to Know Them.*" *Journal of Basic Writing* 18.1 (1999): 21–26. Print.

Liese affirms the need for Marilyn Sternglass's *Time to Know Them: A Longitudinal Study of Writing and Learning at the College Level* [82], which examines nine City College of New York (CCNY) students' academic and personal lives. Liese argues that Sternglass's conclusions (that these students can succeed against overwhelming odds if given the time necessary to learn and if time is taken to know them) are valid. Sternglass contends that political decisions directly affecting the funding available for higher education and the administrative call for writing assessment tests made the situation for basic writers more troublesome in the late 1990s than it was when Mina Shaughnessy wrote *Errors and Expectations* [117] about students at CCNY in the 1970s. *Time to Know Them* is a plea to recognize the possibility of success and what can be done to foster that success.

72   Lunsford, Andrea A. "Cognitive Development and the Basic Writer." *College English* 41.1 (1979): 38–46. Print.

Based on her study of basic writers at The Ohio State University, Lunsford argues that basic writers have not attained the level of cognitive development required to succeed at college-level work. Because they have not developed the cognitive ability to decenter themselves to perform tasks that require synthesis and analysis, basic writers have difficulty forming abstract concepts. Lunsford recommends that basic writing teachers use various strategies, ranging from grammar and sentence-building activities to essay assignments, to engage students in inferential reasoning rather than in isolated drill exercises and rule memorization. Working in small group workshops, basic writing students should be allowed to practice analyzing, generalizing, and then abstracting, all of which are skills that they need to succeed in college.

73   Minot, Walter S., and Kenneth R. Gamble. "Self-Esteem and Writing Apprehension of Basic Writers: Conflicting Evidence." *Journal of Basic Writing* 10.2 (1991): 116–24. Print.

The notion that self-esteem and writing apprehension can define basic writers as a distinct homogenous group is challenged by the results of an empirical study. Basic writing programs do not seem to acknowledge that basic writing students are a heterogeneous population with diverse, individual writing difficulties; instead, it labels them as a predictable, constant group. This study looked at sixteen sections of regular composition and three sections of basic writing, and the data gathered indicate the potential that self-esteem and writing apprehension may have in writing situations. Remarkably, one basic writing section "had lower writing apprehension and higher self-esteem than sixteen classes of regular composition" (121). These results suggest that conflating self-esteem and writing apprehension limits the affective, cognitive, developmental, social, and cultural influences and expectations that basic writers bring to their writing. Rather than dismissing self-esteem and writing apprehension, however, this study calls for more research and writing on the "emotional atmosphere" (122) that surrounds the different writing situations of basic writers and on the role of teachers within this affective space.

74 Mutnick, Deborah. *Writing in an Alien World: Basic Writing and the Struggle for Equality in Higher Education.* Portsmouth: Boynton, 1996. Print.

Mutnick profiles four older, urban, minority basic writing students who take an intensive six-credit basic reading and writing course for two terms. Each case study focuses on a piece of writing the student chooses and on related interviews with the student, the instructor, and sometimes other instructors. The papers, handwritten or typed, are reproduced in the book with instructor comments. Both students and teachers are asked to read the paper aloud and comment on the text while reading. Thus a dialogue "between the written texts and the 'metacommentary'" (xxi) is created. Student writers and writing teachers are asked similar questions about their family backgrounds, educational experiences, roles as student or teacher, and what "being a writer" and "learning to write" mean to them. Mutnick also describes her own background and attitudes. In essence, the study compares the "readings" of the various participants: the basic writing students who composed the texts, instructors' readings of those texts, and Mutnick's readings of the texts and of the overall situation.

75 Piorkowski, Joan L., and Erika Scheurer. "'It Is the Way That They Talk to You': Increasing Agency in Basic Writers through a Social Context of Care." *Journal of Basic Writing* 19.2 (2000): 72–92. Print.

The authors conducted interviews and designed a questionnaire to portray two kinds of basic writers: those who became more confident in acquiring agency over their work and those who remained relatively distrustful of available assistance. Susan McLeod's work on the role of affective factors in writing and Chris M. Anson's interpretation of William Perry's categories of cognitive development of college-level students are used to back up the authors' findings that students' perception of their instructors' care is as important to students' success as their understanding of feedback and acceptance of assistance with their work. The study also reveals how students use other sources (friends, peers) when they do not trust the ones that are available in writing centers. Students' responsibility for their writing, the authors conclude, comes in response to a surrounding context that includes care.

76 Rose, Mike. "Narrowing the Mind and Page: Remedial Writers and Cognitive Reductionism." *College Composition and Communication* 39.3 (1988): 267–300. Print.

Rose summarizes trends in cognitive science—field dependence and independence, brain hemispherics, Jean Piaget's stages of cognitive development, and orality and literacy—and discusses their implications for writing instruction. His social constructivist perspective drives this analysis, and he reveals severe limitations for the practical application of any of these cognitive theories, which have caused stereotyping and the privileging of certain styles because of cultural biases, to writing instruction. Rose's research clarifies the problems associated with attempting to read writing through the limited lens of clinical psychological research. Class, race, gender, and other differences must be considered in the results, since social factors such as these "should not automatically be assumed to reflect 'pure' cognitive differences but rather effects that may well be conditioned by and interpreted in lieu of historical, sociopolitical realities" (297).

77 Rossen-Knill, Deborah, and Kim Lynch. "A Method for Describing Basic Writers and Their Writing Lessons from a Pilot Study." *Journal of Basic Writing* 19.2 (2000): 93–123. Print.

Rossen-Knill and Lynch present a holistic method for describing basic writers and their writing to encourage classroom research at two- and four-year colleges and to enable comparisons of basic writers across institutions. Their method grew out of a pilot study of basic writers and writing at two community colleges and one four-year private college that centered on a survey of the basic writers' backgrounds; "back talk," through which students respond to the authors' preliminary interpretations of the survey; and analysis of student writing for use of conventional discourse features and for rate, type, and seriousness of error. Rossen-Knill and Lynch offer some preliminary results from their pilot study to illustrate the type of findings their approach yields and to highlight the importance of such findings to classroom instruction.

78 Shaughnessy, Mina P. "Diving In: An Introduction to Basic Writing." *College Composition and Communication* 27.3 (1976): 234–39. Print.

In the partnership between teachers and basic writers, the basic writer is perceived as the party who progresses. Discussion thus centers on student needs and attitudes rather than teacher changes that may be the key to student progress. Teacher transformation at various stages of working with basic writers is described through metaphor in a developmental scale. In the stage called Guarding the

Tower, teachers are committed to protecting academic tradition from unprepared interlopers; in Converting the Natives, teachers come to perceive basic writers as empty vessels capable of learning the mechanics of language and essay structure; in Sounding the Depths, teachers shift from studying the students to studying writing as a behavior, error as a revealing logic, and the role of teacher as pedagogical planner; and in Diving In, teachers realize and accept the need to remediate themselves regarding the needs and learning styles of basic writers.

79   Stenberg, Shari. "Learning to Change: The Development of a (Basic) Writer and Her Teacher." *Journal of Basic Writing* 21.2 (2002): 37–55. Print.

Using Joseph Harris's discussion of metaphors for teaching, Stenberg asserts that teachers must consider how they construct their own identities. Regardless of pedagogy, most instructors still adopt in some measure the posture of "expert, authority, hero" (37). Using her work with a student, Linda, Stenberg explores two questions — "How do particular basic writers construct their own identities?" and "How do we teachers construct our own identities in relation to basic writers?" — to present a "two-way dynamic" in which both teacher and student undergo "revision" together (38). Stenberg tracks her own assumptions about and responses to Linda's self-definition as a writer, Linda's race and cultural position, and Linda's attitude toward help with grammar. Stenberg states, "I was trying to name and respond to her identity apart from her when, in fact, my pedagogy needed to be made *with* her" (46). Teachers, then, must strive to create pedagogies that focus on students' self-definitions — on what students bring to writing rather than on what teachers posit is lacking. A shared process will emerge that will certainly be "messier" than conventional processes but also will foster the development of students, teachers, and responsive pedagogies (53).

80   Sternglass, Marilyn S. "The Changing Perception of the Role of Writing: From Basic Writing to Discipline Courses." *BWe: Basic Writing e-Journal* 2.2 (2000): n. pag. Web. 11 Aug. 2009.

Drawing on a six-year longitudinal study at an urban university, Sternglass uses the comments of several students to show how they used writing to learn. Students revealed that writing was helpful to memory tasks. Writing, they reported, helped them with critical tasks, such as criticism, analysis, and assessment. Students' comments and results from the study suggest that critical abilities develop gradually. Exposing the students to and having them use academic language helped basic writing students develop the analytical abilities expected in upper-level courses. When students commented on how the process of learning through writing helped throughout their college years, they discussed how early reliance on textbook language led to their later ability to put their own ideas into words. Sternglass suggests writing assignments that allow basic writing students to practice analytical tasks. She also suggests reading assignments that relate general issues to students' own experiences and writing tasks that help students understand concepts as well as language.

81 Sternglass, Marilyn S. "Students Deserve Enough Time to Prove They Can Succeed." *Journal of Basic Writing* 18.1 (1999): 3–20. Print.

Sternglass uses a six-year study of a basic skills student from the City College of New York to argue that, given sufficient time and support, students who begin college in a basic writing program have the potential to succeed and in fact do succeed. The study's findings show that colleges must provide opportunities for students to obtain the skills and knowledge necessary for academe.

82 Sternglass, Marilyn S. *Time to Know Them: A Longitudinal Study of Writing and Learning at the College Level.* Mahwah: Erlbaum, 1997. Print.

Sternglass's book is a six-year study of college writers enrolled in one of three courses at the City College of New York in the fall of 1989: two levels of basic writing and one first-year composition course. Fifty-three students initially agreed to participate in the study. Sternglass provides extensive background information for nine students and detailed case studies of five of these students. In a heartening report that counters negative assessments of at-risk students' success rates, Sternglass reports that by June 1996, 66 percent of these students had either graduated from college or were still enrolled. The case studies focus both on the complex, arduous path that students must take through college and on students' encounters with writing and learning in their college courses. Based on these observations, Sternglass encourages composition teachers to develop courses and assignments that fully articulate how facts and details support claims. The institutional and instructional contexts for student learning also receive careful attention. Sternglass demonstrates the importance of teacher commentary that addresses surface-level issues but also focuses on the rhetorical realms of content, ideas, and complexity. Sternglass observes courses across the disciplines and suggests that supportive but rigorous instruction will encourage students to succeed.

83   Stygall, Gail. "Resisting Privilege: Basic Writing and Foucault's Author Function." *College Composition and Communication* 45.3 (1994): 320–41. Print.

Michel Foucault's author function becomes a conceptual structure to show how basic writers are constructed and inscribed by institutions. Teachers of basic writers should resist reinscription of institutional norms through questioning and challenging how the author function positions basic writers in the English department and in the university. Specifically, Stygall explores how certain discursive practices support the academically privileged and how those discursive practices are ignored or used specifically to privilege a certain group. Stygall describes a research project that studied correspondence between graduate student teachers in the author's teacher development class and basic writing students from a different university. This research began with the hope that teachers could avoid reinscribing basic writers by becoming aware of the discursive practices that reinforced this notion. The research explored the social and institutional pressures that basic writers and the teachers faced with such a correspondence. Stygall concludes the essay with a reflection on the research project as well as some information about what the teachers in this study have done to change their perceptions of basic writers.

84   Tinberg, Howard. "Teaching in the Spaces Between: What Basic Writing Students Can Teach Us." *Journal of Basic Writing* 17.2 (1998): 76–90. Print.

Tinberg points out that both the political right and the intellectual left have criticized the basic writing enterprise. Basic writing students are largely silent during these debates, even though the outcomes directly impact them. In writing about literacy and education, Tinberg's basic writers demonstrate an understanding of the complexity of the terms and teach him to "reconsider the value of nonschool learning" (83). Basic writing instruction must challenge and respect the unique knowledge and logic that basic writers bring to the classroom. A productive turn for basic writing research, Tinberg suggests, would be to begin asking the crucial question, "Whose responsibility is it to promote broad-based literacy in this nation?" (89).

85   Villanueva, Victor. "Theory in the Basic Writing Classroom? A Practice." *Journal of Basic Writing* 16.1 (1997): 79–90. Print.

Villanueva argues that teachers should view their basic writers not as cognitively deficient but, instead, as individuals who need to connect what they know with what the academy wants them to know. When Villanueva began scholarship in composition, most studies of basic writers reflected a cognitivist perspective. This research made claims about basic writers, suggesting they were basic because of their lack of cognitive abilities. The author questions this notion and considers how he could encourage basic writers, help them believe in their abilities with writing and language, and show them respect for who they are as learners, thinkers, and writers. To demonstrate his approach to basic writing, he provides a script of the first day of class. He is careful to show various student responses to his script and hopes that the ones who stay realize that, as college students, they need to learn certain conventions.

86   Virtanen, Beth L. "Brad, Sean, and James: Saying What They Mean in Voices That Sound Like Themselves." *Open Words: Access and English Studies* 1.1 (2006): 9–26. Print.

Virtanen shares a case study of three students in order to foreground an otherwise silenced and erased perspective from higher education—that of working-class students. Virtanen traces the students' entrance to college after earning GEDs; all three students attended open-enrollment institutions and then later transferred to four-year universities. Working-class students, as Ira Shor and Mike Rose attest, often undergo negotiations between home culture language use and the middle-class discourses and argumentation they encounter in higher education. For Brad, Sean, and James, negotiation enables them to experience a process of becoming accepted members of higher education, partly a process of self-acceptance, without having to erase their home histories and values. Virtanen raises important questions about curriculum design, student audience, and access to higher education. He asks how teachers can function as a bridge between curriculum and students to make the classroom meaningful to multiple learners, including those who have historically been denied access to higher education.

Literacy and Basic Writing

87   Bernstein, Susan Naomi. "Material Realities in the Basic Writing Classroom: Intersections of Discovery for Young Women Reading *Persepolis 2*." *Journal of Basic Writing* 27.1 (2008): 80–104. Print.

At the end of open admissions in the University of Cincinnati, students in a first-year, first-quarter Basic Writing class explore the intersectionality of their own lives as they relate to Marjane Satrapi's experience portrayed in *Persepolis*. The article begins by looking at literacy and reading in the work of Deborah Hicks and Tami K. Dolan in studying younger girls' reading practices near the university. It highlights and discusses the work of five women in the class who find recognition of their own narratives through close reading, writing, and designing curricula with the instructor. Although similarities between Marjane and the students in this class are hard to find, the resonance of her character as one of "resilience and resistance" allows students to make assertions about their own identity and how they move within the larger world of family, work, and the academy through writing.

88   Biser, Eileen, Linda Rubel, and Rose Marie Toscano. "Be Careful What You Ask For: When Basic Writers Take the Rhetorical Stage." *Journal of Basic Writing* 21.1 (2002): 52–70. Print.

The authors argue that if basic writers are to effect social change through their writing, they must be taught how to read critically the range of social, economic, political, cultural, and ideological perspectives of their audiences—intended and unintended—and how to explore the limitations and benefits of textual forms available for response. Noting that basic writers are also basic readers who apply only a personal interpretive frame to texts, the authors analyze a deaf student's failed attempt to effect social change on her campus and conclude that the student's attempt failed because they, her instructors, failed pedagogically to move beyond a romanticized notion of effecting public change through public rhetorical acts.

89   Brammer, Charlotte. "Linguistic Cultural Capital and Basic Writers." *Journal of Basic Writing* 21.1 (2002): 16–36. Print.

Brammer suggests that basic writers are linguistic outsiders who lack the cultural capital for success in academe because they use oral-discourse patterns that reveal their ethnic, geographic, and economic backgrounds. She argues that instructors should accept Standard Written English as a dialect and mine second-language acquisition studies and literacy studies to better teach linguistic variations. Brammer contends that students need explicit instruction in language variation and in rhetorical strategies that are part of academic discourse but that might be different from students' own oral strategies. She recommends that writing instructors focus on metacognitive activities; strategies at the essay, paragraph, and sentence levels that will support students; and critical reading and analysis, syntactic cohesion, and grammar.

90   Bruch, Patrick, and Thomas Reynolds. "Critical Literacy and Basic Writing Textbooks: Teaching toward a More Just Literacy." *BWe: Basic Writing e-Journal* 2.1 (2000): n. pag. Web. 11 Aug. 2009.

Bruch and Reynolds examine two texts (*Creating America: Reading and Writing Assignments*, by Joyce Moser and Ann Watters, and *Cultural Attractions/Cultural Distractions: Cultural Literacy in Contempo-*

rary Contexts, by Libby Allison and Kristine L. Blair) to assess the possibility for a "more just literacy" (par. 2) through the influence of cultural studies on basic English. Calling on the definition and discussion of critical literacy put forward by James Berlin and Michael Vivion in *Cultural Studies in the English Classroom*, they suggest that cultural studies theory provides the means to discover gaps in cultural representation but does not automatically provide a satisfactory remedy. Turning to the two selected textbooks, Bruch and Reynolds contend that they and many others fail to examine "institutionally valued literacies and justifications for racial hierarchies" (par. 19). Adding material to a textbook is insufficient if literacy itself, or the valued forms of writing taught to students, remains unexamined. Thus Moser and Watters's addition of minority authors, for example, does not change what counts for literacy.

91 Carter, Shannon. "Redefining Literacy as a Social Practice." *Journal of Basic Writing* 25.2 (2006): 94–125. Print.

In this essay, Carter deplores the pervasive skills-based instruction in basic writing classes, as well as the ubiquitous "teach to the state-mandated standardized test" pedagogy that all too many basic writing classes have. She proposes a "pedagogy of rhetorical dexterity," informed by New Literary Studies and activity theory, through which basic writing students "develop the flexibility and skill necessary to negotiate multiple, always changing literacies." The article includes assignments and student writing for those assignments.

92 Collins, James. "'The Troubled Text': History and Language in American Basic Writing Programs." *Knowledge, Culture, and Power: International Perspectives on Literacy as Policy and Practices*. Ed. Peter Freebody and Anthony R. Welch. London: Falmer, 1993. 162–86. Print.

Collins situates a study of two basic writing courses within the broader tensions surrounding the role of education. He begins by tracing the birth of the liberal arts curriculum as an attempt to inculcate students into the values reflected in the curriculum and to stifle public debate. As a result of twentieth-century attacks on this original purpose of the liberal arts, universities have moved to "cafeteria-style" approaches where writing is often the only core "skill" that runs throughout. Yet basic writing courses and programs disrupt the elite character of the university. Next, Collins describes two basic writing classes that reflect the "skill-based" nature of writing and basic writing's potential. In one class, students wrote primarily from and about experience and were confused about vague assignments that provided little guidance about how to read "experience" within broader contextual frameworks. In the other class, the instructor developed assignments rooted in specific experiences of race, and students became invested in the assignments and wrote copiously. This course was also challenging because of the limitations imposed by institutional constraints—both the instructor's time and the limits of acceptable discourse within institutions. Collins then places both approaches within a broader context of literacy and literacy crisis, suggesting that instructors must be attentive to the institutional and social contexts that shape how literacy is defined and enacted in various contexts.

93   Corkery, Caleb. "Literacy Narratives and Confidence Building in the Writing Classroom." *Journal of Basic Writing* 24.1 (2005): 48–67. Print.

The literacy narrative, a familiar genre in many writing classrooms, presents both advantages and disadvantages to student writers. The literacy narrative transitions students to a new form of literacy and enables them to position themselves as participants within an academic field. In doing so, students begin to develop academic identities. Stressing the importance of personal experience, the literacy narrative builds on what students bring to a text and often leads students to a new social and cultural awareness. It provides successful models for students to imitate, and the practice of imitation often motivates students in their writing. Yet the literacy narrative is not without its disadvantages. Teachers may hesitate to encourage imitation. In addition, and perhaps most problematic for the literacy narrative, students who view themselves and their educational experience as "outside" the traditional classroom standards and experiences may not connect to or identify with the texts. If students lack a meaningful experience with a literacy narrative, they fail to develop new academic identities. These students who see themselves as outsiders, as less skilled, or who come from predominantly oral cultures may not trust the "privileged" writing teacher, may not identify with the characters in a text, and are apt to view the literacy narrative as a daunting task. Corkery argues that literacy narratives are powerful and engaging tools but that they must be used with caution and attention to students' needs.

94   Deming, Mary P. "Reading and Writing: Making the Connection for Basic Writers." *BWe: Basic Writing e-Journal* 2.2 (2000): n. pag. Web. 11 Aug. 2009.

Deming views writing and reading as complementary components in basic writing courses. She contends that programs that eliminate the teaching of critical reading from their basic writing curriculum need to reexamine this practice. Drawing from Robert Tierney and P. David Pearson's "Toward a Composing Model of Reading," Deming applies their process model of composition to reading patterns by citing specific classroom examples. The four steps of this reading model—planning, drafting, aligning, and revising—illustrate Deming's argument that the structures of reading comprehension and process writing are too closely linked to be separated. True critical interaction between the students' lives and their worlds is a goal of a college education; for students to achieve this goal, both reading and writing instruction need to be expanded at all levels of college.

95   Dickson, Marcia. "Learning to Read/Learning to Write." *BWe: Basic Writing e-Journal* 1.1 (1999): n. pag. Web. 11 Aug. 2009.

Basic readers in college already know how to read well for pleasure, but they lack the schemata and experience to read challenging non-fiction texts in a critical way. Dickson notes that since many basic college readers approach texts from the formulaic topic sentence/support structural pattern, they often misread or dismiss texts that rely on subtle organization or sarcastic tones. Dickson outlines typical problems that basic readers have with text perceptions and lists practical teaching steps that can help instructors lead students toward more complex and critical reading comprehension. She also includes a helpful list of possible "non-textbook" reading texts and their corresponding classroom goals.

96   Goto, Stanford T. "Basic Writing and Policy Reform: Why We Keep Talking Past Each Other." *Journal of Basic Writing* 21.2 (2001): 1–20. Print.

Goto contends that the argument over the place of basic writing programs in universities is the result of the disparate worldviews of supporters and critics of those programs. Each, he says, espouses a different philosophy of education. Goto suggests that until those who teach basic writing learn to use the language of the policy makers to convey the importance of basic writing classes, programs for basic writers will be cut. Through an analysis of the literature, Goto shows that basic writing critics believe it is not possible to maintain high standards while allowing open access. These critics view education as a vertical or linear construct where students master information at one level before moving on to a higher level of learning. Goto suggests that critics, believing that it is up to the student to adapt to the university, have not attempted innovative practices to help basic writers reach the expected level of writing skills. Equally important, these critics use statistical or quantitative methodologies to assess the success or failure of basic writing students, often analyzing any data they gather in terms of cost benefits. Supporters of basic writing, on the other hand, believe that these programs maintain both access and standards. They see education as horizontal, as a matter of width, not depth. They have instituted new instructional practices because they view students who need remediation not as deficient but as requiring different strategies to learn. They use qualitative methodologies to describe the success rate of basic writing students, and they present the individual success of students as the real benefit of the programs. This new method of viewing the critics and supporters of basic writing programs should be used to improve the discussion of the value of basic writing programs.

97   Hourigan, Maureen M. *Literacy as Social Exchange: Intersections of Class, Gender and Culture.* Albany: State U of New York P, 1994. Print.

In her initial historical review, Hourigan demonstrates that the literacy crises of the 1970s and 1980s were not new phenomena and that paying attention to a history of literacy problems in America can help to avoid repetition of old remedies that did not work. She then argues that academe must more thoughtfully consider the intersections of class, gender, and culture when thinking of basic writers and their various needs. Hourigan explores the field of basic writing as a site where important work gets done in relation to the literacy debate. However, she notes that discussions of basic writers as outsiders often come from researchers at highly competitive institutions where basic writers, who would be mainstreamed in less competitive schools, are often admitted with "special" status. The result is a skewed portrait of basic writers. Hourigan advocates research at two-year schools to provide a more accurate profile of other basic writing students. Hourigan also examines gender as a marginalizing aspect of literacy crises. Here, she argues that pedagogies focused on gender often ignore and further marginalize nontraditional and non-Western students. She then focuses on intersections between feminism and basic writing pedagogies as well as pedagogies that give voice to students from a variety of cultures. She suggests that all compositionists should attend to intersections of race, class, and gender.

98   Lu, Min-Zhan. "Redefining the Legacy of Mina Shaughnessy: A Critique of the Politics of Linguistic Innocence." *Journal of Basic Writing* 10.1 (1991): 26–40. Print.

Despite the importance of Mina Shaughnessy's *Errors and Expectations* [117], Lu argues that Shaughnessy's pedagogical intentions would have been better served by a theory of language that eschews essentialism and the "politics of linguistic innocence" (27). While pedagogies motivated by the idea of an inherent deep structure of meaning successfully pose the dual challenges of becoming familiar with conventions and of gaining authorial confidence, they fail to offer students a chance to respond to "the potential dissonance between academic discourses and their home discourses" (27). Lu observes that the process of writing in a political and linguistic context of academic convention tends to determine the contingencies of meaning produced by a given student writer. Rethinking the essentialist premises of *Errors and Expectations* allows the possibility of extending Shaughnessy's original open-ended purpose of using the writing classroom to respond to social inequality and cultural marginalization. Therefore, the article goes on to criticize the uses to which Shaughnessy's work has been put by E. D. Hirsch in his New Right rhetoric.

99   Lunsford, Andrea. "Politics and Practices in Basic Writing." *A Sourcebook for Basic Writing Teachers*. Ed. Theresa Enos. New York: Random, 1987. 246–58. Print.

Lunsford responds to the so-called literacy crisis with an overview of the history of "literacy crises" in American universities, a review of certain practices that Lunsford views as "unacceptable or harmful responses" (253) in the education of basic writers, and a review of the practices that she believes constitute a more appropriate response to the condition of basic writers. Lunsford explores the way that basic writing practices have, for more than a century, been overdetermined by "economic, social, and political power" (253) and that, indeed, the so-called current literacy crisis is hardly more than a historical practice of domination and hegemony. Her critique of "bad practices" focuses on a mistaken oversimplification of basic writing courses and an overattention to correctness, error detection, and unethical labor practices. She endorses challenging students, collaboration, critiquing error within specific writing contexts, requiring smaller class sizes, and customizing the curriculum to learner needs.

100 McCrary, Donald. "Represent, Representin', Representation: The Efficacy of Hybrid Texts in the Writing Classroom." *Journal of Basic Writing* 24.2 (2005): 72–91. Print.

Creatively utilizing techniques from both academic discourses and those discourses too long excluded from our classrooms, such as African American Vernacular, McCrary argues that today's basic writing teachers need to do far more than pay lip service to the value of students' own linguistic competencies. Analyzing popular urban magazines, newspaper articles, scholarly essays, and literary nonfiction, McCrary reveals that we must also make students' home literacies integral components of our writing curricula. To best accomplish this, he contends that more hybrid texts that weave together the autobiographical languages of our popular hip-hop urban landscape with traditional academic languages must be brought into our classrooms. McCrary suggests that doing so will not only go a long way toward actually supporting the linguistic expertise of students long marginalized by the academy; it will also help to foster crucial communities among students from radically different cultural backgrounds. Real basic writing student success will come from hybridization—combining our students' home literacies with those literacies traditionally valued by academic environments, combining popular cultural texts with standard academic texts.

101   Odell, Lee. "Basic Writing in Context: Rethinking Academic Literacy." *Journal of Basic Writing* 14.1 (1995): 43–56. Print.

Writing programs need to rethink instruction in literacy and communication at all levels. Basic writing in particular ignores the complexity of literate activity in various civic and workplace contexts, assuming instead the centrality and value of academic literacy. Practices in nonacademic environments suggest that the academy's notion of literacy is too narrow (summarizing a text, mastering standard usage, etc.). Writing programs, instead, should be informed by an increased amount of research into the best literate practices from diverse contexts. Writing programs, Odell suggests, might then do a better job of preparing students for their lives as workers and citizens. Programs might also broaden their criteria for determining which students have the capacity to accomplish particular goals. He describes a third-grade classroom in which the students planned a children's literature symposium that included a well-designed program and invited speakers. Elsewhere, inner-city high schoolers revised a chamber of commerce handbook.

102   Ong, Walter J. "Literacy and Orality in Our Times." *ADE Bulletin* 58 (1978): 1–7. Print.

Describing differences between speaking and writing, Ong sets up a dichotomy between orality and literacy and uses this distinction to explain some of the challenges that students face when developing skills in literate practices. He describes oral culture as loosely structured and emotional and literate culture as analytical and logical. Additionally, Ong sets up a distinction between primary orality, which has not been affected by literate practice, such as the orality of nonliterate cultures, and secondary orality, which is not separate from literate practices but is dependent on them, such as radio and television. He argues that students must move from the spoken form of thought to the written form of thought and explains that because of the influence of oral culture, student writing might resemble the loosely structured form of conversation. Moving to the written form of thought, however, enables students to participate in intense analysis that is not possible in primary oral culture.

103   Purves, A. C. "Clothing the Emperor: Towards a Framework Relating Function and Form in Literacy." *Journal of Basic Writing* 10.2 (1991): 33–53. Print.

Academic literacy has become separated from the multiple literacy practices of everyday life. Educators carry in their minds a narrow, sociocultural model of literacy that determines what is required for outsiders to join the literate elite and also excludes anyone who is unable to follow the formal, often unexplained model, particularly students labeled "at risk." To remedy the exclusionary nature of academic literacy, teachers can incorporate all forms of literacy into the classroom, from graffiti to junk mail. By examining the functions and forms of the written texts that students are already using, teachers then can put academic literacy into sociocultural perspective and teach it as an additional literacy rather than as a replacement. In this way, students who have previously been marginalized in the classroom can learn the forms and functions of academic literacy.

104   Scott, Jerrie Cobb. "Literacies and Deficits Revisited." *Journal of Basic Writing* 12.1 (1993): 46–56. Print.

Scott identifies two main factors that contribute to the perpetuation of deficit theories in basic writing pedagogy. The first factor is tied to traditional definitions of literacy that focus on the ability to communicate using certain types of privileged discourses. The result of this limited definition is often a pedagogy that oversimplifies content, is boring and irrelevant, and labels marginalized students as deficient. Scott maintains that a broader definition of literacy—one that allows for multiple literacies existing in multiple ways—protects teachers from bringing deficit theories into their instruction. The second factor involves the concept of "uncritical dysconsciousness" (46), the conscious or unconscious "acceptance of culturally sanctioned beliefs that, regardless of intentions, defend the advantages of insiders and the disadvantages of outsiders" (46). Scott argues that there is a resistance to change in pedagogical practices that stems from a lack of change in attitude toward marginalization. She concludes that a "higher level of critical consciousness" (55) can help bring about different approaches to teaching marginalized students that do not focus on deficits. She closes the essay with "think abouts" (55) for readers, intended as strategies for moving toward pedagogical approaches and writing programs that do not depend on deficit models.

105   Soliday, Mary. *The Politics of Remediation: Institutional and Student Needs in Higher Education.* Pittsburgh: U of Pittsburgh P, 2002. Print.

Taking an in-depth look at the history of remediation from the late 1800s through the 1990s, Soliday posits that remediation exists to serve institutional needs and "to resolve social conflicts as they are played out through the educational tier most identified with access to the professional middle class" (1). For students, remedial programs provide extra reading and writing instruction, whereas for institutions, the programs assist with the crisis in admission standards and keep up enrollment when perennial budget problems tighten departmental belts. To illustrate this claim, Soliday constructs her arguments beside a chronological discussion of the transformation of educational institutions, providing relevant examples from her experiences at the City College of New York. In each chapter, she breaks down the history of a central issue while providing the conversation contemporary to each time period. Soliday also brings in other basic writing researchers' work to illustrate the overarching argument that remediation is not new, even when each time period reconceives it as such. Soliday ends the book by raising several more questions to be considered in the field.

106   Stevens, Scott. "Nowhere to Go: Basic Writing and the Scapegoating of Civic Failure." *Journal of Basic Writing* 21.1 (2002): 3–15. Print.

Stevens argues that mandates to reduce remediation rates at California State University campuses have been heralded publicly by administrators as a return to standards but that these mandates result in expelling basic writers. Detailing the local options facing these students, Stevens proposes that the lack of educational choices available to such students is analogous to the institutionalized absence of alternatives for basic writing programs. Moreover, Stevens analyzes the contradictory rhetoric of official policy, linking the elitist return to standards with the ongoing underfunding of public education in California that started in the 1970s and continues today.

Resources

107   Bernstein, Susan Naomi. "BWe 2007: Practice, Professional Development, and Favorite Books." *BWe: Basic Writing e-Journal* 6.1 (2007): n. pag. Web. 11 Aug. 2009.

In this introduction to the issue, Bernstein lists some of the favorite readings of basic writing instructors. Essentially comprising a brief annotated bibliography, texts are listed for use in developmental writing classes, in basic writing pedagogy courses, and in a program of individualized, continued professional development of composition faculty. The annotations themselves are notes from instructors who use the texts, describing the nature of the various successes. Also included is a link to a more extensive list of resources inside CompPile.

108   Carter, Shannon. "Graduate Courses in Basic Writing Studies: Recommendations for Teacher Trainers." BWe: Basic Writing e-Journal 6.1 (2007): n. pag. Web. 11 Aug. 2009.

Carter reviews several graduate-level courses in basic writing studies and finds that one key strategy in designing effective assignments and discussion activities for these classes is to "emphasize both the practical in the theoretical and the theoretical in the practical." She suggests that an "equally important strategy is to present the political in the personal and the personal in the political," and she notes that any involvement in basic writing pedagogy has political implications. Her essay provides overviews of the courses and links to sample syllabi and other materials.

109   Enos, Theresa, ed. A Sourcebook for Basic Writing Teachers. New York: Random, 1987. Print.

This collection of forty-two essays (some previously published; others written specifically for this text) includes essays that focus on issues of literacy and cognition, definitions of what basic writing is and how to teach it, ways that error and grammar fit into basic writing classrooms, and pedagogical strategies. The text includes essays by David Bartholomae, Anne E. Berthoff, Patricia Bizzell, Kenneth Bruffee, Robert Connors, Lisa Ede, Paolo Freire, Karen Greenberg, Patrick Hartwell, Glynda Hull, Andrea Lunsford, Sondra Perl, Mike Rose, Mariolina Salvatori, Mina Shaughnessy, Lynn Troyka, and others. As Theresa Enos writes in her preface, "The Sourcebook aims to build upon Shaughnessy's contributions to the study of basic writing by gathering together the best of contemporary research, theory, and practice on the subject" (v).

110   Fox, Tom. Defending Access: A Critique of Standards in Higher Education. Portsmouth: Boynton, 1999. Print.

Fox argues that contemporary calls for "standards" work against providing broader, more equitable access to higher education. The book is divided into five chapters, with the first three developing a critique of standards in both historical and contemporary contexts and the second two sketching how work for access can be carried out in both pedagogy and writing program administration. The book concludes with a brief comment on the need for perseverance in committed educators—that is, "staying around is half the battle" (114)—and four observations about change: stubborn persistence is necessary; alliances are important; preparation for confrontation helps student survival; and survival is possible with strategic choices about which battles to fight.

111   Halasek, Kay, and Nels P. Highberg. *Landmark Essays on Basic Writing*. Mahwah: Erlbaum, 2001. Print.

The essays in this volume speak directly to the debilitating assumptions that place basic writing students and teachers, and the discipline itself, on the margins of educational, economic, and political localities of influence. The collection is designed to present readers with various previously published essays that depict the fundamental and shifting theoretical, methodological, and pedagogical assumptions of basic writing instruction over the past two decades. Beginning with essays published between 1987 (after the publication of *A Sourcebook for Basic Writing Teachers* [109]) and 1997, the book is arranged roughly chronologically, from Adrienne Rich's 1979 "Teaching Language in Open Admissions" [114] to Jacqueline Jones Royster and Rebecca Greenberg Taylor's 1997 "Constructing Teacher Identity in the Basic Writing Classroom" [37]. The collection seeks to historicize the preceding decades of scholarship and also anticipate the future of the field. Essays examine such issues as defining basic writers, the phenomenology of error, cognitivism and writing instruction, the social construction of remediation, and the politics of basic writing pedagogy in a postmodern world. They collectively speak to some of the most enduring and important debates in the field of basic writing. At the same time, they illustrate that neither the basic writing classroom nor recent scholarship need be intellectually marginalized locations. The contributors claim the "margin"—the basic writing classroom—as a borderland, a site of contention and negotiation that allows for a cultural and pedagogical reflection and critique not available to them in more centrally located sites in English departments.

112   Kasden, Lawrence N., and Daniel R. Hoeber. *Basic Writing: Essays for Teachers, Researchers, and Administrators*. Urbana: National Council of Teachers of English, 1980. Print.

This germinal book provides important perspectives in the history of basic writing research. It includes essays by Sondra Perl, Arthur Dixon, Milton Spann and Virginia Foxx, Patrick Hartwell, Harry Crosby, Nancy Johnson, Rexford Brown, Constance Gefvert, Kenneth Bruffee, and E. Donald Hirsch. Each contributor focuses on different elements of basic writing and basic writers, from cognitive studies to examinations of writing programs and writing center practices.

113   Moran, Michael G., and Martin J. Jacobi. *Research in Basic Writing: A Bibliographic Sourcebook.* New York: Greenwood, 1991. Print.

This text is most useful now as a resource documenting the state of basic writing scholarship in the late 1970s and mid-1980s. Although the book bears a publication date of 1991, its ten bibliographic essays (and appendix) are heavily weighted with research and scholarship considerably earlier than the date of publication. The *Sourcebook* was written when basic writing was experiencing a resurgence; thus it extensively documents the dominant approach to basic writing. Woven into many of the chapters are emphases on linguistics, "new grammars" and sentence combining, cognitive psychology, and the City College of New York "origins" of basic writing interest and instruction, a claim that has been contested. Nevertheless, the *Sourcebook* constitutes a useful artifact of a certain period in basic writing scholarship.

114   Rich, Adrienne. "Teaching Language in Open Admissions." *Landmark Essays on Basic Writing.* Ed. Kay Halasek and Nels P. Highberg. Mahwah: Erlbaum, 2001. 1–13. Print.

Rich brings a narrative vision and quality rarely found in scholarship on basic writing. Through her experiences, we see the "graffiti-sprayed walls of tenements" (8) and "the uncollected garbage" (3) on the streets of New York, and we witness the lives of students and teachers as they come together to make sense of the circumstances of their collective educational endeavors in the Seek for Evaluation, Education & Knowledge (SEEK) program at the City College of New York in 1968. Rich describes the larger social, political, and human contexts of that time and formulates many of the questions that continue to demand attention in basic writing scholarship. Rich articulates a condition of education that is characterized by institutional racism and classism. She cites Paulo Freire, insisting that students need to learn to use language for critical reflection, and calls on educators to reassess their methods and materials for teaching. At the same time, her narrative demands that basic writing scholars work at their own critical self-reflection.

115   Rose, Mike. *Lives on the Boundary: The Struggles and Achievements of America's Underprepared.* New York: Free, 1989. Print.

This examination of the idea of "underpreparedness" in a range of schools and educational systems also explores Rose's own experiences as a student who was erroneously placed in the vocational education track. He suggests that lower-track classes create a self-fulfilling prophecy for most students who might, if challenged to succeed, do well in advanced classes. Among the issues Rose discusses are the problems encountered by students whose backgrounds provide little context for the ideas and language they encounter in the academy. By explaining his personal challenges and his experiences with various mentors, Rose illustrates how he worked to master academic language and ideas. Rose uses his experiences as a student and a teacher as evidence for a critique of conceptions of literacy used in contemporary education. He suggests that students labeled "underprepared" are inexperienced with the expectations of the academy, that literacy crises running through the nineteenth and twentieth centuries were manufactured and deflect other concerns, and that schools must work with students differently.

116   Shaughnessy, Mina P. "Basic Writing." *Teaching Composition: Twelve Bibliographic Essays.* Ed. Gary Tate. 1976. Fort Worth: Texas Christian UP, 1987. 177–206. Print.

Rejecting the medical metaphor, Shaughnessy articulates varied definitions of basic writers and writing among institutions and over time. She establishes 1964 as the year when the "new" remedial English began. The essay defines the population of basic writing students, characterizes instructors and instructor training, and notes that little had been published before 1976 on this rich area of potential research. The essay identifies three major components of research to that point and suggests readings on these: classroom environment, methods of instruction, and focus on prewriting. Throughout, Shaughnessy emphasizes the challenges faced by students who are identified as basic writers and suggests that traditional instructors rethink their approaches to better accommodate these students. The essay closes with an in-depth discussion of selected readings for instructors on classical studies of language, on grammar, on language in various social settings, and on writing. Most of the cited articles remain classics in the field. Shaughnessy sums up the main point of the essay: "The 'remediation' of basic writers' teachers may, in fact, be the most important education going on today" (167).

117   Shaughnessy, Mina P. *Errors and Expectations: A Guide for the Teacher of Basic Writing.* New York: Oxford UP, 1977. Print.

Shaughnessy takes teachers through writing problems such as poor handwriting and punctuation, syntax, common errors, spelling and vocabulary errors, and lack of idea development. While her focus is primarily on error, it is underscored by a sensitive understanding of the reasons behind the rhetorical and linguistic difficulties discussed and a strong belief in the inherent intelligence of learners described as "basic writers." Shaughnessy's claims about the difficulties faced by basic writers are supported by examples from thousands of student papers. Examples of many kinds of errors are provided. Each chapter also includes suggestions for the teacher on how to reduce the particular kind of error discussed in that specific chapter. Shaughnessy also explains why these errors occur by examining the rules that are manifested in students' writing. The book also contains suggestions for placement essay topics and suggested readings for the teacher of basic writing.

118   Smoke, Trudy. "What Is the Future of Basic Writing?" *Journal of Basic Writing* 20.2 (2001): 88–96. Print.

Writing as coeditor of the *Journal of Basic Writing* (first with Karen Greenberg and then with George Otte), Smoke surveys seven years of *JBW* (1994–2001), a time when the journal became "more theoretical and political" (88). Looking back, Smoke highlights some of the most important issues in basic writing: the demise of open admissions at the City University of New York, tracking versus mainstreaming, a reappraisal of Mina Shaughnessy's work, and the elimination of basic writing programs (and hence basic writers). Smoke asserts that research in the field has entered into "meta-analysis" and that scholarship has begun to "historicize" basic writing. Smoke concludes with a tribute to *JBW* and its role as she turns over her editorship to Bonne August.

119   Uehling, Karen S. "The Conference on Basic Writing: 1980–2001." *Histories of Developmental Education*. Minneapolis: Center for Research on Developmental Education and Urban Literacy, 2002. 47–59. Print.

After briefly laying out the politics of basic writing, the diversity of basic writers, and top-down versus skills-focused pedagogies, Uehling outlines the twenty-one-year history of the Conference on Basic Writing, a special-interest group of the Conference on College Composition and Communication (CCCC). Moving from "Early History and Original Goals" and a "Brief Chronology," Uehling devotes most of the essay to CBW's current goals and activities, especially its communicative ones—such as its newsletter, sponsorship of book projects, electronic discussion list, electronic journal, Web site, annual meeting, and workshops at CCCC. Included is a history of the national basic writing conferences that began in 1985 and were eventually cosponsored by CBW.

Pedagogical Issues

Composing Processes

120   Ashley, Hannah. "The Art of Queering Voices: A Fugue." *Journal of Basic Writing* 26.1 (2007): 4–19. Print.

Ashley argues that teaching reported discourse in the traditional way—as a set of conventions for quoting, paraphrasing, and citing sources—encourages basic writers to try to pass as academic insiders by hiding, or "closeting," their outsider status and perspectives. Teaching students how to "queer" reported discourse conventions, by which the writer means how to use them in playful, disruptive, and unexpected ways, offers students an opportunity to develop openly hybrid, insider-outsider authorial voices. Ashley offers a compelling model of what reported discourse looks like when it is queered and a thorough analysis of how queered discourse works. (She refers readers to another article for advice about how to teach it.) The article is written as a demonstration of queered discourse: the academic arguments are collaged with snippets of confessional narrative, dictionary definitions of musical forms, and quotes from the DSM-IV diagnostic manual.

121   Bernstein, Susan Naomi. "Seeing beyond the Ordinary: Imagination and the Work of Teachers and Students in Basic Writing." *Modern Language Studies* 34.1/2 (2004): 84–91. Print.

Bernstein suggests that standardized and skills-based pedagogies at the elementary level operate much the same way in the post-Fordist university. She argues that by the time students reach college, they have been "exposed to basic skills training for years" (87). Thus Bernstein "understand[s] the teaching of writing as a continuum" (86), suggesting that her experiences teaching imaginative writing through metaphor to elementary students helped her to imagine how figurative language might create similar dissonance in her university-level basic writing courses. Bernstein affirms that providing contexts and spaces for students to re-imagine their lives through metaphor and figurative language moves student learning beyond skill and drill to meaningful, critical, and personal engagement with language and the material conditions of the writing classroom.

122   Biser, Eileen, Linda Rubel, and Rose Marie Toscano. "Mediated Texts: A Heuristic for Academic Writing." *Journal of Basic Writing* 17.1 (1998): 56–72. Print.

Mediated text is defined as written text produced with second- and third-party assistance in its drafting and final production. Because the Americans with Disabilities Act requires accommodation for deaf college students, mediated texts produced with second- and third-party assistance help deaf college students successfully complete writing courses. Biser, Rubel, and Toscano identify the function of mediated texts as a useful drafting technique for English as a second language (ESL) students and for basic writers as well. Although they address philosophical and pedagogical implications of second- and third-party participation, mediated texts as heuristic devices may benefit many students in their drafting and revision.

123   Cody, Jim. "The Importance of Expressive Language in Preparing Basic Writers for College Writing." *Journal of Basic Writing* 15.2 (1996): 95–111. Print.

Cody argues that basic writers should develop their own voices and not just imitate others', which will result in language that is "more sensitive to multicultural concerns" (109) and "more openly accountable for the damage caused from academia's privileging of dominant discourses" (109). To this end, Cody urges a move away from "pedagogies of imitation" (108), in which students must adapt to existing formulas and standards, reject familiar discourses, and "hide the evidence" (101) of their lives outside academia—lives that often involve "oppression, marginalization, deprivation, and suppression" (101). Instead, he endorses a pedagogy that encourages students to use their own experiences and discourses in academic writing. This approach also helps students become aware of audience and purpose, affords them the experience of having readers pay attention to their work, and transforms academic language into a more representative discourse. Cody argues that instructors and students can work from such "expressive" language toward more "linear modes" used in academe without betraying their own discourses.

124   Collins, James L. "Basic Writing and the Process Paradigm." *Journal of Basic Writing* 14.2 (1995): 3–18. Print.

Collins contends that an unquestioned acceptance of the process approach to teaching writing may fail basic writers because of the myths that inform the implicit instruction in this paradigm—that "writing development is natural and that teaching is primarily the facilitation of development" (5). Collins also notes that process literature promotes a structuralist, binary approach to writing instruction. He recommends a more poststructuralist appreciation of "differences among discourses" (5).

125   De Beaugrande, Robert, and Mar Jean Olson. "Using a 'Write-Speak-Write' Approach for Basic Writers." *Journal of Basic Writing* 10.2 (1991): 4–32. Print.

The authors begin with a dilemma: linguists emphasize the primacy of speech over writing, but this causes problems with labeling dialects. De Beaugrande and Olson refute the linguistic premise that restricted speech, such as that identified by Basil Bernstein as spoken by the British lower class, is an indicator of psychological and linguistic deficits, and the authors question the connections between speech and writing. They also argue that formal correctness is not a prerequisite for effective communication. They describe a pilot project in which student athletes were asked to create a narrative about three of their games—one week in writing, one week later in speech, and the third week in writing (the Write-Speak-Write Approach). Each student was asked to use the first written draft and an annotated, typed transcript of the speech to compose the final draft. Final drafts were longer and clearer than the initial versions. A change of approach to teaching basic writing in elementary and secondary schools could greatly ease the problems we are now facing at the college level, which often cannot be fully remedied in one or two semesters. Writing instructors should support the human freedom of access to knowledge through discourse.

126   Hebb, Judith. "Mixed Forms of Academic Discourse: A Continuum of Language Possibility." *Journal of Basic Writing* 21.2 (2002): 21–36. Print.

In challenging Patricia Bizzell's negative characterization of hybrid discourses, Hebb claims that instructors should view them not simply as a mix of the academic and nonacademic but as part of a continuum of discourses for which no solid boundaries differentiate academic discourse from others. At one pole of the continuum is mainstream academic discourse, and Hebb argues that privileging "academic discourse" reinforces dominant ideology. At the other pole is the idiosyncratic and unintelligible. Hybrid discourses fall between these two poles, which represent impoverished forms of discourse that "reflect neither the complexity and multi-vocality of group nor the individual voice(s) of self" (28). Instructors can help their students negotiate their passage into various academic discourse communities by assuming no hierarchy of value, offering students linguistic resources rich in their ideational and expressive possibilities, and encouraging them to produce hybrid discourses that perform intellectual work.

See: Patricia Bizzell, "Basic Writing and the Issue of Correctness" [5].

127   Hull, Glynda, and Mike Rose. "'This Wooden Shack Place': The Logic of an Unconventional Reading." *College Composition and Communication* 41.3 (1990): 287–98. Print.

Contemporary pedagogies that call for an integrative approach to reading and writing in the "remedial" classroom increase the likelihood of divergence between students and instructors along the lines of literary interpretation. Instructors' readings tend toward conventions socialized by training during their undergraduate and graduate study of English, while personal history strongly influences the logic of a basic writer's response to literary texts. To show that basic writers benefit from immersion in the intellectual task of generating new interpretive perceptions, Hull and Rose analyze the discourse surrounding one student's reading of "And Your Soul Shall Dance," a poem by Garrett Kaoru Hongo. The ensuing reinterpretation of the poem demonstrates that "deficit-oriented assumptions about the linguistic and cognitive abilities of remedial students" (296) need reexamination. The more student-centered and "knowledge-making" model of pedagogy that would result might create moments of uncertainty or hesitancy for the instructor, who must nevertheless stand ready to provide guidance, focus, structure, and accountability.

128   Hunter, Paul, and Nadine Pearce. "Basic Writers: The Writing Process and Written Products." *Teaching English in the Two-Year College* 14.2 (1987): 252–64. Print.

Focusing on studies utilizing transcribed audiotapes as a method of researching basic writers' writing processes, Hunter and Pearce question if those processes could be understood by an analysis of think-aloud protocols. After observing the writing processes of eight basic writers, the authors conclude that writing assignments should be designed to minimize "premature editing" (stopping and starting) and that many basic writers do not have at their disposal the kinds of knowledge or language "to respond comfortably and effectively to traditional academic writing tasks" (263).

129   Kirch, Ann. "A Basic Writer's Topoi for Timed Essay Tests." *Journal of Basic Writing* 15.2 (1996): 112–24. Print.

Basic writers have difficulty generating ideas while taking timed essay tests. Patterned after James Berlin's approach—a "positivistic, behavioral epistemology that focuses on steps in processes and descriptions of external reality" (113)—Kirch advocates that basic writers respond to the essay's prompt by asking themselves how other people might respond to the topic. This pedagogy helps students examine the topic more objectively, including their and others' insights, thus making them better able to respond to the topic. Through this technique, basic writers are enabled to "discover the political and social topoi" and "completely reposition the timed writing tests" (123).

130   Krahe, Valerie Ann. "The Shape of the Container." *Teaching Developmental Writing: Background Readings.* Ed. Susan Naomi Bernstein. Boston: Bedford, 2001. 138–42. Print.

Asserting that composition teachers should shape the content of their courses around the needs of their adult students, Krahe draws on David Kolb's experiential learning model and delineation of learning styles to teach writing courses focused on the concept of rhetorical situation. Krahe values Kolb's learning theory over others because it "acknowledges that learning is lifelong" (138), a concept critical to teachers of adult learners. Krahe develops her course content in accordance with Kolb's four learning styles: the converger (learns by thinking, analyzing, and doing), the diverger (learns by intuiting, planning, and reflecting), the assimilator (learns by thinking, analyzing, planning, and reflecting), and the accommodator (learns by intuiting and doing) (139). As Krahe works to teach the concept of rhetorical situation, something she considers critical to composition instruction, she creates assignments that allow students with these learning styles to succeed. Krahe also offers an overview of her course content and assignments as an example.

131   Kroll, Barry M., and John C. Schafer. "Error-Analysis and the Teaching of Composition." *College Composition and Communication* (1978): 242–48. Print.

Process-based error analysis from ESL studies offers insights into the errors native speakers make in written composition. The process-analytic approach views errors as necessary stages in all language learning, the product of intelligent cognitive strategies, and potentially useful indicators of the processes a student uses. The error analyst investigates the sources of error to help students reach target forms and levels of discourse. Like Mina Shaughnessy's work, this approach sees errors as the product of learning and thinking. Error analysis does not dictate any single teaching device, and instructors should avoid simple exercises or explanations. Instead, they should view teaching as hypothesis testing, look for systematicity and pattern in student error, individualize materials and strategies for particular errors, and explain sources of errors to students.

132   McAlexander, Patricia J. "Developmental Classroom Personality and Response to Peer Review." *Research and Teaching in Developmental Education* 17.1 (2000): 5–12. Print.

McAlexander conducted a study of two developmental writing classes to investigate which form of peer review—oral or written—most benefited students. The class she describes as composed of intermediate developmental writers reported a strong preference for oral feedback, with students stating that oral review comments were far more helpful and enjoyable than written comments, especially those written by classmates they did not know. In contrast, students from the class that McAlexander notes demonstrated lower levels of academic and social skills reported that neither method was helpful or enjoyable. McAlexander concludes that the personality of the class is largely responsible for student experiences with peer review. Thus instructors cannot make assertions about student experiences with peer review without first taking into consideration the levels of student self-confidence and motivation and the level of social interaction observed in the particular classroom.

133   Miller, David. "Developmental Writing: Trust, Challenge, and Critical Thinking." *Journal of Basic Writing* 21.2 (2002): 92–105. Print.

Miller argues that basic writers are likely unaware of their own critical thinking skills and that teachers must demonstrate to them how to apply those skills in their own writing. Because students often distrust their own experiences and abilities, Miller suggests that teachers have an obligation to validate students and give them a sense of safety within the physical space of the classroom, for only when students feel safe will they partake in the cognitive activities associated with critical thinking. Miller also stresses the importance of challenging students and describes his own use of difficult texts by Annie Dillard and Mark Twain. Miller concludes by suggesting that engaging students in critical thinking about their own work and the work of others leads them to experience and understand critical thinking as a more "natural" process.

134   Nixon-Ponder, Sarah. "Using Problem-Posing Dialogue in Adult Literacy Education." *Teaching Developmental Writing: Background Readings*. Ed. Susan Naomi Bernstein. Boston: Bedford, 2001. 144–50. Print.

Nixon-Ponder promotes the use of problem-posing dialogue in adult writing classes to strengthen the self-esteem and analytical skills of students. The technique consists of five parts. First, the instructor presents students with a "code"—a photo, a text, or some other item that is to be the central focus of the unit. Students study the code and begin to answer questions to familiarize themselves with it. Second, students identify a problem associated with the code. Third, students personalize the problem. Fourth, the class discusses the personal and social aspects of the problem. Finally, students discuss possible solutions to the problem. Nixon-Ponder concludes that using this problem-posing dialogue technique is effective for adult learners because it shows them that their life experiences are relevant and important to academic tasks, thus empowering them and strengthening their self-esteem as students.

135   Parisi, Hope A. "Involvement and Self-Awareness for the Basic Writer: Graphically Conceptualizing the Writing Process." *Journal of Basic Writing* 13.2 (1994): 33–45. Print.

Basic writing students benefit from conceptually mapping their own writing processes. This activity gives students the opportunity to identify and classify, spatially, their own writing behaviors. Writing students of all ability levels often do not recognize the correlation between their successes and failures as writers and the decisions they make when writing, but this problem is experienced most frequently by students who are less acculturated to the college learning environment. As a metacognitive task, mapping highlights the movement from idea to idea or from task to task that all writers undertake, both independently and through collaboration. Various student experiences of mapping are presented in detail. Examples of student maps are also provided.

136   Perl, Sondra. "The Composing Processes of Unskilled College Writers." *Research in the Teaching of English* 13.4 (1979): 317–36. Print.

Perl summarizes her 1975–1976 study of the composing processes of five unskilled college writers at Eugenio Maria de Hostos Community College of the City University of New York. Perl argues that, prior to this work, little was done to study basic writers and their "observable and scorable behaviors" (318) in the composing process. One specific goal of the study was to provide a mechanism for documenting composing processes: research in a "standardized, categorical, concise, structural, and diachronic" (320) format. Perl developed a code for what students do in their composing processes. "Miscues" in students' own reading and writing work were also noted in a standardized format. The discovery that the students' composing processes were consistent, even when the resultant writing appeared to have been done in a haphazard or arbitrary manner, supports the research Shaughnessy did in the late 1970s. Perl argues that basic writing faculty must look at students' internalized processes to make decisions about instruction.

137   Perl, Sondra. "A Look at Basic Writers in the Process of Composing." *Basic Writing: Essays for Teachers, Researchers, and Administrators.* Ed. Lawrence N. Kasden and Daniel R. Hoeber. Urbana: NCTE, 1980. 13–32. Print.

Perl used Janet Emig's 1969 work on "composing aloud" to set up this study of five students at Eugenio Maria de Hostos Community College of the City University of New York in 1975 and 1976 and to create a formal, standardized approach to viewing the work that basic writers do as they complete writing assignments. The findings show that the student writers, though often unskilled, had consistent strategies for composing. While the students spent little time on prewriting, there was no indication that this created subsequent problems. Students discovered meaning as they wrote in a process that was recursive, discursive, and decidedly nonlinear. Editing created most of the problems for the students, as they often hypercorrected or began to correct before writing enough to untangle what they wanted to say. Perl argues that these students do know how to write and have stable composing processes. She suggests a "loosening" of the writing process: "readying oneself to write, sustaining the flow of writing, shaping the discourse for oneself, readying the discourse for others" (31–32) as a consideration for basic writing instruction.

138   Purves, Alan. "Teaching People Who Don't Write Good." *Journal of Basic Writing* 14.1 (1995): 15–20. Print.

Purves suggests that composition is a complex business that is in a constant state of change. We expect students to come to the university with a certain level of prowess with composition, but perhaps that expectation is unrealistic. Part of the problem is that we are sometimes unsure of what we should teach students. What genres are important? Are we more concerned with grammar or content, style or voice? Do we want students to challenge the academy or become part of its discourse community? Technology complicates the matter further. Composition is evolving into a complex manipulation of images for a rhetorical effect — images including graphemes, punctuation marks, paragraphs, typefaces, illustrations, pictures, and sound effects. Perhaps in this new digital world we are all neophytes. Rather than worry about teaching students how to write well, Purves says, perhaps we should question the very nature of writing.

139   Rose, Mike. "Rigid Rules, Inflexible Plans, and the Stifling of Language: A Cognitivist Analysis of Writer's Block." *College Composition and Communication* 31.4 (1980): 389–401. Print.

This study of students and writer's block finds important differences among writers. Five case studies form the basis of the study, which includes a thorough discussion of writer's block and the challenges student writers face when their performance as writers does not accurately reflect their abilities. Rose concludes that the blocking these writers faced was caused by "writing rules or . . . planning strategies that impeded rather than enhanced the composing process" (390). Acknowledging the complexity of the writing process, Rose proposes that writer's block can in many cases be alleviated if the rigid rules and plans that seem to control writers' performances can be discovered. The essay contains both interview data and writers' self-reports of their composing processes. In interdisciplinary fashion, the essay also contains a survey of "several key concepts in the problem-solving literature" (390) that undergird Rose's analysis.

140   Ryden, Wendy. "How Soft Is Process? The Feminization of Comp and Pedagogies of Care." *Journal of Basic Writing* 20.1 (2001): 53–63. Print.

Through a narrative of her personal experiences, Ryden explores the metaphors of "hard" and "soft" that are often used to describe pedagogical approaches. As a young female instructor at a predominately male school, she avoided pedagogical approaches that might make her appear "soft" and thus vulnerable. Later in her career, she discovered a composition model based on community and process, which necessitated a "softer" approach. Working through the evolution of her pedagogy from "hard" to "soft," she observes, "In order to enact a pedagogy of process, I had to enact a pedagogy of care" (58). However, this pedagogy of care also concedes to certain gender stereotypes. Ryden examines whether process and care are really "soft" and questions whether current pedagogical metaphors "rely on an ethic of care that itself relies on a naturalization of the maternal role of women" (59).

141   Shafer, Gregory. "Negotiating Audience and Voice in the Writing Center." *Teaching Developmental Writing: Background Readings.* Ed. Susan Naomi Bernstein. Boston: Bedford, 2001. 354–64. Print.

Shafer addresses the fundamental tension between students' self-expression and the conventions of academic discourse taught in composition courses. Shafer compares vivid examples of three students' emotionally charged yet nonstandard writing with the correct but bland academic writing often said to be valued in composition courses. In doing so, he critiques David Bartholomae's pedagogy by asking, "Who is really being served in a pedagogy that elevates prescription over critical dialogue?" (359). Shafer refers to Paolo Freire, bell hooks, Mina Shaughnessy, Louise Rosenblatt, Peter Elbow, and Donald Murray as he develops an argument against "a contrived discourse that serves to exult the academic community over the students it is supposed to empower" (357). He also supports students' efforts to accommodate their writing to the instructors' and institutions' requirements, even if these tend to stifle voice, by helping students focus on audience analysis.

See: David Bartholomae, "Inventing the University" [2].

142   Shaughnessy, Mina P. "Some New Approaches toward Teaching." *Journal of Basic Writing* 13.1 (1994): 103–16. Print.

In general, writing teachers are people who did well in school, enjoyed English, and got high grades on everything they wrote. They use internalized models of their past composition successes to evaluate the work of their students, a system that always puts the basic writing student at a disadvantage. Students learn to write by writing, and the teacher who interferes with this process by imposing too many conditions must recognize that the goal of instruction is to guide students to be self-sufficient. Teachers must be sensitive to the details of the various difficulties students may have in handwriting, spelling, punctuation, grammar, and making and ordering sentences. Each student is an individual who will follow a unique, nonlinear path of development. The teacher-student relationship is best described as one in which two people learn from each other.

143   Sirc, Geoffrey. "*The Autobiography of Malcolm X* as a Basic Writing Text." *Journal of Basic Writing* 13.1 (1994): 50–77. Print.

Sirc addresses several issues: subject positions, student ability, and the debate about whether basic writing should focus on teaching "academic writing" or recasting the academic standards of appropriate writing. Mentioning composition's stringent focus on writing process, Sirc endorses the last choice from the above list. The power of revision—both by readers and writers—in the tweaking of meaning forces writers into closure. Sirc prefers Malcolm X's flexible philosophy from the end of his autobiography to be used as a model for basic writing instruction. Most students began reading Malcolm X's story with a fairly stable notion of identity, a closed notion of who people are and how they engage with the world. Sirc claims that most students remained in that mind-set. However, some students demonstrated change, and Sirc believes that many will not remain solely within that reductionist framework. By endorsing this approach to the classroom, Sirc opens the possibility for students to learn the positive force that literacy can have in their lives.

144   Yood, Jessica. "Present-Process: The Composition of Change." *Journal of Basic Writing* 24.2 (2005): 4–25. Print.

Yood finds the process theory of writing to be in a state of "paradigm-paralysis" (8–9), a problem she traces back to Maxine Hairston's misreading of Thomas Kuhn. Proposing the term *social movement* as an alternative to *paradigm*, Yood attempts to resurrect process, not as a "big theory," but as a way of "understanding knowledge making in our complex world as a circular, feedback loop" (13). She endorses "autopoesis," or observing systems and making processes visible, as a conceptual way for writing scholars to reflect upon the "how" of composing (13) and to enact change. As an example of a "present-process movement," Yood highlights the new Writing Across the Curriculum (WAC) program at the City University of New York, a program that took shape after basic writing and remedial writing were dispensed with along with open admissions.

Invention, Reading, Prewriting, and Collaboration

145   Brookfield, Stephen D. "Understanding Classroom Dynamics: The Critical Incident Questionnaire." *Teaching Developmental Writing: Background Readings*. Ed. Susan Naomi Bernstein. Boston: Bedford, 2001: 181–88. Print.

Brookfield draws on his personal experiences with the Critical Incident Questionnaire (CIQ), a weekly evaluation that prompts students to provide specific details about personally significant classroom occurrences. Brookfield argues that the CIQ has several advantages as a diagnostic tool for teaching and learning: it gives the instructor a running commentary of students' feedback about classroom instruction, encourages students to reflect on class activities, and provides a forum for discussing classroom miscommunications or points of confusion. In advocating the use of CIQs in the classroom, Brookfield cites advantages such as increasing student and teacher awareness of problems before disaster develops, encouraging reflective learning, and building the case for diversity in teaching.

146   El-Hindi, Amelia E. "Connecting Reading and Writing: College Learners' Metacognitive Awareness." *Journal of Developmental Education* 21.2 (1997): 10–18. Print.

El-Hindi analyzes the effects of introducing metacognitive awareness strategies through reading logs to a group of thirty-four high school graduates who were participating in a six-week summer reading and writing program before their matriculation as freshmen. Students learned strategies that corresponded to the planning, drafting, and responding stages of reading and writing; responded to questionnaires about their own reading and writing skills; and produced reading logs on their reading, understanding, and analysis of class texts. El-Hindi concludes that metacognitive awareness should aid developmental writers by giving them the skills necessary to analyze and synthesize readings. She also finds that activities asking students to become more aware of their active participation in an assigned task should lead students to be better readers and writers.

147   Emig, Janet. "Writing as a Mode of Learning." *College Composition and Communication* 28.2 (1977): 122–28. Print.

Emig argues that there is a significant difference between speaking and writing. Combining writing and speaking can help develop higher cognitive functions such as analysis and synthesis. Writing requires that we employ learning by doing, learning by depiction in an image, and learning by restatement in words. Writing also requires establishing connections and conceptual relationships.

148   Gardner, Susan, and Toby Fulwiler, eds. *The Journal Book for Teachers of At-Risk College Writers*. Portsmouth: Boynton, 1999. Print.

Incorporating journal writing into a course's curriculum can be beneficial for students at risk of dropping out of their college writing courses and, subsequently, out of college. Sixteen essays provide examples of and reflections on the integration of journal writing into writing courses. Essays focus on subjects such as how and why journals were effective and which innovative ways of envisioning and using journals were effective with diverse student populations. The volume also includes an essay on why one author stopped using journals and an essay on issues connected to assessing journals.

149   Launspach, Sonja. "The Role of Talk in Small Writing Groups: Building Declarative and Procedural Knowledge for Basic Writers." *Journal of Basic Writing* 27.2 (2008): 56–80. Print.

Focusing on a case study, Launspach explores the role of talk in underprepared students' acquisition of academic discourse. Conversation analysis as a linguistic framework is used to examine the interactions of students participating in a small writing group. Tracing the progress of one student's paper, the essay explores how students' participation in small writing groups allows them, in Claus Faerch and Gabriele Kasper's terms, to build declarative knowledge and negotiate strategies they can apply to their procedural knowledge of writing. The small writing groups, led by a teaching assistant, expose underprepared students to the practices and values of the academic discourse community. A systematic look at how students' talk is structured and what topics they focus on offers important insight to instructors into aspects of student writers' learning processes and suggests additional pedagogical approaches.

150 Shafer, Gregory. "Using Letters for Process and Change in the Basic Writing Classroom." *Teaching Developmental Writing: Background Readings*. Ed. Susan Naomi Bernstein. Boston: Bedford, 2001. 46–59. Print.

Wanting his assignments to be informed by real-world relevance, Shafer had his students write personal letters to anyone of their own choosing. Shafer participated in the assignment by sharing a letter he wrote to his recently deceased father and came to understand the anxieties that students feel when sharing their writing with others. As an audience, his students broke free of their normal error seeking, evaluated his letter's essence, and revised instead of edited. The next class meeting demonstrated that students themselves were becoming writers. Many arrived in class with letters that had been revised multiple times. Letter writing, Shafer argues, paired with a writing or literacy club, is "invaluable not only for its short, holistic character but also for the many political and liberating opportunities it offers" (53).

151 VonBergen, Linda. "Shaping the Point with Poetry." *Journal of Basic Writing* 20.1 (2001): 77–88. Print.

VonBergen argues that expressivism does not belong in the basic writing classroom because students have not internalized a sufficient array of narrative models and are likely to produce expressive essays that are heavy on extraneous detail and light on main point. Drawing on David Bartholomae's "Inventing the University," she claims that allowing students to write without making a point is a disservice and that instructors should help students to imitate and appropriate the forms of academic discourse. To that end, VonBergen suggests using poetry to provide students with a model on which to base their essays. Key for VonBergen is that the discursive aims of this assignment are not expressive (emotional) but referential (referring to a concrete reality). She provides a sample assignment that uses Countee Cullen's poem "Incident" as a model for a personal essay. The three stanzas of the poem, she says, are models for three parts of an essay: the context for the incident, the events that happened, and the author's reactions to those events. Using this model, she contends, students are much less likely to produce personal essays in which no point is made or in which a point is made but only incidentally.

See: David Bartholomae, "Inventing the University" [2].

Response and Revision

152 Bartholomae, David, and Peter Elbow. "Interchanges: Responses to Bartholomae and Elbow." *College Composition and Communication* 46.1 (1995): 84–92. Print.

In these responses to each other's longer *College Composition and Communication* articles (also published in issue 46.1), Bartholomae and Elbow further explain their differing views of how to teach students and respond to their writing. Bartholomae advocates teaching students to take a critical stance toward dominant discourses and taking a critical stance when responding to students' papers. His goal is to help see "the ways their writing constructs a relationship with tradition, power and authority—with other people's words" (86). Elbow advocates "hold[ing] back" criticism of students' work to "let them make as many decisions as they can about their writing" (90). He recognizes that they "may be written by the culture" (90), but he values "the long-range benefits of helping students achieve their goals" (91).

153   Butler, John. "Remedial Writers: The Teacher's Job as Corrector of Papers." *A Sourcebook for Basic Writing Teachers*. Ed. Theresa Enos. New York: Random, 1987. 557–64. Print.

Butler suggests that the markings that a teacher puts on a basic writer's paper mean little to the writer. The writer already knows that he or she is a weak writer, and these marks confirm this fact. While the comments are meaningful to the instructor, they are not meaningful to the writer. This essay encourages instructors to use comments on each student essay as a chance to encourage the writer and to meet one-on-one with students to help the student with specific problems in his or her writing.

154   Conrad, Susan M., and Lynn M. Goldstein. "ESL Student Revision after Teacher-Written Comments: Text, Contexts, and Individuals." *Journal of Second Language Writing* 8.2 (1999): 147–79. Print.

The authors analyze the effect written feedback has on the revision processes of three ESL college students. Researching drafts of student papers, written comments by teachers, and transcripts of teacher-student conferences, Conrad and Goldstein conclude that "the crucial variable that influenced the effectiveness of revisions was the type of problem students were asked to revise" (160). Students generally seemed to successfully revise problems related to lack of details or examples, coherence, cohesion, purpose, paragraphing, or lexical choice. Students were usually unsuccessful, however, in revising problems related to explanation, explicitness, and analysis. Additionally, the authors identify contextual factors that affect the revision process (teacher and student beliefs, roles and assumptions, content knowledge, and time constraints). Three pedagogical implications are drawn: the need for different instructional strategies appropriate to the context, the benefits of explicitness when giving feedback, and the benefits of composition classrooms that are designed around the content about which students will write (174).

155   Gay, Pamela. "Dialogizing Response in the Writing Classroom: Students Answer Back." *Journal of Basic Writing* 17.1 (1998): 3–17. Print.

Teacher commentary on student-written texts usually yields emotional reactions from students. For teachers to gain perspective on how students react to their comments, Gay advocates a written dialogic interaction between teacher and student. Students should respond to teacher commentary immediately upon receiving their drafts, even if their reactions include anger, frustration, or confusion. In addition, students should be encouraged to initiate teacher commentary by writing a letter to the teacher in which they identify their goals for their text and their own perceived weaknesses and strengths as writers. Through this exercise, students learn to appreciate the dialogic nature of language and to appreciate a range of reader reactions to their written texts.

156   Gray-Rosendale, Laura, and Raymona Leonard. "Demythologizing the 'Basic Writer': Identity, Power, and Other Challenges to the Discipline." *BWe: Basic Writing e-Journal* 3.1 (2001): n. pag. Web. 11 Aug. 2009.

Gray-Rosendale and Leonard focus on one student, Leonard, who had successfully completed Northern Arizona University's STAR (Successful Transition and Academic Readiness) summer program and subsequently took Gray-Rosendale's English 105 class. The authors detail each assignment and cite examples from Leonard's writing. Along with an analysis of these texts, there are examples from and comments on both the teacher's and the student's responses. In many ways, this essay outlines a dialogue between teacher and student writer as each responds—and continues to respond—to the other about the student's work. Carrying on such ongoing dialogues with our basic writing students, the authors say, "we will learn a great deal more about what students labeled as such think about their own writing, about Basic Writing as a discipline, and about the kind of scholarship we produce" (par. 62). Gray-Rosendale and Leonard call not only for the inclusion of student voices in our research and scholarship but also for a "place where student intervention and query is in fact the very foundation of our scholarly inquiry" (par. 66).

157   Grobman, Laurie. "Building Bridges to Academic Discourse: The Peer Group Leader in Basic Writing Peer Response Groups." *Journal of Basic Writing* 18.2 (1999): 47–68. Print.

Basic writers are traditionally located outside the realm of academic discourse, which makes peer-response activities problematic for them because they do not feel that they have sufficient authority to criticize other writers' work. Grobman attempts to correct this problem by introducing a peer-group leader—a sophomore who offers assistance and guidance to the students—into her first-year class's peer-response activities. Grobman concludes with a discussion of the pros and cons of employing such a leader in the basic writing classroom.

158   Hanson, Sandra Sellers, and Leonard Vogt. "A Variation on Peer Critiquing: Peer Editing as the Integration of Language Skills." *A Sourcebook for Basic Writing Teachers*. Ed. Theresa Enos. New York: Random, 1987. 575–78. Print.

Students entering universities under open admissions typically did not possess the language skills necessary to participate in the analysis of writing required in traditional peer critiquing. Therefore Hanson and Vogt created a model of peer editing that develops language skills through the integration of speaking, listening, reading, and writing. Although the peer-editing procedure begins with a focus on content and structure, three-member peer groups spend extensive time on editing. Each writer reads his or her paper aloud, stopping after each sentence for peer comments on grammar and mechanics. Through the process of peer editing, reviewers and writers begin to recognize discrepancies between the writer's verbal representation of his or her text and the text itself and thus learn to catch their own errors. The integration of language skills involved in the process of peer editing allows writers to see the changes they need to make in their writing. The ability to distinguish one's own errors gives basic writers a critical voice and autonomy in their own learning.

159   Horner, Bruce. "Rethinking the 'Sociality' of Error: Teaching Editing as Negotiation." *Rhetoric Review* 11.1 (1992): 172–99. Print.

Compositionists generally agree that what counts as an "error" in writing is often a failure to adhere to a set of arbitrary conventions— socially agreed-on ways to make notations that create meaning. However, the history of the regularization of these conventions suggests that they favor the syntactic form of dialects spoken by the dominant social groups; that correctness in writing has to do with power, status, and class; and that pedagogies can contribute to a sense of powerlessness in speakers of nonstandard dialects. It might be more productive, then, to understand errors as representing flawed social transactions and a failure on the part of both the writer and the reader to negotiate an agreement about the significance that should be attributed to the written notations offered. Such an understanding would allow power to operate dialectically, and basic writers would make changes not to appease their instructors but to communicate particular meanings to particular readers.

160   Hull, Glynda. "Research on Error and Correction." *Perspectives on Research and Scholarship in Composition.* Ed. Ben W. McClelland and Timothy R. Donovan. New York: MLA, 1985. 162–84. Print.

Hull surveys research on and attitudes toward error and suggests pedagogical approaches to error. Acknowledging that the role of research in this area is to help provide access for underprepared students, Hull discusses the changes in attitudes toward error that make possible an informed pedagogy focused on inclusion. Revision is reformulation rather than surface polishing. Research is beginning to focus on error as a cognitive process. Hull identifies key articles on the history of attitudes toward error; the relationships among power, status, race, and class; and the desire of inexperienced writers to conform to conventions. There has been "a movement away from a concern solely for correctness and toward an interest in rhetoric" (171). The article categorizes and analyzes research on the mental processes involved in making errors. It includes research on error counts, error categories, and possible sources of error, arguing that errors should be treated from a developmental perspective. Another subtopic is research on editing, which typically includes protocol analysis and interviews. Research demonstrates that "students can learn to edit through repeated acts of locating errors and imagining alternatives to them in contrast to learning about errors in the abstract in hopes of somehow inhibiting them" (181). The article ends with recommendations for further research on error that will increase the access of "outsiders."

Reading and Using Texts

161   Bernstein, Susan N., and Pete Johnson. "Writing to Learn: The Nickel and Dimed Project." *Research and Teaching in Developmental Education* 20.2 (2004): 59–75. Print.

The participant inquiry research of a critical literacy project in a linked developmental reading and writing course suggests that students engaged in real-life mathematics, reading, and writing can gain content knowledge, critical literacy, and appreciation of the roles math and literacy may play in their lives. The assignments for the linked classes were based on Barbara Ehrenreich's book, *Nickel and Dimed.* Literacy lessons included multiple, guided close readings and rereadings of the book as well as note-taking lessons and writing assignments, such as reactions to insights gained while rereading the book. Mathematical lessons included a re-creation in the students' Houston area of Ehrenreich's efforts to survive on a minimum wage salary. Students combined mathematical and literacy insights, and the authors offer poignant evidence of students' maturation.

162 Falk, Jane E. "Shaped by Resistance: Work as a Topical Theme for the Composition Classroom." *Open Words: Access and English Studies* 1.2 (2007): 49–61. Print.

Falk traces the use of work as a topical theme through several semesters of first-year composition at The University of Akron. A former manufacturing hub, Akron experienced severe decline in its rubber industry, and a high percentage of University of Akron students reported having at least one part-time job while they attended the university. In her composition classroom, the author utilized summer reading texts such as Barbara Ehrenreich's *Nickel and Dimed*, Yvonne Thornton's *The Ditchdigger's Daughters*, and Joyce Dyer's *Gum-Dipped*. Assignments ranged from personal narratives of a work experience, rhetorical analyses of American Dream narratives, critical analyses of employer-employee relationships, and comparisons between student work experiences and those of fictional characters in film and television. Collaborative projects involving field research furthered the inquiry into work issues. While many students showed critical thinking and raised awareness of issues, student resistance often acted as a catalyst for assignment revisions and prompted the use of reflective journals. In particular, students debated the depressing nature of some work-related topics, their perceptions of the summer reading texts, and the ethical issues involved in conducting research in one's own workplace. Falk concludes that, "despite initial resistance to the topic, I believe that the study of students' working lives enables growth, furthers lively discussion and critical thinking about the commodified and class stratified world in which we live, and has present and future relevance for students at The University of Akron" (60).

163 Jones, Billie J. "Are You Using? Textbook Dependency and Breaking the Cycle." *BWe: Basic Writing e-Journal* 2.1 (2000): n. pag. Web. 11 Aug. 2009.

Jones argues that while textbooks stabilize courses often organized at the last moment for adjunct instructors, help instructors link reading and writing, and are safe in their familiarity, they also often place needless philosophical and monetary restraints on teachers and students alike. These textbooks rarely fit an instructor or class population completely and are often directed at traditional-age first-year college students rather than returning learners. Jones calls for close analysis of textbook dependence in basic writing classes and a knowledgeable choice about when to use them. The author suggests that by examining often unconscious dependencies on textbooks in basic writing classrooms, instructors will be able to creatively reexamine classroom activities and more closely approach course goals.

164   Maxson, Jeffrey. "'Government of da Peeps, for da Peeps, and by da Peeps': Revisiting the Contact Zone." *Journal of Basic Writing* 24.1 (2005): 24–47. Print.

Maxson discusses ways to advance contact-zone pedagogy for basic writing students. Based on his teaching of a hybrid basic/first-year writing class at a midsize public university, Maxson focuses attention on the subject matter of a writing classroom: academic language and students' (assumed) position of outsiders to academic discourse. In the first exercise, students translate a challenging text into a recognized form of slang. In the second exercise, students compose a parody of academic language and genre. The students' writing explores the power dynamics at play in both academic texts and writing classrooms. Maxson argues that these two exercises challenge the idea that basic writing students cannot participate in productive critiques of academic discourse.

165   Moran, Mary Hurley. "Connections between Reading and Successful Revision." *Journal of Basic Writing* 16.2 (1997): 76–89. Print.

Moran explores the hypothesis that students who read their writing aloud produce more successful drafts than students who do not. Moran notes a correlation between reading ability and the efficacy of this activity. Reading drafts aloud was beneficial to students with adequate or good reading skills but did not make any significant difference in the case of poor readers. The first stage of the research involved investigating students' writing processes. Poor writers often wrote a single draft of a paper and made only superficial changes during the revision process. Stronger writers, by contrast, completed more drafts, revised more thoroughly, and began by revising content and style before looking at issues of mechanics and structure. The second stage involved secondary research about the relationship between drafting and revising aloud, and Moran mentions that the findings of much of the research agree with her hypothesis. In the third stage, Moran describes a classroom experiment that was designed to test the validity of her hypothesis that the more proficient readers would read their drafts aloud and score higher on the essay and that the experimental group would read their drafts aloud more often than students in the control group. The first assertion was not definitively proven; however, the second seems to have been correct. As a result of her experiment, Moran was convinced that reading essay drafts aloud is beneficial to basic writers who are also proficient readers but is not beneficial to students who do not engage in reading with any degree of frequency.

166   Salvatori, Mariolina. "Reading and Writing a Text: Correlations between Reading and Writing Patterns." *A Sourcebook for Basic Writing Teachers.* Ed. Theresa Enos. New York: Random, 1987. 176–86. Print.

Basic writers tend toward what Wolfgang Iser calls "consistency building" (179), seeking main ideas and familiar concepts rather than attending to multiple interpretations and textual inconsistencies. Thus reading instruction that includes analysis of how readers construct meaning and interact with texts is integral to the basic writing class. As writers become more actively involved in constructing textual meanings through reading, their writing begins to exhibit recognition of inconsistencies, alternative interpretations, and disagreement. Salvatori's research suggests that reading has a greater impact on writing than previously thought.

167   Spigelman, Candace. "Taboo Topics and the Rhetoric of Silence: Discussing *Lives on the Boundary* in Basic Writing." *Journal of Basic Writing* 17.1 (1998): 42–55. Print.

Spigelman explores basic writing students' resistance—expressed largely through silence—to Mike Rose's *Lives on the Boundary* [111]. Using Rose's text, Spigelman encouraged her students to explore and critique educational and institutional inequities such as those Rose faced and that many of the students likely also faced. While in their essays many students identified personally with Rose's struggles, they resisted larger cultural critique: they rejected any notion that the system was to blame and read *Lives on the Boundary* as an American success story. Interpreting her students' refusal to speak about the failures and exclusions of education as rhetorics of silence, Spigelman argues that despite students' confusion and discomfort, compositionists should not abandon the ethical and political implications of writing instruction, but neither should we ignore the implications of those silences. Finally, citing a discussion she had with Rose, Spigelman urges compositionists to address these contradictions and conflicts through creativity and imagination—first by helping students to see inequalities and then by helping students re-imagine alternatives.

Style, Grammar, and Usage

168   Briggs, Lynn, and Ann Watts Pailliotet. "A Story about Grammar and Power." *Journal of Basic Writing* 16.2 (1997): 46–61. Print.

The authors combine a self-reflection on how grammatical instruction can be used to reinforce institutional hierarchies at several levels with a close analysis of the words preservice students use to respond to perceived student errors to demonstrate how grammatical instruction remains a locus of power and control in English instruction at any level. Briggs and Pailliotet study undergraduate preservice students' responses to student errors on a test. Despite at least two semesters of writing courses taught from a process or postprocess approach to language conventions, these preservice students overwhelmingly linked usage errors with student incompetence and carelessness and did not focus on the cognitive aspects of these errors. While these responses were frustrating in light of the exam's wording and these preservice students' class work, Briggs and Pailliotet were not surprised because of the institutional and cultural responses to language conventions. Further, the authors recognize that they participate in linking grammar and power by participating, however reluctantly, in administering and correcting the test. English educators at all levels are encouraged to continue to broaden their approaches to working with students, especially preservice students, on how to address surface-level error and grammatical instruction.

169   Connors, Robert J., and Andrea Lunsford. "Frequency of Formal Errors in Current College Writing, or Ma and Pa Kettle Do Research." *College Composition and Communication* 39.4 (1988): 395–409. Print.

In their analysis of three hundred samples of writing from first- and second-year college composition courses across the United States, Connors and Lunsford wanted to identify the most common patterns of student writing errors and the patterns that were marked most consistently by American teachers (397). Topping the list of 54 identified types of errors were spelling (450 errors), no comma after introductory element (138 errors), comma splices (124 errors), and wrong words (102 errors). They found that "what constitutes a serious, markable error var[ies] widely" from teacher to teacher and that "teachers do not seem to mark as many errors as we often think they do" (402). In addition, what constitutes an error is largely an individual judgment, the kinds of errors students make may be a result of cultural trends, and students are probably not making any more errors in their writing than they did decades ago.

170   D'Eloia, Sarah. "The Uses—and Limits—of Grammar." *Journal of Basic Writing* 1.1 (1977): 1–20. Print.

The analytical study of grammar is of limited value for basic writers, but D'Eloia suggests that other approaches to grammar are useful. Basic writing instructors benefit from grammatical expertise since it gives them tools to identify, explain, and design appropriate exercises for student error. Students benefit when they are taught grammar economically and as part of the writing process. Instructors should use minimal, simple terminology to teach students as much grammar as they need to make standard English predictable. Students should complete grammar exercises that help them transfer abstract principles into the production of correct writing, such as dictation, focused proofreading, paraphrasing, and imitation. A discovery approach, in which students move inductively to grammar rules, can be more helpful, though time consuming. D'Eloia provides sample exercises and a syllabus for teaching the verb phrase.

171   Fearn, Leif, and Nancy Farnan. "When Is a Verb? Using Functional Grammar to Teach Writing." *Journal of Basic Writing* 26.1 (2007): 63–87. Print.

This article outlines the result of teaching two sections of tenth-grade students with a focus on what words do in sentences, rather than on the more traditional focus on what those words are called. Fearn and Farnan compare their results for those two sections with another section taught with a focus on identification, description, and definition (IDD). Their results indicate that while all students scored about the same on mechanical accuracy and a grammar test, their two classes did better on holistically graded writing.

172   Gray, Loretta S., and Paula Heuser. "Nonacademic Professionals' Perception of Usage Errors." *Journal of Basic Writing* 22.1 (2003): 50–70. Print.

Gray and Heuser update the survey that Maxine Hairston created for her groundbreaking article, "Not All Errors Are Created Equal: Nonacademic Readers in the Professions Respond to Lapses in Usage." Hairston correctly assumed that readers would consider some errors more egregious than others. To determine what errors would be the most bothersome, Hairston surveyed professionals who were not English teachers. The survey consisted of sixty-six sentences, each with a single mistake. Nonacademics were to choose from the following options: "Does not bother me," "Bothers me a little," or "Bothers me a lot." Gray and Heuser added a "No Error" answer and some grammatically correct sentences to the survey and represented each error by at least two sentences. The survey revealed that respondents were often inconsistent or incorrect in applying grammar rules. Overall, the revised study results suggest that while nonacademics are less bothered by usage errors, the errors that they find most bothersome are still common dialectical features. Gray and Heuser argue for a comprehensive grammar curriculum so that students may learn metalinguistic skills to understand the ways that language usage norms vary among communities.

173   Harris, Muriel, and Katherine E. Rowan. "Explaining Grammatical
      Concepts." *Journal of Basic Writing* 8.2 (1989): 21–41. Print.

      Harris and Rowan suggest that editing is a complex problem that is
      perceived as having many steps, especially for basic writers. While
      such students do not "need to be able to spout grammatical *terminol-
      ogy*," they do need to "understand fundamental grammatical *con-
      cepts*" to successfully edit their writing (22). Harris and Rowan
      suggest drawing on "concept learning research"—an approach that
      focuses on explaining a student's "most frequent misunderstandings"
      (23). The authors explain and outline in detail four key steps to
      understand and explain concepts: recalling background knowledge,
      controlling all the critical features of a concept, recognizing new
      instances of a concept, and discriminating apparent from real in-
      stances of a concept. The authors also make suggestions on how to
      implement their ideas. They conclude that no one method works
      for all students and all problems; however, they suggest using a com-
      bination of approaches.

174   Hartwell, Patrick. "Grammar, Grammars, and the Teaching of
      Grammar." *College English* 47.2 (1985): 105–27. Print.

      To demonstrate how misunderstandings in the debate over grammar
      instruction have rendered it largely useless for producing effective
      strategies for teaching writing, Hartwell identifies five definitions of
      grammar: the arrangement of words, the study of rules about the
      arrangement and use of words, judgments based on the use and
      arrangement of words, school grammar, and stylistic grammar. He
      argues that instructors often confuse the more useful definition
      of grammar (how language works) with power-imbued definitions of
      grammar (school rules for writing correctly). Too often, teachers
      conclude that students are poor writers because they don't know the
      school rules for writing when, in fact, students often have great
      command over how language works. Hartwell concludes that our
      theories and research studies should teach us that student involve-
      ment with language is always preferable to any direct instruction on
      the "rules" of that language.

175   Kenkel, James, and Robert Yates. "A Developmental Perspective on
      the Relationship between Grammar and Text." *Journal of Basic Writ-
      ing* 22.1 (2003): 35–49. Print.

      Citing the long-standing awareness of the limitations of teaching for-
      mal grammar to developmental students, Kenkel and Yates propose
      viewing student errors from a developmental perspective—not as
      evidence of ignorance or carelessness but as "principled attempts to
      manage information" (45). Expanding on the earlier work of Charles
      Fries, Mina Shaughnessy, Patrick Hartwell, Robert De Beaugrande,

Rei Noguchi, Charles Coleman, and Eleanor Kutz, the authors suggest that some nonstandard constructions can be explained as students' "difficulty fitting complex ideas into the correspondingly more complex syntactic structures" (39). The authors assert that assignments should be constructed to encourage mature shifting of focus (something that a personal narrative, for example, does not do) and "making explicit comparisons between student texts and mature texts" (46). These types of nonstandard constructions are not performance errors, they contend, cannot be easily self-corrected, and will not disappear after extensive reading and writing.

176   Lees, Elaine O. "Proofreading as Reading, Errors as Embarrassments." *A Sourcebook for Basic Writing Teachers*. Ed. Theresa Enos. New York: Random, 1987. 216–30. Print.

Lees argues that a social view of proofreading and error explains why basic writers have difficulty correcting their own writing. Joseph Williams's work on the complexities of perceiving error shows that errors are located not in texts or writers but in the reader's experience. Proofreading is not a mechanical process of correcting the physical features of a text but a critical interpretation carried out within a cultural group. Skilled proofreaders use texts to construct meanings that support conventional judgments of literacy. Unsuccessful proofreaders do not possess the interpretive frameworks to organize the features necessary for revealing errors. Errors are flaws in social display that embarrass writers by revealing their imperfect mastery of behaviors considered appropriate in communities they wish to join. Some basic writers have trouble leaving behind their original interpretive community for that of Standard Edited American English and might always need help when editing their work.

177   McAlexander, Patricia J. "Checking the Grammar-Checker: Integrating Grammar Instruction with Writing." *Journal of Basic Writing* 19.2 (2000): 124–40. Print.

Following advice from Rei Noguchi's *Grammar and the Teaching of Writing* [180], McAlexander implemented a short course in grammar followed by a grammar-checker project and experienced success in her academic assistance composition classes as a result. The project provided a review of the grammar lessons, applied many grammar rules specifically to the students' writing, and taught students the effective use of the grammar checker.

178   Neuleib, Janice, and Irene Brosnahan. "Teaching Grammar to Writers." *Teaching Developmental Writing: Background Readings*. Ed. Susan Naomi Bernstein. Boston: Bedford, 2001. 91–97. Print.

Neuleib and Brosnahan argue that for teachers to use approaches like sentence combining and error analysis in the classroom, the teachers themselves must know grammar better than they currently do. The authors tested twenty-four teacher-certification students in a required upper-level grammar course and found that most of these prospective teachers had had grammar instruction at three or more levels (elementary, junior high, high school, and college) but that few knew grammar as well as they thought they did. Neuleib and Brosnahan attribute this gap in perception to fuzzy definitions of grammar that are not informed by the history of language. To help students edit for grammar, teachers "need to be able to work out exercises of the types illustrated by Shaughnessy and D'Eloia, exercises patterned to individual students' language problems" (118). Better grammar instruction at the teacher-training level will enable teachers to apply grammar instruction effectively in their own classrooms.

See: Sarah D'Eloia, "The Uses—and Limits—of Grammar" [170].

179   Newman, Michael. "Correctness and Its Conceptions: The Meaning of Language Form for Basic Writers." *Journal of Basic Writing* 15.1 (1996): 23–38. Print.

Basic writers are sometimes overly preoccupied with grammatical concerns because they are "trying to send the message that they belong to the academic world they have come to join" (35). Surface-level errors are best approached with students through acknowledging this perspective and working with them on how their texts might fit in best with the expectations of register or genre. Newman posits that teaching language conventions from a perspective that views many usage edicts as based on logic or another language's grammatical rules does students little good; nor does denying the appropriateness of the above-mentioned usage edicts, as so many sociolinguists do. These edicts carry weight because they are based on myth, not science, and the myths of prescriptivism are an attempt to make clear what is not. Instead, instructors may do best by focusing on register variations, approaching tasks with students by working with them to best fit their texts into those already in the genre. In this way, instructors would not just be teaching grammar but would be focused on helping students "acquir[e] a new way of meaning" (38).

180   Noguchi, Rei R. *Grammar and the Teaching of Writing: Limits and Possibilities.* Urbana: NCTE, 1991. Print.

Citing a long line of research from anti- and pro-grammarians, Noguchi suggests that writing teachers navigate the middle ground by using grammar in a way that works to improve student writing. This sort of grammar instruction addresses a manageable collection of a select few rules and rubrics based loosely on generative grammar and commonsense editing models that can help writing students help themselves. Noguchi addresses grammar more as an editing tool than as a generative tool. To further circumvent a reductive traditional approach, Noguchi suggests an editing and revising model based on students' innate and cultural grammatical and syntactic knowledge.

181   Truscott, John. "The Effect of Error Correction on Learners' Ability to Write Correctly." *Journal of Second Language Writing* 16.4 (2007): 225–72. Print.

In the last decade, much research about error correction has presented one-sided discussions, offering a favorable view of error correction. In this small-scale meta-analysis of the effect of error correction on learners' ability to write accurately, Truscott comes to the conclusion that error correction actually has a small negative effect on learners' ability to write accurately. Error correction is defined as correcting errors of all types, such as spelling errors and grammatical errors. Six controlled and six uncontrolled experiments are selected for synthesis. All of the controlled experiments suggest that correction has small harmful effects on students' ability to write accurately, and the uncontrolled studies indicate small gains in accuracy made by correction groups. However, Truscott points out two biasing factors that may lead to the gains shown in correction groups in the uncontrolled studies: (1) the same setting of correction and testing and (2) avoidance. The first factor means the break between the correction and the measurement of accuracy is very short, and thus long-term effects remain unknown. The avoidance factor explains the phenomenon that students tend to avoid using situations corrected before, thus leading to deceptive gains in accuracy. A discussion of factors that may have biased previous studies as well as meta-analysis of key studies of controlled comparisons between those who received correction and those who did not and of absolute gains made by correction groups reveal the ways that previous studies have overestimated the effectiveness of correction and underestimated the harmfulness of correction.

182   Weaver, Constance. *Teaching Grammar in Context*. Portsmouth: Boynton, 1996. Print.

Weaver explains that grammatical concepts taught in isolation have not been effective in improving students' writing. Noting that "students can learn and apply many grammatical concepts without learning to analyze the parts of speech and various other grammatical constructions" (25), she urges the teaching of grammar through example rather than through the memorization of rules. She addresses reasons for teaching grammar and reviews research studies from 1936 on, providing a tour of research on the efficacy of grammar instruction. Weaver illustrates how English speakers learn complex English grammar without direct instruction, and she posits that errors in writing are "evidence of thinking" and that teachers need strategies that will teach students to "edit effectively" (59). Her recommendations include envisioning the writing process as truly recursive, using editing checklists, and modeling editing. Weaver also argues that editing should be linked to college-level writing, calling for teachers to narrow their focus and concentrate on teaching only those grammatical concepts and terms that are truly necessary for effective editing and revising, and she further advocates setting such an approach in the context of learning theory.

183   Weaver, Constance. "Teaching Style through Sentence Combining and Sentence Generating." *Teaching Developmental Writing: Background Readings.* Ed. Susan Naomi Bernstein. Boston: Bedford, 2001. 119–29. Print.

Weaver offers four mini-lessons for preservice and in-service teachers in a course on grammar or the teaching of grammar. The lessons help teachers to view themselves as writers and to model techniques of teaching grammar in context. The first lesson encourages students to include narrative and descriptive details in their writing. The second lesson encourages students to write "I am" poems that metaphorically equate themselves with things that reflect their interests. The third lesson encourages students to identify present participle phrases, past-participle phrases, and absolute phrases and to use all three of these free modifiers in their writing. The fourth lesson encourages students to find effective examples of absolute constructions in literature and to appreciate absolute constructions as a means of conveying descriptive detail.

184   Williams, Joseph. "The Phenomenology of Error." *College Composition and Communication* 32.2 (1981): 152–68. Print.

Williams explores how educated readers read and react to perceived errors based on the complex interplay of text, reader, and intention. Williams shows how differently texts are read when they are read not for error but for their message. He does this by highlighting passages taken from style guides that break the very rules they posit. He argues that error cannot be defined only as either a violation of a grammatical rule or a breach of social expectations because the significance of an error depends on our response to it. Williams challenges his readers to realize that "if we read any text the way we read freshman essays, we will find many of the same kind of errors we routinely expect to find and therefore do find" (159). Williams discusses the range of responses we have to "errors" that are often lumped together in style guides and common wisdom as "nonstandard," showing how errors that mark class (nonstandard verb forms, for example) provoke much higher negative responses than errors of usage (the use of *irregardless*, for example).

Curriculum Development

Course Development

185 Bartholomae, David. "Facts, Artifacts, and Counterfacts: A Basic Reading and Writing Course for the College Curriculum." *A Sourcebook for Basic Writing Teachers.* Ed. Theresa Enos. New York: Random, 1987. 275–306. Print.

This article details how Bartholomae and Anthony Petrosky came to design a course for basic writers. It discusses their approach to the course (one based on close reading and written responses to specific texts), the ways in which such reading strategies are critical for basic writers, and the specific curriculum goals of their basic reading and writing course. Their course concentrates on literacy and writing from a social constructionist perspective and seeks to teach academic discourse to basic writers. Bartholomae offers a critical synopsis of their textbook, outlining the methodologies and pedagogical philosophies surrounding Bartholomae and Petrosky's course. He takes up questions of epistemology in basic writing pedagogy and examines issues of authority as they are presented within basic writers' prose.

186 Bartholomae, David, and Anthony Petrosky. *Facts, Artifacts, and Counterfacts.* Portsmouth: Boynton, 1986. Print.

Bartholomae and Petrosky present curriculum, theoretical framework, and rationale for teaching "students outside the mainstream — students unprepared for the textual demands of college education" (4). Their course disrupts many of the previous constructions of basic writing courses by suggesting that basic writers be challenged intellectually rather than given rote exercises. Drawing from contemporary theory and social constructionist philosophies, the authors reveal how teaching thoughtful, critical reading can help basic writers to utilize and comprehend academic discourse. The book includes a brief discussion of the problems basic writers face, pragmatic suggestions about how to teach reading and writing skills to basic writers, the procedures basic writers undertake when completing reading and writing, a case study of one basic writing student, an explanation of the implications of reading and writing assignments, and a discussion of error and editing and the complexities teachers face while teaching these issues to basic writers.

187 Bruch, Patrick L. "Universality in Basic Writing: Connecting Multicultural Justice, Universal Instructional Design, and Classroom

Practices." *BWe: Basic Writing e-Journal* 5.1 (2004): n. pag. Web. 11 Aug. 2009.

Bruch addresses the challenges of reinvigorating universality for basic writing by bringing together the notions of multicultural justice and Universal Instructional Design. He "proposes an understanding of universality that links the work of Basic Writing to recent political philosophy and the pedagogical movement Universal Instructional Design." (The term *Universal Instructional Design* comes from architecture and refers to the movement to make buildings accessible to those with physical disabilities while enhancing the quality of the design for all users.) Bruch presents assignments created for his basic writing class that his students have redesigned and enhanced to address their diverse needs as learners. Bruch suggests that implementing Universal Instructional Design to the theory and practice of basic writing pedagogy "is a way of equipping ourselves to explain the project of Basic Writing—the project of enabling participation in transforming cultural and material obstacles to educational equity." He offers an example of the ways in which Universal Instructional Design provides opportunities for him to collaborate with his students in revising a summary assignment so that it is more inclusive of students' multiple learning styles, emphasizing opportunities for students "to participate in creating alternative designs for texts." Such strategies, Bruch argues, offer students insight into conversations generated by texts and give students a chance to "lear[n] about literacy work by doing the work of literacy."

188   Carter, Shannon. *The Way Literacy Lives: Rhetorical Dexterity and Basic Writing Instruction.* Albany: State U of New York P, 2008. Print.

Drawing on activity theory and New Literacy Studies, Carter advocates teaching rhetorical dexterity, "a meta-awareness of the ways in which literacy functions in a familiar community of practice as a first step in reading and negotiating an unfamiliar one" (63). Carter proposes a basic writing curriculum whose subject is literacy itself, as students analyze their own literacies of work and leisure before studying the rules for academic literacies. She begins by contextualizing her own institutional position as a composition director in Texas and by examining how high-stakes testing has shaped her university's writing program. She then illustrates the implications of reductive definitions of literacy with a compelling narrative of how her brother's highly literate behaviors remained unrecognized and invisible in Texas public schools. Claiming that the era of accountability has limited the effectiveness of the kind of critical pedagogy proposed by David Bartholomae and Anthony Petrosky, Carter argues that bringing high-stakes testing and schooled literacy into the classroom for critique can be both politically and pedagogically effective. Later chapters demonstrate what a course teaching rhetorical dexterity would look like. The book includes a course overview, classroom materials, and analyses of student writing.

189 Cohen, Samuel. "Tinkering toward WAC Utopia." *Journal of Basic Writing* 21.2 (2001): 56–72. Print.

Cohen begins with an extended metaphor that connects Thomas Pynchon, Voltaire's *Candide*, and the 1999 World Trade Organization protests in Seattle. Through the lens of concerns over globalization, Cohen examines the history of Writing across the Curriculum (WAC), its relationship to basic writing, and its possible future path. Cohen then outlines classroom workshop techniques that attend to students' basic skills without neglecting critical thinking or a postmodern perspective. He contends that instructors should not abandon the utopian ideals of WAC simply because they have failed to work perfectly in the past. Taking small steps, such as tinkering with individual classes and then with programmatic issues, he argues, is a path that offers much promise.

190 Connors, Robert J. "Basic Writing Textbooks: History and Current Avatars." *A Sourcebook for Basic Writing Teachers.* Ed. Theresa Enos. New York: Random, 1987. 259–74. Print.

Textbooks specifically for developmental writers first appeared in the 1890s, as mainstream composition authors such as A. S. Hill and John Genung responded to growing cultural and institutional concerns about linguistic correctness with basic treatments of college-level writing. By the advent of open admissions policies in the late 1960s, basic writing texts had slowly developed into standardized forms such as the simplified rhetorics and basic handbooks and workbooks, still seen in large numbers today. Simplified rhetorics as a whole portray the sentence and paragraph as the primary units of discourse and reduce writing to an algorithmic, rule-governed process. Basic writing handbooks and workbooks offer prescriptive lessons on mechanics and pages of fill-in-the-blank and multiple-choice exercises for which students provide correct answers. By isolating and diagnosing discrete grammatical problems through repetitive drills and simplified rules, these texts ignore most of what compositionists currently know about the phenomenon of writing—that it consists of saying something to someone in context. They also reflect a basic writing community that has not progressed as much as a reading of professional books and journals would indicate.

See: Joseph F. Trimmer, "Basic Skills, Basic Writing, Basic Research" [45].

191   Curtis, Marcia, and Anne Herrington. "Writing Development in the College Years: By Whose Definition?" *College Composition and Communication* 55.1 (2003): 69–90. Print.

Curtis and Herrington examine their book, *Persons in Process: Four Stories of Writing and Personal Development in College* (2000), to "explore more closely" their invocation of development and the relationship between writing development and personal development. At a moment when postmodern theories that figure the individual as constructed by discourses, or as shaped by biological or environmental factors, have placed the entire developmentalist project in question, the authors align themselves with theorists who view development as "multidirectional, not unidirectional" and who are interested in the "interplay between the individual and historical/contextual factors in shaping change" (70–71). In response to cautions about college writing focused on personal matters and attention to self, Curtis and Herrington focus on the five-year journey of a student featured in their longitudinal study to show that both writing development and personal development are characterized by "positive change that carries with it into the present clear threads of the past . . . and [an] inescapable link between public and private" (73). They focus on six essays written by "Lawrence/ Steven" to illustrate that when writers are provided with opportunities to write about personal/private concerns, they can discover and explore public/academic interests. For the students in their study, "writing development and personal development were furthered by class projects" that provided "specific and varied frames that gave a focus to students' self-reflections as well as connection with public interests" (85). In answer to the question posed in the title, Curtis and Herrington question an emphasis on skills assessment that narrows the concept of development and its measurement to a focus on grammar and syntax and on expository or argumentative writing. Concerned that measurement of skills might become confused with measurement of development, the authors argue for a broad, multidimensional view of writing curricula that draws on several developmental models of writing (they name Applebee's "Alternative Models of Writing Development").

192   Darabi, Rachelle L. "Basic Writers and Learning Communities." *Journal of Basic Writing* 25.1 (2006): 53–72. Print.

The positive impact of learning communities on student success and retention is well established, but there has been minimal examination of composition courses in such contexts. Darabi's study focuses on a Learning Community Pilot Program implemented at Indiana University–Purdue University Fort Wayne (IPFW), where the retention rate between the first and second year had been at 65 percent. A study by the IPFW Office of Academic Affairs found a strong correlation between passing basic writing and remaining in school. The pilot program was designed to structure a first-year learning community experience that linked together three skills-based courses that included basic writing. Attendance improved, Drop-Fail-Withdrawal (D-F-W) rates markedly decreased, and retention rates for students who participated in the program increased to 82 percent. Given these findings, Darabi suggests that basic writing courses may produce better results when taught within a learning community than in isolation. Students make strong connections with each other in the learning community context. This bonding carries over into their work with basic writing on many levels: the improved quality and completion of assignments as well as enhanced ownership of the writing process. In turn, collaborative work with writing strengthens the quality of student interactions in other classes, helping to make the shift from the more socially based interaction of high school to the learning-based interaction of college.

193 Davi, Angelique. "In the Service of Writing and Race." *Journal of Basic Writing* 25.1 (2006): 73–95. Print.

Davi argues that the incorporation of service learning allows underprivileged students to develop the necessary critical reading and writing skills needed in college. But more important, service learning also provides these students with the opportunity to recognize their own contributions to the community while simultaneously learning how to speak critically about race, class, and gender. Using her own experience as a teacher of underprivileged and underperforming students, she explores the benefits and drawbacks to service learning, pointing out that one of the common criticisms of this approach is that many students view service learning as their way of "feeling good about themselves," which prevents them from engaging in critical thought. To avoid this patronizing sentimentality, she asks her students to talk about what was difficult about service learning rather than just telling the "feel good" stories. By writing about their experiences in service learning and in the educational system, students learn to think critically about race, class, and gender.

194 Delpit, Lisa. "The Silenced Dialogue: Power and Pedagogy in Educating Other People's Children." *Landmark Essays on Basic Writing.* Ed. Kay Halasek and Nels P. Highberg. Mahwah: Erlbaum, 2001. 83–101. Print.

Delpit uses the process versus skills debate, as well as other examples, to uncover and critique larger societal and educational cultures of power that inform U.S. classrooms. Progressive and liberal educators,

Delpit argues, do significant and irreparable damage to black and poor students who are not participants in the culture of power by ignoring or denying that cultures of power exist and, in turn, by not articulating for students the rules of that culture. Delpit, however, does not advocate a simple, unself-reflexive return to direct instruction. She recognizes that students need to use their knowledge and to write for real audiences and purposes at the same time that they are taught and use the conventions and expectations of academic discourse. Delpit's narrative analysis, coupled with the chorus of teachers she quotes, constructs a look into the cultural divide that exists in classrooms in which white teachers, even those with the best of intentions, do not recognize themselves as part of the institutional and cultural forces constructed to ensure the continued success of middle-class and white students at the cost of further disenfranchisement of poor students and students of color. The pedagogical divide is articulated nowhere more strongly than in Delpit's contrastive descriptions of democratic and authoritarian classrooms.

195 Fleck, Andrew. "Instructional Note: 'We Think He Means . . .': Creating Working Definitions through Small-Group Discussion." *Teaching Developmental Writing: Background Readings*. Ed. Susan Naomi Bernstein. Boston: Bedford, 2001. 220–25. Print.

Fleck became frustrated while teaching a course structured around "The Arts of the Contact Zone" by Mary Louise Pratt and an excerpt from Stephen Greenblatt's *Marvelous Possessions*. In his analysis, his students were not arriving at understandings of these complicated texts. His solution was to create discussion groups of three to five students because research in the use of small discussion groups claims that students can better modify and clarify ideas through discussions with other students. Fleck reports that students who had never talked in class participated in the small-group conversations and that students used key-term definitions created by the group while discussing Greenblatt to write more sophisticated essays. Fleck concludes that small-group discussions release students from the anxiety of speaking to the entire class, help them to ask questions and clarify their thinking, and encourage them to engage in more sophisticated discussions of complicated texts.

See: Mary Louise Pratt, "Arts of the Contact Zone" [240].

196 Gleason, Barbara. "Returning Adults to the Mainstream: Toward a Curriculum for Diverse Student Writers." *Teaching Developmental Writing: Background Readings*. 3rd ed. Ed. Susan Naomi Bernstein. Boston: Bedford, 2007. 214–38. Print.

Based on her argument that returning students should not be placed in remedial courses, Gleason presents a case for creating writing courses specific to the working adult student and particularly for using ethnographic writings in these courses. She describes what she does in her courses at the Center for Worker Education, a program within the City College of New York. In addition, Gleason discusses the diversities within an adult population, especially at her academic institution, and how these academic and cultural diversities help the students and teacher to learn from one another and to expose their different levels of abilities and expectations in the academic world. Gleason demonstrates, through the case studies she presents, the connection between older adult students' conversational and oral presentations and their writing skills. She argues that their writing skills often contradict their true abilities and intellects, which are demonstrated in their oral skills. Once students recognize that they are able to tell stories about their own literacy development, they can begin writing ethnographic papers by incorporating their oral interviewing skills; these papers develop into a writing project. Via the sequenced writings, students learn academic writing abilities and forms and gain knowledge that should assist them in becoming successful in their college careers. Gleason argues that adult students do not need to be in remedial courses but need to experience a writing curriculum that allows them to be successful while expanding their literacies.

197   Goode, Dianne. "Creating a Context for Developmental English." *Teaching Developmental Writing: Background Readings*. Ed. Susan Naomi Bernstein. Boston: Bedford, 2001. 71–77. Print.

To motivate learners, Goode asserts, it is necessary to provide a real context for their reading and writing. Goode describes the CONCUR ("CONtextual CURriculum") program at Piedmont Community College in rural North Carolina. The purpose of the program is to provide developmental English students with a context for reading and writing. The CONCUR program models the workings of a publishing house: students choose what to read and what to write, and the term's writing is collected into a class-designed anthology that is published and shelved in the school library. Simply knowing that their writing will be published spurs the students to attend carefully to their coursework. Students read fifty to seventy-five pages each week and "reflect, analyze, speculate, [and] evaluate" their reading in a journal shared with the instructor (75). Students also participate in silent reading, book discussions, vocabulary sharing, mini-lessons on reading strategies, and literature circles.

198   Grobman, Laurie. "(Re)Writing Youth: Basic Writing, Youth Culture, and Social Change." *Journal of Basic Writing* 20.1 (2001): 5–26. Print.

Grobman attempts to carry into practice Henry Giroux's call for educators to consider carefully "the crisis of youth" and the ways that youth culture is depicted in the media. She therefore takes a cultural studies approach in working with her basic writing students to help them gain the critical and rhetorical skills "to write across and against their socially inscribed identities" (9). Grobman learns about public sites where her students can publish their views, but she also comes to question the implications of Giroux's call, particularly educators' responsibility to provide an ethical discourse in the classroom that might allow students to use their voices to assert their identities and to challenge existing ones. Grobman finds that she and her students got caught up in the contradictions of accepting and rejecting these representations, and she concludes that this ethical discourse is difficult to negotiate in practice. The difficulty she experiences raises some key questions for educators: How does the teacher encourage critique and at the same time not subtly direct students to engage in critique that is ideologically aligned with the instructor's? And at what point does the instructor accept students' views, even though these views support negative representations of young people, particularly representations that involve race?

199   Harris, Joseph. "Beyond Community: From the Social to the Material." *Journal of Basic Writing* 20.2 (2001): 3–15. Print.

This revised version of a talk given at the 2001 meeting of the City University of New York Association of Writing Supervisors continues a line of thinking that Harris set forth in A *Teaching Subject: Composition since 1966*, which critiqued the current use of metaphors of community in teaching writing as both utopian and confining. Harris argues that instructors need to avoid the kind of easy reliance on the idea of community that permeates discourse about writing classrooms. Instead, he suggests that instructors adopt alternate ways of imagining writing and teaching as taking place in more open, contested, and heteroglot spaces, proposing three counterconcepts to community: public, material, and circulation.

See: Mark Wiley, "Response to Joseph Harris's 'Beyond Community'" [211].

200   Harris, Joseph. "Negotiating the Contact Zone." *Journal of Basic Writing* 14.1 (1995): 27–42. Print.

Harris examines the problems that emerge from the growth, initiation, and conflict metaphors that have become dominant in the field of basic writing. While acknowledging differences in discourse, these metaphors fail to recognize the problems that occur for students. Harris discusses Mary Louise Pratt's theory of contact zones and suggests how a more expansive view of this theory could be helpful in basic writing. He maintains that if these conflicts are allowed to emerge in a natural way that encourages students to choose their own positions, this atmosphere would be more beneficial because it would be less artificial and would present differences in a more meaningful way.

See: Mary Louise Pratt, "Arts of the Contact Zone" [240].

201 Hidalgo, Alexandra. "Group Work and Autonomy: Empowering the Working-Class Student." *Open Words: Access and English Studies* 2:2 (2008): 3–23. Print.

Working-class students often face difficulties when attending college and may feel alienated from academic discourse. Unlike their middle-class counterparts, they may feel as if they do not belong in university classrooms and may feel frustrated in courses like freshman composition. Hidalgo draws on the experiences of scholars like Barbara Mellix, who, as a nontraditional, working-class, African American student, felt she was not "meant to be in those classrooms" and feared her peers and instructors would see her as an "imposter who should not be there" (5). In typical composition classrooms, discussions, writing assignments, and academic language can be quite daunting and intimidating for some working-class students. To empower these students and to make them feel comfortable as members of the academic environment, Hidalgo suggests group work to foster discussion of relevant readings, drafts of assignments, and ideas for improving writing. Group work reflects "community," which is "important in working-class culture" (10). Utilizing group work in writing classes creates a more comfortable atmosphere for working-class students to express themselves, gives them a sense of belonging, and helps them to become a part of the academic discourse community. This leads to success in future classes.

202 Lazere, Donald. "Back to Basics: A Force for Oppression or Liberation?" *Landmark Essays on Basic Writing.* Ed. Kay Halasek and Nels P. Highberg. Mahwah: Erlbaum, 2001. 121–34. Print.

Lazere asks whether liberatory pedagogy, which has come to be defined in the United States in generally Freirean terms, serves the needs of students better than a basic skills approach. "Leftists," he writes, "err grievously in rejecting . . . a restored emphasis on basic skills and knowledge which might be a force for liberation — not oppression — if administered with common sense, openness to cultural pluralism, and an application of basics toward critical thinking, particularly about sociopolitical issues" (123). In arguing his case, Lazere undertakes a Marxist critique of both liberal and conservative motives for pedagogical choices. Lazere launches a critique of James Sledd, Andrew Sledd, and Richard Ohmann, among others, for their refusal to see beyond their own assumptions about the relative value of various approaches to literacy education.

203   Leary, Chris. "'When We Remix . . . We Remake!!!' Reflections on Collaborative Ethnography, the New Digital Ethic, and Test Prep." *Journal of Basic Writing* 26.1 (2007): 88–105. Print.

Leary challenges the common notion in basic writing curricula that students must be taught low-level skills that will merely help them to "pass." Such curricula, he argues, confine students and leave their valuable voices out of the conversation on composition studies. Drawing from his own experience with leading a "collaborative ethnography" project in a basic writing course designed to prepare students to take the ACT writing exam, Leary illustrates two ways in which he worked to resist traditional approaches to teaching basic writing. First, he involved students with the composition of one of his graduate school essays in composition studies, engaging them in the critical reading of scholarly texts and in the written correspondence with another composition theorist, and eliciting their feedback in the writing and revision process of the essay itself. Leary later invited his students to experiment with the ACT writing exam by collaboratively drafting their responses to practice prompts, posting their responses online and hyperlinking their text to related Web sites, and comparing prompts across exams for their cultural implications. These two projects, he found, helped students not only to get involved in an academic conversation about the culture of composition but also to gain access to and be critical about higher-level composition issues, such as textual and digital remixing. This approach to basic writing, he argues, not only helps to foster students' success with the ACT, but it also helps them to reimagine writing as relevant, creative practice.

204   Maas-Feary, Maureen. "Attitude Is Everything, a Developmental Writing Instructor Finds While Teaching Freshmen English." *Research and Teaching in Developmental Education* 17.2 (2000): 83–85. Print.

Maas-Feary explores the difference in students' attitudes toward College English (a developmental writing class) and Freshman English (the writing class required for all students at her community college). Students in College English do not take pride in their work and believe that the class should be easy to pass, whereas Freshman English students take the class seriously and produce thoughtful work. Maas-Feary believes these attitude differences can be attributed to the stigma assigned to College English at her school. She concludes that the instructor needs to infuse the developmental writing class with an attitude of purpose by assigning college-level work that challenges students' views of themselves as well as the class.

205   Peele, Thomas. "Writing about Faith: Mainstream Music and Composition." *BWe: Basic Writing e-Journal* 6.1 (2007): n. pag. Web. 11 Aug. 2009.

Peele reminds readers that composition (and academe writ large) tends to devalue faith and formal religion—particularly when used as evidence. He argues for the inclusion of faith traditions within the curricula of the first-year composition classroom, asserting that the practice of discouraging students from writing about their faith diminishes their potential for examining their beliefs in context with people of other faith traditions. He feels that many basic writing students, in particular, need to have their faith-based experiences affirmed by the academy. To bring discussions of faith into an appropriate academic setting, Peele outlines a pedagogy in which students write about how popular music represents religion and faith—a pedagogy he finds valuable in part because students learn how various discourse communities conceptualize and value religion and faith. He presents a writing project he assigned in one of his classes; the assignment sequence has students use critical discourse analysis as a lens through which to consider issues of intertextuality and tone in lyrics that take up spiritual issues. Ultimately, Peele concludes that this sequence's focus on textual analysis, interpretation, and consideration of multiple perspectives allows students to develop and practice the kinds of intellectual and rhetorical proficiencies valued in the academy. Included in the article are several student responses, as well as links to PowerPoint presentations, thirty-second audio clips of songs used in the writing projects, and the writing assignment sheet given to students at the beginning of the project.

206   Raymond, Richard. "Building Learning Communities on Nonresidential Campuses." *Teaching Developmental Writing: Background Readings.* Ed. Susan Naomi Bernstein. Boston: Bedford, 2001. 204–18. Print.

Raymond describes the process that he and colleagues from the speech and anthropology departments went through to develop and implement a learning community on a campus with a substantial population of commuter and working students. Raymond discusses how the instructors gathered support, planned their classes, and underwent assessment by the college's assessment expert, students, and faculty. He also discusses the assessment tools that he and his colleagues used and includes student writing samples and excerpts from his own assessment journal. Raymond concludes that linked courses can help to demonstrate students' reading, writing, and critical thinking abilities and can help to facilitate student retention.

207   Remler, Nancy Lawson. "The More Active the Better: Engaging College English Students with Active Learning Strategies." *Teaching Developmental Writing*. 3rd ed. Boston: Bedford, 2007. 239–45. Print.

Using Charles Bonwell and James Eison's definition of active learning, Remler draws on her own classroom experiences to argue for an approach to teaching college English that emphasizes active learning strategies as the most effective means of facilitating student engagement and fostering understanding of course concepts. She discusses her successes with active learning strategies in both her sophomore literature course and her first-year composition course, where students engage with course material by working in groups and by constructing their own discussion questions using Bloom's taxonomy. When students take on the role of professor and instruct one another, Remler argues, they also take ownership of the class and thereby invest more heavily in the material.

208   Rustick, Margaret Tomlinson. "Grammar Games in the Age of Anti-Remediation." *Journal of Basic Writing* 26.1 (2007): 43–62. Print.

Rustick responds to the ambiguity surrounding grammar instruction for developmental writers, citing a necessary shift in the way basic writing teachers consider contextual differences between written and spoken language. She suggests supplementing grammar instruction with the use of creative games that require students to consider the way sentences are constructed and focus on how meaning and function shift when certain parts of a sentence are rearranged. Rustick argues that her games help students build metalinguistic knowledge through the manipulation of words and sentence syntax that can change the meaning and function of specific elements in a sentence.

209   Uehling, Karen S. *Starting Out or Starting Over: A Guide for Writing*. New York: Harper, 1993. Print.

"Starting out" refers to those "traditional" college students, eighteen to nineteen, who are entering college for the first time; "starting over" refers to nontraditional students returning to college to complete studies started years ago or attending college for the first time in search of a new career. A third target audience for the book is basic writers. The book is designed to break away from a skill-and-drill mode of worksheets and "objective" instruments to help students learn how to write better. Unlike other approaches, which publish complete student essays in tandem with "professional" writers' essays, this text employs student writing of various types, lengths, and quality. Uehling uses these assorted texts to illustrate many of her pedagogical points. For instance, she argues that distinctions between modes of discourse are an artificial way of examining composition because outside the artificial world of the classroom, few paragraphs and virtually no compositions are written exclusively in one mode. Uehling advises student writers about developing a positive attitude, accepting suggestions, letting go of the text and allowing others to read it, building their confidence as writers, and allaying fear. Uehling also spends some time discussing "critique anxiety" and ways to overcome this serious impediment to joining the conversation of the classroom (120–22).

210   Wiley, Mark. "Rehabilitating the Idea of 'Community.'" *Journal of Basic Writing* 20.2 (2001): 16–33. Print.

Wiley argues that composition studies, and in particular basic writing, can benefit from the present educational reform movement involving learning communities. Practically speaking, learning communities provide environments of peer collaboration and relationship building and can thus facilitate learning and writing development. Moreover, Wiley counters Joseph Harris's conception of the basic writing classroom as a "city" that privileges conflict over consensus and that positions the student as a developing public intellectual. Learning communities help students acquire the "discourse about being a student" (30) through social networks that do not ignore conflict but instead aid students' negotiation of consensus at their "point[s] of need" (31).

211   Wiley, Mark. "Response to Joseph Harris's 'Beyond Community.'" *Journal of Basic Writing* 20.2 (2001): 34–37. Print.

Wiley responds to Joseph Harris's critique of "community" in the Fall 2001 issue of the *Journal of Basic Writing* by emphasizing the materiality of learning communities, the need for both dissent and compromise, and the complementary natures of the concepts of community and public. Wiley rejects the notion that community implies a regressive, naïve, or enclosed space. Rather, he argues that communities, especially learning communities, offer new possibilities for thinking, learning, and writing.

See: Joseph Harris, "Beyond Community" [199].

212   Williams, Mark T., and Gladys Garcia. "Crossing Academic Cultures: A Rubric for Students and Teachers." *Journal of Basic Writing* 24.1 (2005): 93–119. Print.

The authors contend that a process-guided rubric, based on Kenneth Burke's dramatist pentad, is especially useful to transition students from the position of *outsider* to academic writing to the preferred position of *insider*. Relying heavily on Burke's "pentad of act, scene, agent, agency, and purpose," Williams and Garcia illustrate through student essays and subsequent analysis the many ways that student writers function as either *outsiders*, *crossers*, or *insiders* to the writing style that the academy demands (96). Acknowledging that traditional rubrics for writing assessment do not allow for cultural differences, the authors propose the process-guided rubric. They write, "We use the rubric to characterize student writers who may be crossing into the more critical terrain of academic culture and to invite fellow teachers to reconsider the values and viewpoints that underwrite our position within the academy" (95). An understanding of the process-based rubric that Williams and Garcia propose is realized through the in-depth analysis of student essays in terms of *outsider*, *crosser*, and *insider* writing. Detailed analyses acknowledge not only the strengths of each stage of writing but also the weaknesses of each stage. Furthermore, the authors suggest ways that those teaching basic writing may proceed in integrating the process-based rubric, support student writing, and learn from their students' writing.

213   Winslow, Rosemary, and Monica Mische. "The Hero's Performance and Students' Quests for Meaning and Identity: A Humanities and Writing Course Design." *Journal of Basic Writing* 15.2 (1996): 76–94. Print.

Winslow and Mische describe a thematic course they developed for at-risk students. The course is centered "around the idea of the hero as one put into a position of difficulty and who must then decide whether to act to overcome obstacles, to establish a new position for himself in society, and perhaps to renew society in the process" (77). Initially, students examine the archetype of the hero by reading Carol Pearson's *The Hero Within: Six Archetypes We Live By* and Homer's *Odyssey*. Classes are organized into seminar, large-group lecture, small-group workshop, and tutorial formats, and students are placed in a combination of these types of classes to work on their writing and their understanding of complex texts.

Essays and Personal Writing

214   Bartholomae, David. "Writing with Teachers: A Conversation with Peter Elbow." *College Composition and Communication* 46.1 (1995): 62–71. Print.

Based on ongoing exchanges between Peter Elbow and David Bartholomae, this essay critiques the ideology of expressive writing and Elbow's 1969 text, *Writing without Teachers*. Bartholomae defends his definition of academic writing and defines expressive writing in an attempt to distinguish between the two. While Bartholomae acknowledges ambiguity in the term *academic writing*, he constructs a definition by distinguishing academic writing from what it is not. He claims that since "academic writing is the real work of the academy," there can be no writing that is "without teachers" (63). Bartholomae further asserts that Elbow's text ultimately works to preserve the authority of the student as well as the assumed value of expressive writing. Instead, Bartholomae argues that basic writing as well as other college classes should be spaces in which we investigate the "transmission of power" (66). College writing courses, he says, should teach students about intertextuality as well as the dialogic nature of reading and writing, helping them to recognize that they are writing "in a space defined by all the writing that has preceded them" (64).

215   Berthoff, Ann E. "What Works? How Do We Know?" *Journal of Basic Writing* 12.2 (1993): 3–17. Print.

Berthoff attacks the idea of the five-paragraph essay and writing instruction that focuses on error. Instead, she advocates an approach that "preach[es] the gospel of the uses of chaos and the making of meaning" (5). Using the "us-against-them" approach (the writing instructors versus the deans), she comments that the deans want students to write beautiful, well-organized prose but give little or no thought to how students get there. She argues that students will come to that beautiful, well-organized prose only by combining personal and public discourse.

216   Bloom, Lynn Z. "The Ineluctable Elitism of Essays and Why They Prevail in First-Year Composition Courses." *Open Words: Access and English Studies* 1.2 (2007): 62–78. Print.

Based on an analysis of freshman composition readers published from 1946 to 1996, this article argues that the essay as a genre reflects elitist attitudes and education. Bloom isolates 175 authors who are "canonical essayists" (63) and suggests that they write to an upper-middle-class to middle-class audience, whose intellect and education make sophistication in prose and allusion a given. These canonical essays, even when they include journalism and excerpts from autobiographies, assume that the reader is "along for the pleasure of the ride itself as the essay meanders into engaging byways and scenic overlooks rather than sticking to the superhighway to the main idea" (64). A "common cultural repertoire" (64) among these authors and the anticipated audience constructs a barrier for working-class students to overcome. Bloom notes the lack of innovation in form and the adherence to standard written English in contemporary and canonical essays reproduced in textbooks that focus on working-class culture, feminist thought, and ethnic perspectives. She believes that the goal for both textbook publishers and writing programs is to "ensure that the essays, however elitist in form, may be understood in terms of middle-class values and experiences, even those that discuss working-class lives" (70). The glut of textbooks espousing middle-class values accompanies the teaching of first-year writing courses, which is "by and large a middle-class endeavor" (72). She feels that as long as the academy remains middle class, "there will be little incentive to re-orient composition pedagogy to challenge these middle-class values and aims" (73). Yet she concludes that "students' cultural horizons" cannot help but be broadened by the readers available for first-year writing courses (73), even though the essays within are written in standard written English. This merely reflects the dominant method of writing instruction in college-level reading and writing courses, which Bloom feels is as it should be.

217   Elliot, Norbert. "Narrative Discourse and the Basic Writer." *Journal of Basic Writing* 14.2 (1995): 19–30. Print.

Many experts in the field of basic writing use narrative in their own academic discourse but do not allow their students to use narrative in the classroom. An examination of the academic discourse about basic writing indicates that narrative is used widely as a way to make academic issues relevant to our lives. In light of this, perhaps we should reconsider our skepticism about the value of narrative discourse in the basic writing classroom. Narrative has attributes that foster many of the academic skills we seek to nurture in our students. For one thing, it serves as a form of legitimization — a way for students to establish a position before those who might otherwise dismiss them. Furthermore, narrative can facilitate metacognition. By asking students to distinguish between the story and the presentation of the events, we encourage them to think about the process of thinking. Perhaps most important, narrative can provide access to the mysterious, the spiritual, and the awe-inspiring. Through narrative, students can explore themselves and their place in the world, including the academy. They can discover the relationship between their lives and their ideas.

218   Mlynarczyk, Rebecca Williams. "Personal and Academic Writing: Revisiting the Debate." *Journal of Basic Writing* 25.1 (2006): 4–25. Print.

Hearkening back to a "defining moment in composition studies" (8) — the Peter Elbow–David Bartholomae debates over personal versus academic writing — Mlynarczyk juxtaposes their ideas with the work of psycholinguist Jerome Bruner and linguist James Britton. She argues that there is widespread disagreement today about what type of writing is most appropriate for the composition classroom and the academy. After outlining Bruner and Britton's language theories and reviewing Elbow and Bartholomae's 1995 debate, Mlynarczyk illustrates the similarities between Elbow and Britton's emphasis on expressive language and Bartholomae and Bruner's preference for transactional language. Mlynarczyk sides with Elbow and Britton: if basic writing students are to become comfortable with and adept at academic writing, they are more likely to reach that point via assignments that promote personal writing. To support her stance, Mlynarczyk cites a qualitative study she conducted on the journal writing experiences of five multilingual students. In particular, one ESL student exemplifies that the personal and expressive writing appropriate to journaling can lead to self-confidence and ability in traditional academic writing. Forming and expressing thoughts in a personal language helps students become more proficient at forming and expressing thoughts in the language of the academy. Mlynarczyk admits there are "caveats" (18): some students do not learn to embrace journal writing; some are uncomfortable with it for cultural reasons; and some do not transcend the inauthenticity of calling what is actually a public product (the journal) private and personal. Nevertheless, Mlynarczyk asserts that the Britton-Elbow concept of expressive language, especially through journaling, is better suited to helping basic writers acquire the thinking and writing discourses expected of them at the academy and beyond.

See: David Bartholomae and Peter Elbow, "Interchanges" [152].

See: David Bartholomae, "Writing with Teachers" [214].

219   Moran, Molly Hurley. "Toward a Writing and Healing Approach in the Basic Writing Classroom: One Professor's Personal Odyssey." *Journal of Basic Writing* 23.2 (2004): 93–115. Print.

Moran outlines how her experience of writing a book about a personal tragedy led her to investigate the fledgling interdisciplinary field of writing and healing. She redesigned her basic writing class to ask students to start by writing on personal and often painful issues, but also to move toward academic genres of writing, connecting those experiences to larger societal issues. Initial survey results indicate that such an approach may help improve students' attitudes about and confidence in their writing; it also appears to help basic writing students develop a "stronger prose style and more authentic voice." Anecdotal reports also indicate a significant level of student engagement from the approach.

Gender, Race, Class, and Ethnicity

220   Adler-Kassner, Linda. "The Shape of the Form: Working-Class Students and the Academic Essay." *Teaching Working Class*. Ed. Sherry Lee Linkon. Amherst: U of Massachusetts P, 1999. 85–105. Print.

Adler-Kassner argues that some students' issues with the expository essay "extend to a disjuncture between students' own values, reflected in their literacies, and the values and literacy reflected in the shape of the essay itself, as a genre" (86). She traces the history of the form of the expository essay through the work of Progressive Era compositionists like Fred Newton Scott. She notes that while they helped to transform expository writing into an act at least somewhat related to students' experiences, they also insisted that the form (and language) of the essay reflect particular conventions, which themselves reflected particular values of their culture. These conventions and their accompanying values remain intertwined with the expository essay to the current day, but students who do not share these values sometimes have issues with the expository essay for this reason. To make this point, Adler-Kassner examines writing by working-class students and proposes three possible solutions to pedagogical problems arising from this clash between cultures: move toward hybrid texts, design assignments that invite student experience, and allow hybrid language and form into the essay.

221   Agnew, Eleanor, and Margaret McLaughlin. "Basic Writing Class of '93 Five Years Later: How the Academic Paths of Blacks and Whites Diverged." *Journal of Basic Writing* 18.1 (1999): 40–54. Print.

Agnew and McLaughlin report on the results of a five-year longitudinal study of sixty-one students originally enrolled in developmental reading and writing classes. The authors followed the academic progress of the students through interviews with the students, interviews with their English instructors, analyses of the students' writing, and analyses of students' academic transcripts. Based on the results of the study, they conclude that the students did not do well overall in college, no matter what their performance was in the developmental English class, but they also found that African American students did worse than their white counterparts: 57 percent of the white students graduated by the end of the fifth year, but only 22.5 percent of black students graduated within that same time frame. The authors found that students' reading ability was more of a predictive factor than their writing ability in their overall academic success. They also conclude that minority students need more institutional support to be successful at a predominantly white university.

222 Agnew, Eleanor, and Margaret McLaughlin. "Those Crazy Gates and How They Swing: Tracking the System That Tracks African-American Students." *Mainstreaming Basic Writers: Politics and Pedagogies of Access.* Ed. Gerri McNenny. Mahwah: Erlbaum, 2001. 85–100. Print.

A seven-year longitudinal study that tracked the academic progress of sixty-one basic writers provisionally admitted in 1993 to a rural southeastern regional university found that the basic writing course itself did not negatively affect students' lives as much as the invalid assessment system that framed the program did. Although a poorly designed assessment system is detrimental to any student writer at any level, the results of this study suggest that unreliable and invalid writing assessment may contribute to the widely recognized cycle of academic failure and high attrition rates for black students who, on the basis of one timed, impromptu exit essay, can become trapped in noncredit courses. The subjective nature of creating and scoring single-method holistic essays—an assessment system that lacks conceptual validity and interrater reliability—led to a gatekeeping process that was most damaging to African American basic writers whose home speech is African American Vernacular English (AAVE). Excerpts from students' exit essays and a description of the arbitrariness of one holistic scoring session are included as a possible explanation for why almost twice the percentage of black students (31 percent) as white students (17 percent) did not exit basic writing after four attempts. Four failures to pass the exit essay excluded students from enrolling in any state-supported postsecondary institution for the next three years.

223 Balester, Valerie M. *Cultural Divide: A Study of African-American College-Level Writers.* Portsmouth: Boynton, 1993. Print.

Balester examines the spoken and written discourse of eight Black English Vernacular-speaking African American students at the University of Texas. Although Balester acknowledges a cultural divide between her informants and mainstream academic culture, she does not consider these students disadvantaged or deficient in any way. While she calls on composition teachers to help students learn the conventions of academic discourse, she also calls on academic discourse to change in response to the rhetorically effective practices of students like these because an emphasis on African American rhetoric in the academy "would be an opportunity to expand and enrich our academic discourse that, under a paradigm of white, middle-class, male domination, has traded flexibility for stability and has thus become more rigid than it need be" (159).

224   Bean, Janet, et al. "Should We Invite Students to Write in Home Languages? Complicating the Yes/No Debate." *Composition Studies* 31.1 (2003): 25–42. Print.

The authors work with a variety of populations, including students who speak African American Vernacular English and immigrant and international students, and take "[a shared] interest in helping all [their] students to produce effective and appropriate writing in English for academic contexts and purposes" (26). The authors state that "writers will feel more confident as language-users when their home language is valued and respected" (26). While the article recommends that teachers experiment with assignments that offer students a variety of opportunities for using their home language, the authors review a "list of variables" that complicate writing situations and can derail an instructor's best intentions. The authors consider the differences between home language and home dialect and suggest how the conditions shift, depending on whether (or to what degree) the home language is considered stigmatized. In addition, the authors point to circumstances when it might be valuable for students to use their home dialects for something not converted into standardized English. They emphasize the significance of inviting students to use their own dialects and the possible consequences of that decision. "Linguistic richness and bilingualism" should be valued, the writers argue (37). The article closes with an important reminder from Lucille Clifton, who writes in a poem titled "defending my tongue" that, "what i be talking about/can be said in this language/only" (38).

225   Bloom, Lynn Z. "Freshman Composition as a Middle Class Enterprise." *College English* 58.6 (1996): 654–75. Print.

Bloom argues that freshman composition addresses a number of the major aspects of social class to get students to write and think as good citizens of the academic community and the workplace. One major reason that freshman composition is the only course required of all students remains its reproduction of middle-class values that are thought to be essential to proper functioning of students in the academy. Bloom likens students in freshman composition to swimmers passing through a chlorine footbath before plunging into the pool. Bloom names self-reliance and responsibility, respectability (middle-class morality), decorum and propriety, moderation and temperance, thrift, efficiency, order, cleanliness, punctuality, delayed gratification, and critical thinking as the hallmarks of middle-class identity. Working-class students are often placed in so-called remedial courses like developmental writing because of an unspoken supposition that they will not be successful in freshman composition classes requiring such virtues. In addition, developmental writing teachers are encouraged to move their students in the direction of these virtues.

226   Cochran, Effie P. "Giving Voice to Women in the Basic Writing and Language Minority Classroom." *Journal of Basic Writing* 13.1 (1994): 78–90. Print.

Examining the ways that language affects sex roles, Cochran concentrates on women in English as a second language (ESL) and basic writing classes. She contends that they are often disadvantaged because they do not possess the language skills that allow them to succeed. In addition, males in these classrooms often make it difficult for women to participate. To facilitate women in ESL and basic writing classrooms, Cochran has four suggestions for teachers: use dramatic scenarios or dialogues, become conscious of the nonverbal communication of the instructor and the student, model the use of nonsexist language, and become familiar with the "literature on the topic of sexism and language" (85).

227   Coles, Nicholas, and Susan V. Wall. "Conflict and Power in the Reader-Responses of Adult Basic Writers." *College English* 49.3 (1987): 298–314. Print.

Coles and Wall discuss a study of students enrolled in a course modeled on the one described in David Bartholomae and Anthony Petrosky's *Facts, Artifacts, and Counterfacts* [186]. Early in the semester, students' responses were typically tied to their understanding of success. They admired those who refused to give up, and they believed education would provide the way to a better life. They treated books as repositories of self-evident facts rather than as arguments constructed by writers to be interpreted by readers. The students "fail[ed] to see . . . how the 'facts' are selected, sorted, and marshaled in the service of particular interests and viewpoints" (302). Later, students were able to identify with the characters' interpretations and explanations of their common experiences and even to move to a recognition of the race, class, gender, and group memberships that might explain the individual's social condition. The students could leave behind a simple identification with the individual and move on to making generalizations across categories. Coles and Wall argue that academic literacy is more than acquiring a set of rhetorical conventions or simply moving from one discourse community to another, and they stress the importance of allowing students to construct their understanding of the texts through their own histories, even if this approach results in conflict.

228   Counihan, Beth. "Freshgirls: Overwhelmed by Discordant Pedagogies and the Anxiety of Leaving Home." *Journal of Basic Writing* 18.1
(1999): 91–105. Print.

This study was based on an ethnographic study of three female freshmen who enrolled at City University of New York's Lehman College.
Counihan began with high hopes for her subjects, whom she called
freshgirls, but she went on to see them fail to pass most of their classes.
She wonders why this happened—if the girls failed or if the institution failed them. She centers her study around a description of their
classrooms to illuminate the problems facing the freshgirls. Counihan explains the background that produced the freshgirls and the
problems that they encountered growing up in one-parent or unsup-
portive homes. In college, these subjects hoped to find a way into the
comforts of the middle class, but none wanted to submit to the workings of the educational institution to make that happen. Instead,
they bucked the system, and their own grades suffered as a result of
their nonconformity. The freshgirls did not possess academic literacy,
and they resisted their teachers' efforts to educate and engage them.
Based on her observations of the freshgirls, Counihan suggests that
"we need a serious reassessment of our rigid views of what a college
experience 'should' be" (103). She hopes for the adoption of a flexible pedagogy that might help students like the freshgirls succeed. She
concludes her article by explaining what has happened to the freshgirls since their semester at Lehman in fall 1995.

229   DiPardo, Anne. *A Kind of Passport: A Basic Writing Adjunct Program
and the Challenge of Student Diversity.* Urbana: NCTE, 1993. Print.

DiPardo examines the successes and failures of a peer-teaching program at "Dover Park University," a largely white university grap-
pling with issues of racial and cultural equity throughout the campus.
She focuses on workshops led by two peer teachers (adjuncts)
for students enrolled in a faculty-taught course in basic writing.
Through observations, interviews, and teaching logs, DiPardo studies and reports on the dynamics between adjuncts and student writers working together in an intimate workshop setting. The book
captures challenges faced by undergraduates who are becoming educators with pedagogical uncertainty and minimal preparation and
the development of their teaching self through the day-to-day experiences of working with struggling writers. While she sometimes
asserts that both the peer teachers and the university were not curious enough, DiPardo finds that by welcoming equity students and
beginning the task of transforming basic writers into mainstream
achievers, the students, the teachers, and the institution itself will
all be slowly but unquestionably changed.

230   Dunn, Patricia A. *Learning Re-abled: The Learning Disability Contro-versy and Composition Studies*. Portsmouth: Boynton, 1995. Print.

Dunn presents an overview of current understandings of learning disability theory and a rich discussion about the ways that institutions, writing programs, composition scholars, and faculty privilege certain ways of understanding students' writing problems. Dunn grounds her research in her observations of the extreme difficulty that some students have in learning to use written language proficiently. She notes that composition theory does not fully account for the kinds of errors that some students make, and she suggests that the field has largely ignored neurological causes of writing difficulty and privileged instead research and theory that considers writing difficulty to be a primarily socioeconomic challenge. According to Dunn, "[e]ven if only one student—. . . who may have a difference in learning not related to dialect, social class, or educational background—appears in a composition class, the instructor owes it to that student to be informed" (43). The book focuses on perspectives on and controversies about learning disabilities, the ways that composition has understood writing difficulties, multimodal pedagogies for students with learning disabilities, interviews with learning disabled (LD) students who describe their frustrations and experiences, and the ways that instructors and administrators can best help LD students demonstrate their intelligence and communicative competence.

231   Gaskins, Jacob C. "Teaching Writing to Students with Learning Disabilities: The Landmark Method." *Teaching English in the Two-Year College* 22.2 (1995): 116–22. Print.

Gaskins discusses teaching methods he learned during a week-long training institute at Landmark College, a school for students with learning disabilities. He presents and briefly discusses ten principles that constitute the "Landmark Method" for teaching writing to students with dyslexia, dysgraphia, attention-deficit disorder, and other learning disabilities. Approaches are phrased as imperatives ("exploit the inter-relatedness of reading, writing, speaking, and listening"; "foster meta-cognition"; "teach to the student's strengths and accommodate learning styles"). Citing the institute's training materials, Gaskins suggests ways that these principles can translate into specific classroom practices.

232   Gilyard, Keith, and Elaine Richardson. "Students' Right to Possibility: Basic Writing and African American Rhetoric." *Insurrections: Approaches to Resistance in Composition Studies*. Ed. Andrea Greenbaum. Albany: State U of New York P, 2001. 37–51. Print.

Gilyard and Richardson survey the core ideas of the 1974 "Students' Right to Their Own Language" (SRTOL) resolution and contend that empirical models of how to implement SRTOL pedagogically are needed. The authors offer a model in the form of a study conducted by Richardson that was designed to evaluate the practicality of using SRTOL principles to teach academic writing to African American students who are placed in basic writing courses. The study asked "to what extent African American speech styles can be instrumental to the development of critical academic writing" (39). Richardson designed and taught a basic writing course focusing on Afrocentric topics and African American rhetoric. Drawing on a modified version of Geneva Smitherman's 1994 typology of black discourse features, the authors perform quantitative and qualitative analyses of forty-seven student essays from this course to conclude that "making the African American rhetorical tradition the centerpiece of attempts to teach academic prose to African American students, especially those characterized as basic writers . . . increase[s] the likelihood that they will develop into careful, competent, critical practitioners of the written word" (50).

233   Gleason, Barbara. "Returning Adults to the Mainstream: Toward a Curriculum for Adult Student Writers." *Mainstreaming Basic Writers: Politics and Pedagogies of Access.* Ed. Gerri McNenny. Mahwah: Erlbaum, 2001. 121–43. Print.

Mainstreamed writing courses are especially suitable for returning adults at the City College of New York Center for Worker Education. As is often the case in similar programs, the Center for Worker Education aims to speed up students' academic progress with convenient schedules, life experience credits, and no remedial classes. At the center, all students are placed directly into credit-bearing courses, regardless of their skills or test scores. The curriculum for a first-year writing course is designed for students who have highly diverse competencies. This curriculum features sequenced multitask assignments that offer appropriate challenges for strong writers and opportunities to experience success for weaker writers. Students' oral-language fluencies are the foundation for assignments such as interviewing and ethnographic research. Case studies illustrate the benefits of this curriculum for one weak student and one strong student. Both students wrote ethnographic research reports in the same course, and both experienced growth as writers and success in the classroom.

234   Gunner, Jeanne, and Gerri McNenny. "Retrospection as Prologue." *Journal of Basic Writing* 16.1 (1997): 3–12. Print.

Gunner and McNenny present their differing views of the 1997 Conference on College Composition and Communication/Conference on Basic Writing preconference workshop. Gunner discusses her opinion of how mainstreaming affects educators and students of basic writing. For her, the role of the workshop was to provide "professional synthesis" (4). Mainstreaming basic writers into composition programs motivates writing program administrators to take the students into consideration, lifting the status of basic writing professionally. McNenny focuses on the role of class as a "site of struggle" (7) for regaining "a sense of empowerment" (7). Noting that the existence of class tends to be denied in American culture and that basic writers want to believe the mythology of classless equality, she expresses the need for basic writing teachers to encourage students to scrutinize the class system and its assumptions.

235   Lu, Min-Zhan. "Conflict and Struggle: The Enemies or Preconditions of Basic Writing?" *College English* 54.8 (1992): 887–913. Print.
      Contemporary theorists of writing, such as Gloria Anzaldúa, Mike Rose, and many others, celebrate the idea that writing takes place at a site of painful yet constructive tension between the academy and the student's original culture. Nevertheless, much basic writing instruction still centers on the relatively isolated mastery of "skills" and discursive conventions, thus failing to acknowledge the inevitable process of ideological repositioning implied in poststructuralist models of language. Lu examines the roots of the basic writing movement that followed the introduction of open admissions at the City University of New York to historicize the conceptual role of conflict and struggle in the writings of numerous educators, including Kenneth Bruffee, Thomas Farrell, and Mina Shaughnessy. In the 1970s, the arguments of other thinkers and writers—Lionel Trilling, Irving Howe, and W. E. B. Dubois—contextualized the emergence of basic writing instruction as a discipline. Only by accepting conflict and struggle as important parts of the scene of composition can basic writing teachers hope to empower their students to make an authentic move toward the rhetorical position that Anzaldúa characterizes as the "borderlands."

236   Marinara, Martha. "When Working Class Students 'Do' the Academy: How We Negotiate with Alternative Literacies." *Journal of Basic Writing* 16.2 (1997): 3–16. Print.
      Adult learners generally have experience, training, and knowledge but may be labeled "basic" if they lack knowledge valued within academia. Furthermore, they frequently have not "named" or "claimed" their own knowledge (4). To bring together her students'

knowledge and academic ways of knowing, Marinara designed a basic writing class that focused on work. Marinara argues that such reflexive curricula can help students to construct "political identities" that "can take action in the world" (14) and that if universities integrate students' own "outside" literacies with academic literacy, what is considered to be academic literacy will change.

237   McCrary, Donald. "Speaking in Tongues: Using Womanist Sermons as Intra-cultural Rhetoric in the Writing Classroom." *Journal of Basic Writing* 20.2 (2001): 53–70. Print.

McCrary offers a model and a rationale for analyzing womanist sermons in writing classrooms. Womanist theologians construct sermons that reinterpret biblical texts, utilize standard and nonstandard rhetoric, and challenge white male-oriented interpretations. The sermons are examples of intracultural rhetoric that employs traditional African American rhetorical effects to achieve the goal of empowerment among a primarily African American audience. In this sense, the sermons are intended not to cross cultural boundaries but to operate within the African American community, challenging the multiple oppressions that women of color face. Other-literate students (whom McCrary describes as literate in discourses other than standard) especially benefit from the culturally hybrid structures of womanist sermons because they can recognize rhetorical maneuvers that are rooted in nonmainstream cultures. McCrary's analysis of his class's discussions of womanist sermons and of examples of student-generated "secular sermons" shows how using intracultural rhetoric draws on and expands students' abilities to interpret and produce both standard and nonstandard texts.

238   Newton, Stephen. "Teaching, Listening, and the Sound of Guns." *BWe: Basic Writing e-Journal* 4.1 (2002): n. pag. Web. 11 Aug. 2009.

De-romanticizing the notion of a multicultural classroom as one full of exotic voices, Newton's experiences in a Brooklyn open enrollment university increased his awareness of the confessional discourse that developmental writers produce. When Newton asked his students to "write about a turning point in their lives" and to include only examples that they would be comfortable sharing with him and the rest of the class, they wrote detailed accounts of their families' painful struggles with poverty and disease. He defines developmental students as having histories that have caused them to create academic personas separate from their authentic selves because "[t]he weight of institutional authority had superseded the reservations they had about revealing the intimate details of their lives" (par. 21). Thus his example serves as a call for teachers to recognize these students' perceptions of the academy and to discover their students' histories so that they do not assume or underestimate the narratives they will produce. Newton also warns against critical pedagogies that ask for such writing because he believes that there is a "very real danger, indeed likelihood of objectifying them, and by doing so dehumanizing the very people we are claiming to serve" (par. 26).

239   Norment, Nathaniel, Jr. "Some Effects of Culture-Referenced Topics on the Writing Performance of African American Students." *Journal of Basic Writing* 16.2 (1997): 17–45. Print.

Norment examines whether and how culture-referenced topics affect the writing of eleventh- and twelfth-grade African American students in response to an urban university placement exam. In this study, "culture-referenced" refers to any topic or prompt that incorporates values, attitudes, or information relevant to African American culture. Further, the topics incorporate a combination of culturally, socially, linguistically, and historically determined aspects of African American culture. The study considers both the overall quality of writing produced by students (for example, its development, content, usage, and mechanics) and the syntactic complexity, organization, and length of resulting essays. Trained raters scored 711 essays holistically, and the essays of twenty-five students were analyzed using an analytical scale measuring the number of words, sentences, and paragraphs; average words per sentence and paragraph; and number of sentences per paragraph. Norment concludes that culture-referenced topics do, in fact, elicit essays of higher quality and should therefore be considered in the development and implementation of writing pedagogies, curricula, and assessment measures.

240   Pratt, Mary Louise. "Arts of the Contact Zone." *Profession* 91 (1993): 33–40. Print.

This germinal essay introduces the term *contact zone*, which has seen widespread use and application in postcolonial and cultural studies, among other fields. Pratt defines *contact zones* as "social spaces where cultures meet, clash, and grapple with each other, often in contexts of highly asymmetrical relations of power, such as colonialism, slavery, or their aftermaths as they are lived out in many parts of the world today" (34). Pratt's essay discusses the bilingual literacy and biculturalism of fifteenth-century Incan Guaman Poma, whose twelve-hundred-page letter to the king of Spain chronicles and critiques the Spanish presence in Peru. Pomo's text is an "autoethnographic" text, "a text in which people undertake to describe themselves in ways that engage with representations others have made of them" (35). These texts often speak from the margins of cultures. Pratt also discusses the ethnographic term *transculturation*, noting that the term "describe[s] processes whereby members of subordinated or marginal groups select and invent from materials transmitted by a dominant or metropolitan culture" (36). Many composition theorists have invoked these terms in discussions of disempowered student writers, including basic writing students. Pratt acknowledges that our best opportunities for teaching and learning may take place in the contact zones. The pedagogical arts of the contact zone, based on cultural mediation, must be developed.

241   Reagan, Sally Barr. "Warning: Basic Writers at Risk—The Case of Javier." *Journal of Basic Writing* 10.2 (1991): 99–115. Print.

Instead of defining the basic writer, which usually only generalizes or oversimplifies the complex situations of basic writers, we should begin to examine our intentions and methods as teachers of basic writing, especially the work we do with at-risk students, those lower-level basic writers whose reading and writing practices are shaped by social and cultural forces that create problems outside writing. The case study of Javier represents "the multitude of idiosyncratic factors which may influence our students' feelings and behaviors" (101) about reading, writing, and learning. Moreover, the study suggests that "failure" may not be a student's fault at all. Rather, the "problem may lie more significantly on the approach to teaching and the assumptions behind it" (113). This article suggests that the number of at-risk students will continue to grow as America becomes more diversely populated and that our approaches and assumptions must be reflected upon and revised according to the needs of at-risk students like Javier.

242   Richardson, Elaine. *African American Literacies*. New York: Routledge, 2003. Print.

Richardson explores what it would mean to center African American rhetorics and discourses on individual writing classrooms and on composition curricula at large. She argues that African American students are attempting to learn in an educational system that is still dominated by American standardized English and by the cultural hierarchy that it symbolizes and reinforces. Richardson draws on educational research and the rich history of African American rhetorics to explain how students of African American heritage use African American Vernacular English (AAVE) as a "technology" through which to learn and utilize other languages and literacies, including college-level critical literacies. Because African American students are overrepresented in basic writing courses, Richardson argues that teachers of basic writing need to learn and teach the history and linguistic features of AAVE rhetorics and discourses in their writing classrooms. Richardson contends that, "for the most part, America continues to teach us to accept the status of lower achievement for Black students as the norm. Under the present system, we are set in motion to replicate the paradigm and the results" (8).

243   Ryden, Wendy. "Bourgeois Realism or Working-Class Kitsch? The Aesthetics of Class in Composition." *Open Words: Access and English Studies* 1.2 (2007): 4–23. Print.

Our understanding of the aesthetic affects our judgments as respondents and graders of student writing. Ryden advocates theories of kitsch as ways to "understand the rhetoric of student texts (and our reactions to them) as products of a conflicted academic terrain," one where "questions of subjectivity and development" must be "negotiated" (5). Following Celeste Olalquiaga, Ryden relates the class implications of kitsch and argues against the simplistic division of kitsch into the nostalgic, reflected in much student writing, and the melancholic, favored by most instructors. She suggests that "it is easy enough to celebrate loss and irony in a text we consider literary and impersonal but far more difficult to rail against sentimentality in a text we read as a representation of a student's life. . . . [A]n English professor might find rebelliousness and irreverence interesting in literature while taking a dim view of these qualities when they show up in student work" (15). She questions whether students in nonelite institutions know what to present to writing instructors in papers: passion that might appeal to an artistic aesthetic or "bourgeois politeness" that reflects the civilization of working-class qualities (21). The danger to critical rhetorics lurks in the answer.

244   Ryden, Wendy. "Conflicted Literacy: Frederick Douglass's Critical Model." *Journal of Basic Writing* 24.1 (2005): 4–23. Print.

Ryden calls the literacy narrative, a common assignment in basic writing, into question as a tool for critical pedagogy. Frederick Douglass's slave narrative, she notes, is commonly used as an urtext of the genre, but she goes on to critique its representation to students by teachers. She argues, through a discussion of numerous writers, that it is the literacy myth—that literacy is the bedrock of empowerment, self-actualization, and economic progress—that is often presented to students rather than Mary Louise Pratt's notion of a complex transculturation whereby marginalized groups "select and invent from materials transmitted" by a dominant culture (17). Ryden ends with a word of caution about overstating the claims about the power of the literacy narrative to produce critical awareness in writing students.

245   Severino, Carol, J. C. Guerra, and J. E. Butler, eds. *Writing in Multicultural Settings*. New York: MLA, 1997. Print.

This essay collection discusses the theory and practice of teaching writing in an environment that embraces multiculturalism and views writing as an artifact of both personal and cultural expression. The conflict and cooperation between academic discourse and multicultural student discourses are explored through essays that address linguistics, literacy studies, and English as a second language students and their teachers. Essays are grouped into four sections: "Linguistic and Cultural Diversity," "The Roles of Teachers and Texts," "ESL Students in Multicultural Classrooms," and "Social and Pedagogical Tensions."

246   Shepard, Alan, John McMillan, and Gary Tate, eds. *Coming to Class: Pedagogy and the Social Class of Teachers*. Portsmouth: Boynton, 1998. Print.

In this collection of twenty-one original essays by working-class academics, the common goal was to uncover unspoken class suppositions and strictures at play in the culture of academe. The authors offer a book that focuses on how social class shapes the ways teachers work in their classrooms, while the individual essays approach this topic from differing theoretical positions, subject positions, and socioeconomic realities. Essays address issues connected with the role of working-class affiliation in academe, the inattention to class in course content, and the ways that composition is seen in some English departments as "second class" or "service."

247   Soliday, Mary. "Towards a Consciousness of Language: A Language Pedagogy for Multicultural Classrooms." *Journal of Basic Writing* 16.2 (1997): 62–75. Print.

Soliday describes efforts to help students understand that language can help to shape reality in addition to conveying information about that reality. While working on a pilot project at the City College of New York, where as many as sixteen languages may be spoken within a single classroom, Soliday and partner Barbara Gleason developed the Enrichment Approach to Language and Literacy. Soliday concludes by explaining her goals for first-year writing courses, one of which is for her students to become researchers of their own language. Only by doing so, according to Soliday, will her students develop a fully literate attitude about language and its usage.

248   Tassoni, John Paul, Richard Lee Walts, and Sara Webb-Sunderhaus. "Deep Shit: A Dialogue about Rhetoric, Pedagogy, and the Working Class." *Open Words: Access and English Studies* 1.2 (2007): 24–47. Print.

The authors share their after-class e-mail list conversations from a graduate seminar in the Histories and Theories of Rhetoric and Composition. For all three members of the class, one instructor and two students, identified as "working class academics," the term *shit* became a dialectical and rhetorical term as they considered how they took or did not take any shit, but gave shit, stepped into deep shit, and questioned shitty cultural ideologies. The dialogue frequently returned to discussion of one of Webb-Sunderhaus's students, a working-class woman who became pregnant and was struggling with the first-year writing course. To what extent should instructors get involved in the "deep shit" of students' personal lives? At what point do attempts to help a student cross over into a hero narrative or a banking model in which the instructor has all the answers and fixes the student's problems? The term *shit* opened intersections between class and gender and became a third space for discussing working-class voices in academia.

249 Tate, Gary, John McMillan, and Elizabeth Woodworth. "Class Talk." *Journal of Basic Writing* 16.1 (1997): 13–26. Print.

Laying the groundwork for a discussion from a Conference on Basic Writing workshop, Tate posits four theses: social class has usually been ignored by compositionists and academics in general; this neglect appears to be ending; this neglect must end if we hope to reach all of our students; and we must address our own class status before we can fully address class with our students. McMillan shares his own class narrative to demonstrate the fluidity and complexity of class and the need for storytelling, for "[t]o unstory class is to cease to talk about class" (19). Woodworth recalls the "teaching" portion of the workshop, including the writing prompt given to participants and the written response of one participant. She then reflects on this response, as well as the responses of others during the ensuing discussion, and concludes by stressing the importance of connecting "class-talk" with teaching as a way to alleviate students' feelings of alienation and as a means to give them a safe place to grow as writers.

250 Thurston, Kay. "Mitigating Barriers to Navajo Students' Success in English Courses." *Teaching Developmental Writing*. 3rd ed. Boston: Bedford, 2007. Print.

Reflecting on her experiences teaching at a two-year Native American tribal college, Thurston argues that teachers of writing should look at how "global factors" influence student success rates (356). She identifies five major obstacles that students face: financial difficulties, family obligations, attitudes toward Standard American English (SAE), instructor/faculty ethnocentrism, and ambivalence toward Western education (356). Thurston explains how poverty affects learning in myriad ways, including lack of access to technology and the inability to purchase textbooks. Second, family obligations can easily require a student to miss classes or assignment deadlines more frequently than is acceptable. Additionally, what Thurston calls a "prescriptive attitude" toward Standard American English on the part of instructors makes it such that many Navajo students are not as familiar with SAE as is presumed, and in turn, instructors are not aware of Navajo English conventions (359). Instructors are encouraged to see Navajo English and SAE as different dialects as opposed to competing discourses. Fourth, often-unconscious instructor ethnocentrism disadvantages Navajo students by alienating them and by failing to validate different rhetorical styles. Finally, a sense of ambivalence toward Western education on the part of Navajo students can be misinterpreted as low motivation or ability, but in fact, Thurston argues, students can themselves interpret the teaching of SAE as negating or oppressing their tribal language and culture. Thus instructors should focus on helping students see how SAE can serve their families and communities. Thurston concludes that instructors need to do more to overcome these obstacles because failing to pass composition often means failing to earn a degree.

251   Troyka, Lynn Quitman. "Perspectives on Legacies and Literacy in the 1980's." *A Sourcebook for Basic Writing Teachers*. Ed. Theresa Enos. New York: Random, 1987. 16–26. Print.

Troyka argues for support for the challenges that nontraditional students in college writing classes face. She describes the challenges in terms of positive legacies: students' gregarious and social natures, their comfort with and enthusiasm for oral communication, their holistic thinking patterns, and their ambivalence about learning (particularly that they want to learn but do not know how they feel about the changes that learning will bring to their lives). Troyka reminds readers that these strengths and talents can lead to good self-directed writing. Her strategies and perspectives fit all levels of writing courses; she provides excellent evidence for a constructionist classroom philosophy.

252   Young, Morris. "Narratives of Identity: Theorizing the Writer and the Nation." *Journal of Basic Writing* 15.2 (1996): 50–75. Print.

Nontraditional and at-risk students are participating members of our communities, yet because they are also often part of marginalized and oppressed groups, they are not "allowed" the full benefits of literacy. Even with the recent debates surrounding literacy education, these particular students are still being given their identities by teachers and educational institutions. To realize the power of literacy, students should be encouraged to engage in acts of self-determination when reading and writing texts. True literacy comes out of an understanding of the relationship between individual, textual, and cultural selves. This connection is important because literacy is a nationally forged concept and an identity marker of valued citizenship.

253 Zamel, Vivian, and Ruth Spack, eds. *Negotiating Academic Literacies: Teaching and Learning across Languages and Cultures*. Mahwah: Erlbaum, 1998. Print.

In response to the growing diversity in higher education, instructors need to reconceptualize academic discourse and acknowledge multiple types of literacy and approaches to learning. Students' backgrounds and previous knowledge are important resources. In classrooms where students and teachers of various languages and cultures connect, there is the potential for growth and transformation of the academy. Zamel and Spack advocate for an expanded, pluralistic definition of literacy and challenge assumptions regarding academic discourse. They point to the need for "a dynamic process of negotiation, involving both adaptation and resistance" (xii) between teachers and students. The book includes twenty-two previously published readings that address these issues from various fields — such as composition, English as a second language, anthropology, literature, and education — presented in chronological order, beginning with Mina P. Shaughnessy's "Diving In: An Introduction to Basic Writing" [78] and Mike Rose's "The Language of Exclusion: Writing Instruction at the University" [35]. The included essays discuss the process of writing and constructing an identity in more than one culture, explore issues of language and power, examine definitions of literacy, critique academic discourse, and challenge exclusionary notions of what academic literacy and discourse are.

Second-Language Learners/Special Populations

254 Barber-Fendley, Kimber, and Chris Hamel. "A New Visibility: An Argument for Alternative Assistance Writing Programs for Students with Learning Disabilities." *College Composition and Communication* 55.3 (2004): 504–35. Print.

As educators become involved with teaching students with learning disabilities, the issue of what is "fair" treatment has become more troublesome. Generally, students with learning disabilities have been expected to accomplish exactly what students without them can accomplish and in the same ways. The authors shed light on the injustice of rules for accommodations and other approaches to learning disabilities that often prevent LD students from demonstrating their skills through alternative means. As Susan Ohanian noted years ago, the one-size-fits-all approach rarely fits anyone adequately, and this is Barber-Fendley and Hamel's main issue. They argue against traditional forms of learning disability accommodation and in favor of the creation of an alternative approach to assisting LD students in first-year composition programs. Their approach is a useful one for anyone dealing with the challenges of diversity across a much broader spectrum than learning disabilities alone. There are many disabilities that would benefit from approaching students as unique, and there are many students who come to us without physical or psychological disabilities but who would nonetheless benefit from unique attention in their first-year composition courses, such as students with family problems, homesickness, or financial stresses. We are in a unique position to help our students to become acclimated to college, while increasing the likelihood of their success and retention. The focus of this article on providing a unique experience for individual learners also fits the research done on teaching students with disabilities, as well as the research conducted on access and retention at the University of Minnesota's Center for Research in Development Education and Urban Literacy.

255   Becket, Diana. "Uses of Background Experience in a Preparatory Reading and Writing Class: An Analysis of Native and Non-native Speakers of English." *Journal of Basic Writing* 24.2 (2005): 53–71. Print.

Becket critiques the placement of "so-called Generation 1.5 students," who "moved with their parents to the U.S. when they were young children or adolescents" (54), into ESL settings alongside international students. She cites the ways their placement in these courses often works against their current literacy and social and educational needs. She then studies a group of six students in a developmental reading/writing sequence at an open admissions college at a large university in the Midwest. Three participants are native speakers. The other three are "Generation 1.5" ESL students. Although the study shows significant differences in the ways these two groups of students perceived their literacy and efficacy as writers and communicators, their experience of education at the university and high school level, and how they approached writing tasks, the study also concludes that the ESL-labeled writers are often better at idea development, grammatical fluency, and meeting paper length than their native-speaking peers and that their inclusion in a non-ESL setting is more appropriate than placement with international students in a traditional ESL context. Becket concludes that other factors shared with native-speaker developmental reading/writing students, including motivation, attitude, time-management, and willingness to revise are more significant contributors to success than ESL status and that Generation 1.5 students are most appropriately placed in non-ESL developmental reading/writing settings.

256 Belcher, Diane, and George Braine, eds. *Academic Writing in a Second Language: Essays on Research and Pedagogy*. Norwood: Ablex, 1995. Print.

This collection of sixteen essays explores the problems inherent in empowering college ESL students by allowing them access to the skills necessary to participate in the academic community. From the outset, this project is defined in the broadest sense, using the discipline of composition studies as a springboard into suggestions of various transformative, participatory, and resistant strategies within academic discourse. To help the ESL student feel more welcomed than threatened by the academic discourse community, the overarching aim of this collection is familiarization—on the part of the ESL student and teacher alike. The text is divided into three parts: "Issues," "Research," and "Pedagogy."

257 Blanton, Linda Lonon, and Barbara Kroll, eds. *ESL Composition Tales: Reflections on Teaching*. Ann Arbor: U of Michigan P, 2002. Print.

Inspired by a panel at the 1996 TESOL Colloquium on Writing, several veteran educators of ESL students, including Alister Cumming, Ilona Leki, and Tony Silva, ruminate on their teaching careers, obstacles they have faced, and successes they have achieved. The introduction by Barbara Kroll, "What I Certainly Didn't Know When I Started," combines her personal teaching stories with a history of the panel and the creation of the essays into a text. She notes that framing the text with her introduction and Paul Kei Matsuda's epilogue places these stories into different contexts; the introduction and the epilogue help create a discourse that does not exclude younger generations of ESL educators. Each section of the book focuses on a theme, such as instruction, course creation, or theories of ESL education, culminating with advice for educators in the field. Many of the contributors discuss how research has affected their teaching choices. For example, in "The Best of Intentions," Melinda Erickson develops the idea of the "pendulum swings" that teachers experience throughout their careers, particularly at the beginning when it is easy to lose confidence. Erickson describes a failed classroom assignment that makes her overreact, or "swing," in the opposite pedagogical direction. Leki's "Not the End of History" and Cumming's "If I Had Known Twelve Things . . ." reflect on previous teaching pedagogy and how to improve, and possibly change, what appear to be fixed ideas of instruction methods. In his epilogue, "Reinventing Giants," Matsuda reiterates the importance of ESL education, describes the changes that ESL instruction has gone through institutionally, and reflects on the changes that the writers have experienced in their teaching career. Matsuda reinforces the idea of growth that the writers attest to in their stories: through reflection and by learning from others, one can become a more effective teacher.

258   Brueggemann, Brenda Jo, et al. "Becoming Visible: Lessons in Disability." *College Composition and Communication* 52.3 (2001): 368–98. Print.

Brueggemann and colleagues focus on legitimizing students with learning disabilities as possessing valid disabilities, different from mental retardation, and needing different responses. Along with Kimber Barber-Fendley and Chris Hamel's "A New Visibility" [254], this article reflects the problems of substantiating the very real disabilities of students with various learning challenges, of working with existing standards that demand educational conformities that often further handicap LD students, and of making disability visible in an academic world that privileges those people considered ablebodied. The authors look at the place of disabilities in composition, whether it is teaching disability issues, reading texts in which disability is the primary thematic material, working to help LD students write, or claiming a space for teachers and students with varying disabilities in higher education classrooms. For the issue of disability to be adequately addressed in the twenty-first century, we need to transform how we approach the issue of diversity, as these authors note, by creating a more inclusive definition of "normal" such that people who have disabilities are defined as normal, fully human, whole and capable individuals, regardless of whether they are learning disabled or have some other type of disability.

See: Kimber Barber-Fendley and Chris Hamel. "A New Visibility" [254].

259   Casanave, Christine Pearson. *Controversies in Second Language Writing: Dilemmas and Decisions in Research and Instruction.* Ann Arbor: U of Michigan P, 2004. Print.

Casanave succinctly synthesizes historical studies and arguments in second language (L2) writing. She discusses issues and arguments concerning decision making in L2 writing classrooms, contrastive rhetoric, controversies about fluency versus accuracy in students' writing, the process-product argument, and the issue of explicit versus implicit responses to students' assignments. The assessment dilemma is also raised. The interactions of students' writing to audience (with readers) and to plagiarism (with texts) are asserted as controversies in L2 writing. Casanave also discusses the political issue of whether assigned writings in class reflect the teacher's or the students' needs or help students in being more critical in their thinking and writing. The debate over the use of the Internet is also mentioned.

260 CCCC Committee on Second Language Writing. "CCCC Statement on Second Language Writing and Writers." *College Composition and Communication* 52.4 (2001): 669–74. Print.

Produced by the Conference on College Composition and Communication (CCCC) of the National Council of Teachers of English (NCTE), this policy statement consists of three parts: a general statement, guidelines for writing programs, and a selected bibliography. The general statement describes various types of second-language writers in North American universities. It urges writing instructors and program administrators to recognize the growing number of second-language learners in writing classes, to understand their linguistic and cultural needs, and to develop instructional and administrative practices that are sensitive to these special needs. The statement also urges graduate programs to prepare writing teachers and scholars for working with college writers who are increasingly diverse, both linguistically and culturally, and it stresses the need to include second-language perspective in developing writing theories and studies. The guidelines for writing programs provide recommendations regarding the placement and assessment of second-language writers and discuss issues of class size, academic credit, teacher preparation, and teacher support.

261 Center, Carole. "Representing Race in Basic Writing Scholarship." *Journal of Basic Writing* 26.1 (2007): 20–42. Print.

Center notes that Susanmarie Harrington's detailed examination of essays in the *Journal of Basic Writing* found that most essays focused on pedagogical approaches or basic writing programs, instead of focusing on students. Center examines the journal's essays for evidence of "visibility or invisibility" of race in those essays that do focus on students and argues that "[m]aking race visible in scholarly writing . . . can help basic writing teachers to reflect on the implications of difference." She suggests that "student identities and voices should be seen and heard in all their complexity" and that they cannot be if race is invisible in our scholarship.

262   Clark, J. Milton, and Carol Peterson Haviland. "Language and Authority: Shifting the Privilege." *Journal of Basic Writing* 14.1 (1995): 57–66. Print.

To embrace the linguistic diversity in their classes and shift or expand privilege, Clark and Haviland polled students to discover their non-English reading competencies. Based on these polls, they designed an assignment that aimed to shift linguistic privilege and work toward greater linguistic inclusiveness in the basic writing classroom. The assignment responded to the realization that while many of the texts we use reflect our students' cultural diversity, they ignore students' linguistic diversity because they are written in and privilege standard academic English. For the assignment, groups of five students worked with magazines written in French, Spanish, and Chinese. In the groups, at least two students spoke the language in which the magazine was published. Students worked collaboratively to answer the question: "What can you know about this country from the magazine we've given you?" (60). In these groups, ESL students were the experts; they interpreted the articles while the other students added their observations about the country from their reading of the photographs, ads, and cartoon captions. In this atmosphere of "share[d] power and privilege" (64), students participated in genuine collaboration and, as a result, produced texts "richer for this fuller collaboration" (64).

263   Connor, Ulla. *Contrastive Rhetoric: Cross-Cultural Aspects of Second-Language Writing.* New York: Cambridge UP, 1996. Print.

Connor provides a comprehensive discussion of how contrastive rhetoric relates to the theories of applied linguistics, linguistic relativity, rhetoric, text linguistics, discourse types and genres, literacy (cultural and cross-cultural), and translation (structural analyses and literal translation). Connor acknowledges the value of syntactical concerns, such as those advocated in Chomskyan-like models, and expands on the theory that "linguistic and rhetorical conventions of the first language interfere with writing in the second language" (5). Detailed student examples, instructors' comments, tables, and specific language comparisons illustrate her argument. The extended table of contents, subject index, and author index render this book easily navigable. An exhaustive reference list creates an invaluable source for those interested in contrastive rhetoric as it relates to process rather than product.

264   Dong, Yu Ren. "The Need to Understand ESL Students' Native Language Writing Experiences." *Teaching Developmental Writing: Background Readings.* Ed. Susan Naomi Bernstein. Boston: Bedford, 2001. 288–98. Print.

Dong uses her own ESL students' voices to highlight cross-cultural writing differences. She argues that teachers need to understand the diverse native literacy backgrounds of their ESL students if they are to build on that knowledge and help students develop strategies to improve their proficiency in English reading and writing. She invited twenty-six first-year college students to compose autobiographies describing their native language writing instruction, the writing assignments they were given in their home countries, and the differences between writing in English and writing in their native language. Dong presents the students' stories in their own words, and they illustrate a wide variety of experiences and perceptions. From them, Dong concludes that teachers who ask students to reflect on and share their native-language backgrounds can use this information to expand the ways they identify and address each student's unique needs. Students also become more aware of how their previous experiences affect their expectations and approach to learning English.

265 Ferris, Dana. "One Size Does Not Fit All: Response and Revision Issues for Immigrant Students." *Teaching Developmental Writing*. 3rd ed. Ed. Susan Naomi Bernstein. Boston: Bedford, 2007. 83–97. Print. Ferris challenges the practice of treating all ESL students in the same way when it comes to giving feedback on their writing. She recommends, instead, differentiating between international students and immigrant students (what some today may refer to as Generation 1.5 students); international students have learned English as a foreign language (EFL), and immigrant students have already spent some time in the U.S. academic system. The response to teacher commentary within each of the two populations indicates a difference in motivation and ability to respond to feedback. International students, unfamiliar with the notion of revising and having multiple drafts, may actually become confused by comments that extend beyond the grammar and vocabulary lessons that were the focus of their EFL studies in their native countries. Ferris observes that this confusion can lead to inaction. Immigrant students, on the other hand, take teacher feedback "very seriously" (88), using "a variety of resources to deal with teacher commentary" (89). Ferris goes on to discuss the void in research that compares and distinguishes the L2 writing of the two populations and how teacher feedback in various forms and under various scenarios can lead to revision. She does, however, discuss findings from the research conducted to date, which have significant bearing on pedagogy. She notes, for example, that one form of commentary that leads to improved writing for international students is that which discusses *patterns* of error, with examples highlighted within the student's text and offers suggestions

for remedying those types of errors. Immigrant students, though, do better with an indication of where the errors are; they do not necessarily need suggestions on how to correct them.

266   Ferris, Dana. "Preparing Teachers to Respond to Student Writing." *Journal of Second Language Writing* 16.3 (2007): 165–93. Print.

Because responding to student writing is one of the most challenging and time-consuming aspects of a writing instructor's job, it is an important component of preservice teacher training courses. In her paper, Ferris describes the "approach/response/follow-up" training sequence that the author uses with preservice writing instructors. The "approach" section presents various issues, questions, and options available in responding to student writing based on previous L1 and L2 research on teacher feedback. In the "response" section of the sequence, teachers discuss principles and techniques of responding to L2 writing and participate in hands-on practice activities. The last section of the sequence, "follow-up," includes three components: (1) discussions about helping students utilize commentary effectively and holding them accountable, (2) conversations about qualitative and quantitative ways to evaluate teacher commentary and its effectiveness, and (3) a required project with an L2 student writer. The article concludes with special considerations for language-based feedback and ideas for working with in-service instructors.

267   Ferris, Dana R., and John Hedgcock. *Response to Student Writing: Implications for Second Language Students*. Mahwah: Erlbaum, 2003. Print.

In this book, Ferris and Hedgcock comprehensively survey research on the response to student writing and link the research to detailed descriptions of sound response practices. The book is divided into two main parts: five chapters on research and three chapters on practice. Each part features chapters on teacher response, error correction, and peer response. The research section has additional chapters on the relationship between first-language (L1) writing research and second-language (L2) writing research. Throughout the first five chapters, Ferris and Hedgcock summarize major research studies on the response to writing, noting the type of study (from empirical studies to surveys to case studies, from studies with hundreds of participants to those with only a handful), research questions, and major findings, as well as research limitations. Their use of charts and lists throughout these chapters makes it easy to grasp the major trends at a glance. The final three chapters build on the research to focus on practice. In each of these chapters, Ferris and Hedgcock emphasize the links between sound practices and the research discussed in the earlier chapters. Each chapter offers guiding principles, specific suggestions, and clear examples. The authors use charts and lists effectively and include many examples of assignments, student texts, feedback forms, and teacher responses both in the chapters and in useful appendices.

268   Ferris, Dana, and John S. Hedgcock. *Teaching ESL Composition: Purpose, Process, and Practice.* Mahwah: Erlbaum, 1998. Print.

This comprehensive resource is designed to help prospective and current English as a second language composition teachers to design and implement syllabi and lesson plans, choose textbooks, and confront most of the pedagogical obstacles that such courses present. Charts, samples of ESL student writing, and suggested classroom activities fill each chapter. In addition, the application activities that conclude the chapters provide direct practice in such tasks as developing lesson plans and writing commentary on student papers. Ferris and Hedgcock argue that the ESL teacher really must ascertain the needs of each particular ESL class separately. No two are quite alike in terms of ethnic profile and language capacity, so teachers are at pains to adapt curricula carefully once the term has started. The book then outlines how to do that in terms of text selection, instructor feedback, class activities, and so forth. Included are chapters that focus on theoretical and practical issues in ESL writing, the reading-writing relationship in ESL composition, syllabus design, text selection, instructor feedback, editing, assessment issues (including the use of portfolios), and the uses of technology. Ferris and Hedgcock also examine important research on the relationship between reading proficiency and writing ability for both first-language and second-language students, finding that among both, good readers are good writers.

269   Fredericksen, Elaine, and Isabel Baca. "Bilingual Students in the Composition Classroom: Paving the Way to 'Biliteracy.'" *Open Words: Access and English Studies* 2.2 (2008): 24–40. Print.

Bilingual students grow up learning two languages simultaneously: the languages or dialects spoken at home and at school, either of which can be their dominant language, "the one they feel most comfortable in" (24). However, many bilingual students face challenges in the writing classroom because they "fear writing in English and lack confidence to succeed" in these situations. In freshman composition, these fears can hinder the bilingual student from developing critical thinking skills and the ability to generate ideas. And while instructors aid these students in developing the writing process, from freewriting to drafting to proofreading and so on, they often force the students to complete each of these steps in English. Focusing on students whose dominant language is not English,

Fredericksen and Baca suggest a method that "fosters biliteracy—fluency in reading and writing two languages" (24). Looking at the writing experiences of their students and sharing examples of their writing processes, the authors encourage students to generate ideas, prewrite, freewrite, and write journal entries in their dominant language, allowing for improvement in their writing processes and encouraging biliteracy and success in writing.

270   Friedrich, Patricia. "Assessing the Needs of Linguistically Diverse First-Year Students: Bringing Together and Telling Apart International ESL, Resident ESL, and Monolingual Basic Writers." *Writing Program Administration Journal* 30.1/2 (2006): 15–36. Print.

Friedrich acknowledges the presence of three kinds of students in composition programs: international ESL writers, monolingual basic writers, and resident ESL writers (Generation 1.5 students). Friedrich distinguishes between the three groups of student writers based on twelve "attributes": register, strategies, awareness of linguistic background, language acquisition, oral and written language, level of acculturation, educational history, attitudes-placement, grammatical knowledge, attitudes-errors, learning style, and language and emotions. By separating the three groups of first-year composition students on these twelve counts, the article highlights their differences and then focuses on resident ESL writers. The charted distinctions represent where resident ESL learners stand vis-à-vis the other two groups and suggest their expectations from a writing class. Friedrich deliberates on what can be done to mitigate the lapses in the traditionally set disciplinary practices of first-year composition classes. Among her many suggestions, Friedrich seems to reiterate a call for action on the part of instructors and the institution. Developing need-based teaching and curriculum, improving communication between mainstream and ESL programs, deliberating on the usefulness of maintaining separate sections for mainstream and ESL students, increasing the availability of tutoring centers, and rethinking feedback practices are some of the suggestions that Friedrich offers for customizing and even revamping current ineffective practices, which tend to overlook the needs of resident ESL students.

271   Grandin, Temple. *Thinking in Pictures: My Life with Autism.* New York: Random, 2006. Print.

In Grandin's first book, *Emergence,* we learn about autism as a child or an adolescent might describe it. In this book, the focus shifts to a more scientific and medical explanation of the challenges of working with an autistic student. As the title suggests, students with autism have brains that work somewhat differently than the brains of students who don't have autism. The scientific evidence has yet to fully reveal why this is; however, the very real differences in brain structures and function cause equally real differences in student responses in our classes. Grandin's books remind us that the differences autistic people have do not necessarily mean a lack of intelligence. Many people labeled as autistic can become educated and contribute to the world from their own perspectives, which adds to our insights. In this book, Grandin talks about professors who agreed to work with her on her animal handling research in graduate school. One characteristic shared by her professors, and by her previous teachers, is the willingness to ask how her abilities might aid her education, rather than demanding other abilities more foreign to her. While she thinks in pictures, some less successful professors demanded that she think in words like they do. More successful professors acknowledged her ability to think in pictures and supported her skills in that area, which, she testifies, allowed her to continue to grow and develop as an academic.

272   Grandin, Temple, and Sean Barron. *Unwritten Rules of Social Relationships: Decoding Social Mysteries through the Unique Perspectives of Autism.* Arlington: Future Horizons, 2005. Print.

The boundaries of teaching for many writing instructors can often constrain our understanding of what a child or an adult with autism needs to be taught. Grandin and Barron begin by demonstrating that their path to being well-socialized adults was sometimes fairly smooth and sometimes quite rocky, depending on the situation. For children with autism who may not be as quick to pick up social cues, the path is often difficult, and this can affect overall classroom performance. The authors have created the following rules to help children with autism function with less stress for themselves and for the other people near them: (1) Rules are situation- and person-based. (2) Things have different levels of importance. (3) We all make mistakes, and that's OK. (4) Honesty is different from diplomacy. (5) Politeness is always appropriate. (6) Nice people aren't always our friends. (7) There are differences between public and private behavior. (8) You must learn to recognize when you are turning other people off. (9) It is possible to learn how to fit in. (10) People are responsible only for their own behaviors. In the epilogue, the authors acknowledge that learning to be socially accepted by others remains challenging into adulthood for people with autism, but also that learning does continue to help them to improve how they relate to and work with others. When teachers understand how to help that growth, they can make a real difference in the lives of students who have autism by making clear both the academic and the social expectations for all students, not just those with autism. Today, some students who don't have autism have an equivalent need for classroom rules and clear social expectations.

273   Grandin, Temple, and Kate Duffy. *Developing Talents: Careers for Individuals with Asperger Syndrome and High-Functioning Autism.* Shawnee Mission: Autism Asperger, 2004. Print.

For many academics, this book can evoke a startlingly significant awakening of their awareness of just how often and how powerfully we have set up the processes of higher education to focus solely on the kinds of skills we have, while refusing to educate students who are in some ways different. Grandin and Duffy remind us that we too often focus on what students cannot do, while ignoring what they are able to do. In the foreword, Tony Atwood notes that we must understand that many successful adults with autism achieved their success not by learning to be more like nonautistic learners, although improving people skills did help, but by being themselves. This book contains many examples of adults with autism and Asperger Syndrome who haven't become "wordies," and the overall message it sends is that we need to take students as they are instead of using a scalpel to shape them as we might like them to be. The final chapter looks at the kinds of careers in which adults with autism have succeeded, demonstrating that students with autism can perform many kinds of work if they receive adequate guidance in their choices of majors and courses along with some moderate on-the-job support.

274   Grandin, Temple, and Margaret Scariano. *Emergence: Labeled Autistic.* New York: Warner, 2005. Print.

In stunning fashion, Grandin tells the story of her early years as an autistic child whose mother fought to keep her in a regular school, despite her father's insistence that she go "to a school for the retarded" (90) and despite her outbursts, her fears, and her inability to explain to others why she was behaving in such strange ways. Through her eyes, ears, and voice, readers slowly begin to understand autism from the inside, instead of as outsiders criticizing what they do not understand. Teachers, Grandin tells readers, influenced her profoundly because she encountered some teachers who believed she had much to say and an intellect that would grow to help her say it. Most important, she tells us what those teachers did that was effective in helping her to develop her talents. They believed in her potential to do well. They were patient with her awkward stages of growth and development, which were unlike those of many other children but were equally able to propel her into a rewarding career and eventually a PhD in animal science from the University of Illinois. Her final chapter helps us to further refine our understanding, detailing which classroom activities are helpful to autistic children, and other children too, and which are not as useful or are even harmful.

275   Harklau, Linda. "From the 'Good Kids' to the 'Worst': Representations of English Language Learners across Educational Settings." *TESOL Quarterly* 34.1 (2000): 35–67. Print.

Harklau's case studies follow several long-term U.S. resident language-minority students as they transition from their senior year of high school to their first year of community college. Harklau observes that setting plays a dramatic role in how these students are perceived by their teachers and what the curriculum has to offer them. In high school, these language-minority students were seen as "the kids with determination" (45) and "an inspiration for everyone" (46). At the same time, the students were described as having serious "deficits" with English. Nonetheless, Harklau suggests "the representation of ESOL students as persevering through the hardships of immigration" (46) kept these students positively engaged in classroom learning in high school. Then, based on community college placement tests, three of the students were placed in English for speakers of other languages (ESOL) classes. The community college ESOL curriculum is described as "acculturation to life in America" (53) and is designed for international students and other recent newcomers to the United States. Because the students Harklau studied were long-term U.S. residents, they were soon bored with the curriculum and were perceived by their community college teachers to have acquired "the worst of American students' habits" (52). Harklau concludes that "things we do in classrooms serve not only to teach language but also serve to shape our students' attitudes toward schooling and their very sense of self" (64). She notes that the community college was revising the ESOL curriculum to better acknowledge the life experience and expertise brought by long-term U.S. residents and citizens into their classrooms.

276   Harklau, Linda, Kay M. Losey, and Meryl Siegal, eds. *Generation 1.5 Meets College Composition: Issues in the Teaching of Writing to U.S.-Educated Learners of ESL*. Mahwah: Erlbaum, 1999. Print.

The editors discuss "equitable and appropriate" ways to identify and serve the classroom needs of immigrant, refugee, and permanent-resident populations that do not speak English as a native language. They argue that existing ways of categorizing nonnative or bilingual English speakers do not sufficiently address the range of student backgrounds, experiences, and needs. Institutional curricula and program design need to reconsider the automatic designation of such students as "remedial" or unfamiliar with U.S. language and culture. Chapters explore specific needs of various nonnative English-speaking populations, including social construction of writing, language, identity, and ownership; the preparation of teachers and institutional programs to work with specific cultural and linguistic groups; and strategies for program reform and assessment with a view to incorporating these groups.

277   Hillenbrand, Lisa. "Assessment of ESL Students in Mainstream College Composition." *Teaching English in the Two-Year College* 21.2 (1994): 125–30. Print.

Hillenbrand uses responses from an informal survey of teachers of ESL students on her college campus to identify areas of frustration in the assessment of ESL writing and to offer suggestions for meeting the challenges that ESL writers face. She emphasizes the importance of understanding differences in rhetorical patterns between cultures and explains the difficulty of adapting to the common rhetorical patterns of English. To assist ESL students, she suggests providing writing models or encouraging the use of writing strategies like outlining. In addition, she suggests that teachers respond to ESL student writing as a whole, avoiding the temptation to focus just on grammatical and mechanical errors. She suggests that both holistic and analytical scoring can benefit ESL students as well as one-on-one conferences with the teacher, and she especially encourages writing teachers who work with ESL students to be aware of the unique linguistic challenges that their students face.

278   Hyland, Fiona. "The Impact of Teacher Written Feedback on Individual Writers." *Journal of Second Language Writing* 7.3 (1998): 255–86. Print.

Hyland investigates ESL writers' reactions to and uses of written feedback. Using a case study approach and a variety of data sources, including questionnaires, observation notes, interview transcripts, and written texts, Hyland discusses overall findings on six students' use of written feedback in an English proficiency program course at a New Zealand university. She then focuses on two student writers who showed contrasting patterns of feedback use and who both became much less positive about their writing during the course. The student revisions after receiving teacher written feedback are analyzed and contextual data is used to gain a deeper understanding of the students' motivations and responses to the feedback. The data show that use of teacher written feedback varies due to individual differences in needs and student approaches to writing. It also appears to be affected by the different experiences students bring with them to the classroom setting. Some implications for teachers giving feedback are also given. Because the data suggest that the feedback situation has great potential for miscommunication and misunderstanding, there must be a more open teacher-student dialogue on feedback.

279 Hyland, Ken. "Genre Pedagogy: Language, Literacy, and L2 Writing Instruction." *Journal of Second Language Writing* 16.3 (2007): 148–64.

Hyland examines the emerging field of second-language (L2) writing instruction through the pedagogical lens of focusing on genre. Hyland outlines the two leading schools of thought in genre pedagogy, SFL (Systemic Functional Linguistics) and ESP (English for Specific Purposes), and demonstrates how a teacher would implement the theory into actual practice. According to Hyland, teachers employing genre pedagogy assess the needs of their students and incorporate only real-world genres into the class, therefore narrowing the scope of the course to what students will encounter in their given field of interest. Hyland also stresses the importance of teaching students how pieces of text work as a means of communication, and what rhetorical moves authors are employing to make the reader understand their message. He says, "Teachers of *writing* clearly need to be teachers of *language*, as it is an ability to exercise appropriate linguistic choices in the ways they treat and organize their topics for particular readers which helps students to give their ideas authority" (151).

280 Jurecic, Ann. "Neurodiversity." *College English* 69.5 (2007): 421–42. Print.

Citing the increasing prevalence of autism spectrum disorders and a personal experience teaching a student on the autism spectrum, Jurecic argues that students with neurological differences—and autism spectrum disorders in particular—are likely to begin appearing more frequently in college writing classrooms, creating new pedagogical challenges for writing teachers. Responses to these challenges, she argues, can be informed by both social constructivist theories and cognitive science: that is, while writing teachers must continue to be wary of stereotyping students based on a medical diagnosis, cognitive science can provide useful insight into the way characteristics of autism—such as impairments with empathy and social awareness—make writing and writing classrooms difficult for many students on the autism spectrum. Ultimately, Jurecic calls for writing teachers to seek greater understanding of "neurodiverse" students, finding a middle ground where both scientific knowledge and social constructions of difference and normality can mutually inform their pedagogical approaches.

281   Kasper, Loretta F. "ESL Writing and the Principle of Nonjudgmental Awareness: Rationale and Implementation." *Teaching Developmental Writing: Background Readings.* Ed. Susan Naomi Bernstein. Boston: Bedford, 2001. 277–86. Print.

Kasper argues that a more student-centered, process-oriented approach to writing can demonstrably increase intermediate English as a second language students' (TOEFL score of approximately 350) confidence, motivation, and ability to write well. Noting that both basic writing research and ESL writing research suggest that instructor feedback dramatically affects students' development as writers, Kasper describes how she adapted W. Timothy Gallwey's principle of nonjudgmental awareness—originally developed to train tennis players—to her teaching. Kasper describes how to incorporate Gallwey's principle into writing instruction and feedback by using a series of task-oriented questions that encourage students to reflect on their communicative goals and strengths. After conducting an informal three-semester study, Kasper found that incorporating Gallwey's principle to her method of instruction produced much better results than her earlier product- and error-driven methods did: students' confidence and awareness became more noticeable, and they improved their ability to identify and revise essays for content and grammar.

282   Kroll, Barbara. *Exploring the Dynamics of Second Language Writing.* New York: Cambridge, 2003. Print.

Including the works of numerous scholars such as Paul Kei Matsuda, Alister Cumming, Tony Silva, Liz Hamp-Lyons, William Grabe, and Ilona Leki, this collection contains fourteen readings in five sections: "Exploring the Field of Second Language Writing," "Exploring the Voices of Key Stakeholders: Teachers and Students," "Exploring Writers' Finished Texts," "Exploring Contextualities of Texts," and "Exploring Technology." The readings provide an orientation to the field of second-language (L2) writing and represent a collection of scholarly insights about a range of L2 writing issues, including conducting writing research, curriculum design, assessment and feedback, reading and writing relations, and the impact of computers in L2 writing. Each of the five sections begins with a brief introduction to contextualize specific areas of L2 writing. The book ends with an epilogue that challenges L2 writing professionals to thoughtfully consider the importance and relevance of this field.

283   Leki, Ilona. "Reciprocal Themes in ESL Reading and Writing." *Landmark Essays on ESL Writing.* Ed. Tony Silva and Paul Kei Matsuda. Mahwah: Erlbaum, 2001. 173–90. Print.

Leki describes the many parallels between second-language reading and writing research since the 1970s but notes that they are often kept separate from each other. This, she suggests, is a by-product of institutional pressures and the need for disciplinary legitimacy. According to Leki, this unnatural segregation limits instruction, especially in reading. She argues that writing research emphasizes the recursive and reciprocal processes of constructing meaning but that this understanding is distorted in many second-language reading courses through text selection and pedagogical practices that ultimately make reading much harder. The bigger questions about why the text is being read or how it adds to or complicates students' knowledge is downplayed so that reading becomes more about learning skills than creating and negotiating meaning. Leki explains that bringing the fundamentally integral processes of reading and writing together enables students to work with texts in more realistic and holistic ways. She offers strategies to create a more reciprocal, socially transactional model of instruction that incorporates research findings in both reading and writing.

284   Leki, Ilona. *Undergraduates in a Second Language: Challenges and Complexities of Academic Literacy Development.* New York: Erlbaum, 2007. Print.

Leki demonstrates the complexity of ESL literacy development in this qualitative study, which traces the undergraduate careers of four ESL students, each in a different major: nursing, social work, business, and engineering. Based on a rich collection of data, Leki claims that focusing on academic literacy alone does not allow us to understand student experiences, and she stresses the importance of understanding the social and ideological contexts for developing literacy. Leki finds that the students did not represent academic literacy as a priority in their academic lives; she questions the relevance of first-year writing courses in relation to the "lived experiences" of the students she interviewed. Based on her findings, Leki suggests that we question the rationale behind first-year writing instruction when composition genres may not connect with the genres that students encounter after the first year.

285   Leki, Ilona. *Understanding ESL Writers: A Guide for Teachers.* Portsmouth: Boynton, 1992. Print.

Leki argues that although teaching writing to English as a second language writers is similar in many ways to teaching native speakers of English, ESL writers also bring many unique experiences and characteristics to the classroom. For this reason, writing teachers without much experience or preparation working with ESL writers may find it difficult to imagine the characteristics, needs, and backgrounds of those writers. Leki explains that we cannot conflate the motivational, cultural, and linguistic needs of L2 writers with those of L1 writers, including basic writers. Leki offers a practical introduction to the teaching of ESL writing—especially the teaching of international visa students—for future ESL writing teachers and for practicing writing teachers who are not familiar with second-language issues. The first section of the book provides an overview of historical and theoretical background. The second section explores the characteristics of ESL students, beginning with a comparison of ESL and basic writers. The third and final section focuses on writing issues. While each of the chapters can stand easily on its own (e.g., "Classroom Expectations and Behavior," "Contrastive Rhetoric," "L2 Composing," and "Sentence-Level Errors"), they are better understood within the context of the framing chapters, which synthesize perspectives on the history of L2 writing instruction, L2 acquisition research, and a comparison of ESL and basic writers. In "ESL and Basic Writers," she explains how various student groups bring uniquely different histories into the academic writing classroom. Leki's book predates the research on Generation 1.5 writers, but it is still relevant and still the best choice for a one-stop text for new and developing teachers aiming to better understand their ESL students.

286   Leki, Ilona, Alister Cumming, and Tony Silva. *A Synthesis of Research on Second Language Writing in English*. New York: Routledge, 2008. Print.

For many ESL instructors and researchers, issues related to research teaching in second-language writing have remained an unknown area. To meet the needs of both teachers and researchers, this book synthesizes research in the area of L2 writing in English. Focusing on three main areas—contexts for L2 writing, instruction and assessment, and basic research in L2 writing—it aims to uncover a range of issues, some that have been well researched and others that require additional attention. Section 1 offers a wide range of research in various contexts, including different levels of school (e.g., secondary school, undergraduate level, and graduate level) as well as settings outside school (e.g., professional environments). The last chapter of this section also touches on different dimensions in these settings, such as ideological and political issues. Section 2 uncovers different dimensions of teaching and assessing writing in English. It includes an analysis of curricular issues, such as conceptual foundations and theoretical orientations of L2 writing curricula. It further explores various issues in L2 writing assessment, including different types of assessment and responding to L2 students' writing. The final section explores basic research in L2 writing. Prior work summarized in this section is grouped into four main categories: writer characteristics, composing processes, textual issues of written tests, and grammatical issues of written texts. This section also includes an annotated bibliography presented in both alphabetical and chronological order. This outstanding synthesis of research serves as a reference book for anyone interested in understanding prior work in L2 writing and for those wanting to investigate both pedagogical and future research implications in this area.

287 Mason, Katherine. "Cooperative Learning and Second Language Acquisition in First-Year Composition: Opportunities for Authentic Communication among English Language Learners." *Teaching English in the Two-Year College* 34.1 (2006): 52–58. Print.

Mason asserts that using cooperative learning activities with English language learners (ELLs) in a first-year composition course helps students improve writing and speaking proficiency and allows the instructor to respond "effectively, professionally, and compassionately" (53) to students' linguistic needs. The author advocates using collaborative learning activities with an awareness of Spencer Kagan's four principles of cooperative learning, to help students build confidence, naturally integrate the four modes of literacy, and facilitate "a sense of positive interdependence among classmates, thus reducing the affective filter that hinders language acquisition" (57). Mason discusses a few specific collaborative strategies that she has found effective and notes that teacher feedback is often used to complement or supplement peer feedback during collaborative activities. Overall, collaborative activities are represented as an effective supplement to traditional classroom activities since they encourage ELLs to take linguistic risks while "simultaneously engaging in their composing processes" (58).

288 Matsuda, Paul Kei. "Composition Studies and ESL Writing: A Disciplinary Division of Labor." *College Composition and Communication* 50.4 (1999): 699–721. Print.

English as a second language writing has not been considered part of composition studies since it began to move toward the status of a legitimate profession during the 1960s. Matsuda recovers the histories of teaching English as a second language and composition studies and recounts how the formation of professional identities led to a disciplinary division of labor. He states that the absence of second-language writing discussions is reflected in the way composition studies has been constructed in this historical context, as evidenced in the works of influential historians of composition studies, such as James Berlin, Robert Connors, Susan Miller, and David Russell. He provides possibilities for a cultivated relationship between composition and ESL instructors. For example, composition specialists need to learn about ESL writing and writers by reading relevant literature and by attending presentations, workshops, and special-interest group meetings on ESL-related topics at professional conferences; compositionists need to consider second-language perspectives in their work (empirical research); graduate programs in composition studies should incorporate second-language writing into their curricula; and writing program administrators should provide an ESL-friendly environment.

289   Matsuda, Paul Kei. "Contrastive Rhetoric in Context: A Dynamic Model of L2 Writing." *Journal of Second Language Writing* 6.1 (1997): 45–60. Print.

Although research in contrastive rhetoric (CR) has grown significantly in recent times, the pedagogical implications of CR have not been successfully translated into practice. One of the reasons behind this is an outgrowth of a static theory that implicates limiting views of second-language writing. For example, an underlying assumption of this static theory is that an L2 writer is like a programmed machine, devoid of any agency, that produces L2 texts. Furthermore, the explanation of the production of L2 texts solely based on a writer's linguistic, cultural, and educational background is quite simplistic and inaccurate. A dynamic model of L2 writing, on the other hand, views L2 writing as a product of the interrelationship between various elements, such as the background of both reader and writer, their shared discourse community, and the bidirectional interactions between them. The proposed dynamic model attempts to provide a heuristic about the dynamics of L2 writing and points at the complex processes involved in the construction of L2 texts. Keeping the importance of context in mind, as proposed by the model, both teachers and students can gain a better understanding about L2 writing.

290   Matsuda, Paul Kei. "The Myth of Linguistic Homogeneity in U.S. College Composition." *College English* 68.6 (2006): 637–51. Print.

The curricular "containment" of second-language students is as old as U.S. college composition itself. Matsuda demonstrates that decades of curricular strategies to "contain" language difference (e.g., preadmission filtering, segregated composition tracks, postmatriculation remediation, etc.) have "kept language differences in the composition classroom from reaching a critical mass, thus creating the false impression that all language differences could and should be addressed elsewhere" (648). Not only has the institutional assumption that all postsecondary students are by default native speakers never been true; it is moreover increasingly out of step with demographic reality. Countering the possibility—even the desirability—that the college classroom can be a "monolingual space," Matsuda asks composition teachers to imagine their classrooms as places where "the presence of language differences is the default" (649).

291   Matsuda, Paul Kei. "Process and Post-Process: A Discursive History." *Journal of Second Language Writing* 12.1 (2003): 65–83. Print.

Matsuda sets out to show how the discursive constructions of composition have contributed significantly to the historical constructions of the field. He begins by tracing a brief history of the process movement, based on the centrality of student writing to the course and the empirically driven studies of the composing process, as a deliberative break from the "product model" of composing. Matsuda argues, however, that the process movement was just one in a long series of attempted reforms and that the discursive constructions of the process movement as unified in opposition to current-traditionalism was little more than a convenient way of "creating a daemon for the sake of expelling it" (70). Matsuda then outlines some major tenets of the postprocess movement designed to critique the "grand narrative" of process. Finally, he illustrates how the discursive formations of composition have affected, contributed to, and in many cases been anticipated by developments in the field of second-language writing. Through his historical outlines he argues that broad discursive constructions like "process" and "postprocess" have the tendency to ignore the complexities of pedagogical and theoretical movements, and that "postprocess" thinkers need to be careful not to reject process thinking outright, for doing so risks casting off the beneficial developments that the process movement stimulated.

292   Matsuda, Paul Kei. "Situating ESL Writing in a Cross-Disciplinary Context." *Written Communication* 15.1 (2008): 99–121. Print.

Matsuda deplores the lack of attention paid to the writing needs of the increasing number of ESL students in U.S. higher education. One of the reasons for the unsatisfactory situation lies in the lack of qualified ESL writing teachers (i.e., composition teachers with training in ESL or ESL teachers with specific training in writing). Matsuda attributes this deficiency in teacher preparation to how ESL writing has been constructed in relation to two interrelated disciplines: teaching English as a second language (TESL) and composition studies. He examines two existing models, the division-of-labor model and the intersection model, and identifies the two models' negative effects on the development of the ESL writing field. The division-of-labor model "separates TESL and composition studies completely, positioning ESL writing as part of TESL but not of composition studies" (104). The intersection model brings the two disciplines together and fosters communication and cooperation between the two. However, Matsuda points out the rather restricted space for ESL writing within composition studies in the intersection model. He argues for the symbiotic model where ESL writing is given a more autonomous status and does not belong exclusively to either TESL or composition studies. In the symbiotic model, ESL writing, concerned with both writing and second language, has a metadisciplinary discourse of its own that transcends the two related disciplines. Matsuda argues that only the symbiotic model can be conducive to the field of ESL and truly respond to the writing needs of ESL students.

293   Matsuda, Paul Kei. "Writing and Second Language Writers: Toward an Inclusive Definition." *Journal of Basic Writing* 22.2 (2003): 67–89. Print.

Matsuda questions the generalized notion of basic writers often appropriated by academe. With a diverse body of students coming into basic writing classrooms, it is practically impossible to define basic writers in set terms. Studies have shown that linguistic identity labels like "basic writer" do not give a complete picture of a student's identity. As a result, the student could be placed in a mainstream section of basic writing by one institution and categorized as an ESL learner by another. Matsuda gives a historical overview of the field of basic writing by relating how the literature from the 1960s has classified basic writers. He then focuses on the presence of ESL writers, especially resident nonnative (Generation 1.5) students. Given the broad array of incoming first-year composition students, he suggests that institutional practices should take into consideration the requirements of ESL students while rethinking discussions and decisions on basic writers and how to improve their writing skills. While considering how ESL learners have fared in the conventional "disciplinary practices of basic writing," Matsuda suggests changes in the conceptualization of the field itself. The need for awareness among instructors, coupled with professional help to prepare them for ESL-specific teaching skills, is severely felt in this changing frame of basic writing classrooms. Furthermore, it is essential to encourage channels of communication between basic writing teachers and ESL specialists to devise thoughtful pedagogical skills.

294   Matsuda, Paul Kei, et al. "Changing Currents in Second Language Writing Research: A Colloquium." *Journal of Second Language Writing* 12 (2003): 151–79. Print.

This article, based on a colloquium at the 2002 meeting of the American Association for Applied Linguistics, discusses how second-language writing has evolved into "an interdisciplinary field of inquiry with its own disciplinary infrastructure" (151). The authors provide insight into the changing current of L2 writing, focusing on the emergence of the field, the research that is being conducted, and potential directions for future research. Linda Harklau begins by examining the research on Generation 1.5 writers and the issues associated with these writers in North American high schools and colleges. She suggests that the current perspectives on Generation 1.5 writers need to be transformed to build on students' multilingual talents. Suresh Canagarajah considers the notion of multiliteracies and how it pervades the traditions of writing. He contends that writing is largely influenced by our beliefs, values, and subject positions, and therefore we need to extend how we view multiliteracy. Mark Warschauer discusses the influence of technology on writing and how it has changed the way we interact and communicate. He argues that alternative research, other than short-term classroom-based studies, needs to be conducted, and he points to the potential of ethnographies, longitudinal studies, and corpus studies for future research. Ken Hyland emphasizes the importance of discourse analysis for understanding second-language writing. He suggests that an understanding of discourse would familiarize writers with how the writer-audience relationship changes as the context and purpose for writing changes. Finally, Matsuda explains that the field of L2 writing has begun to develop its own identity and has developed a metadisciplinary inquiry of its own, indicating that L2 writing now has its own status, scope, and characteristics.

295   Matsuda, Paul Kei, et al. *Second-Language Writing in the Composition Classroom: A Critical Sourcebook*. Boston: Bedford, 2006. Print.

This collection of articles by well-known second-language scholars is intended primarily for L2 composition professionals. It brings together some of the most significant, and some of the most current, research involving L2 writers and writing. Divided into five major sections, the book covers areas as diverse as the current position of L2 writing within the broader field of composition studies, the language needs of international students as well as resident U.S. writers, ESL writers and academic writing, the role of students' home language in L2 writing, effective classroom writing assignments for L2 learners, the role of computers in L2 writing, and responding to L2 writing, including error feedback. The essays included are both theoretical and practical in nature, and their wide scope indicates the complexities involved in L2 writing. There is also a very useful list of additional readings at the back that L2 scholars and those interested in multicultural composition issues will find to be a very valuable resource.

296   Matsuda, Paul Kei, Christina Ortmeier-Hooper, and Aya Matsuda. "The Expansion of Second Language Writing." *Handbook of Writing Development.* Ed. R. Beard et al. Thousand Oaks: Sage, 2009. 457–71. Print.

Matsuda and colleagues offer an overview of the field of second-language writing in higher education from its early, marginalized beginnings in the 1960s to its current, widely relevant position in the twenty-first century. The expansion of L2 writing correlates with the shifting population in higher education to include more international students, the prevalence of English as the lingua franca, and the emergence of modern linguistics. In the1960s, discussion addressed the placement of L2 writers in writing courses. The decade also debated fluency or accuracy in L2 writing. At the close of the 1960s and into the 1970s, the work of Jerome Bruner shifted the conversation to focus "more on the production and organization of meaningful text" (6) and ushered in a process movement in L2 writing. By the late 1970s and in the 1980s, the research matured as the field generated its own "communities of practice" and posed questions from the classroom and other studies. Throughout the 1980s, advanced literacy became a central concern, and by the decade's close, the field came of age: the term *second-language writing* emerged, and the *Journal of Second Language Writing* began. The 1990s brought the creation of yet another research outlet: the Symposium on Second Language Writing. And the twenty-first century has also offered its share of "comprehensive overviews of the field" (8). Beyond this decade-by-decade overview, the article considers traits of L2 writers, noting that the research shows that the writing processes of L2 writers differ significantly from those of first-language writers. Further, most L2 writers have had little practice or instruction with writing longer compositions. Then the article discusses the research that has considered the curricular implications, such as the question of whether to separate or integrate second- and first-language writers, writing beyond the writing classroom, the supporting roles of writing centers, and supporting faculty development. In addition to the curricular implications, this article notes the research on pedagogy as it relates to four areas: developing "effective writing assignments and curriculum, teacher and peer response, the treatment of error, and assessment" (15). Finally, a section on new areas of research—early L2 writing, who owns English, World Englishes, English studies in non-English cultures, and teaching writing in other languages—closes the article.

297   Matsuda, Paul Kei, Christina Ortmeier-Hooper, and Xiaoye You, eds. *The Politics of Second Language Writing: In Search of the Promised Land*. West Lafayette: Parlor, 2006. Print.

This collection grew out of the 2004 Symposium on Second Language Writing. The editors use Barbara Kroll's metaphor of the "promised lands" for nonnative English-speaking (NNES) students as an overarching frame for this volume. To envision the "promised lands" of excellence in academic English, the editors bring together a collection of sixteen articles that analyze classroom practices within the framework of institutional policies and politics "because instruction is always shaped by larger institutional contexts" (vii). This volume is designed to help educators, researchers, administrators, and members of second-language writing programs and departments make connections between their individual practices and the institutional policies and politics that influence their practices. Moreover, this collection may foster discussion of the politics of L2 writing in geopolitical areas around the globe, as Xiaoye You suggests. You analyzes an educational decree on college English and its effects in two Chinese universities while urging English educators to participate in the institutional imagination of new literacies in China. This volume is organized in five sections: K–12 education; language support programs in higher education, featuring a study on the role of writing centers; English for academic and professional purposes, including a study on the preparation of international teaching assistants; assessment, featuring arguments on online directed self-placement and positive washback; and the politics of the profession. The editors conclude this volume with Kroll's assertion to address the obstacles that prevent NNES students from reaching the "promised lands." According to Kroll, the obstacles include a lack of identification of NNES students, noneffective placement tests, English courses that do not cater to students' needs, lack of English requirements in other departments and colleges, and higher tuition for NNES students. This collection illustrates how to confront some of these obstacles to get closer to the "promised land."

298   Matsuda, Paul Kei, and Tony Silva. "Cross-cultural Composition: Mediated Integration of U.S. and International Students." *Composition Studies* 27.1 (1999): 15–30. Print.

Matsuda and Silva argue that a cross-cultural composition course of first-year writing should be offered as a placement option to prevent the binaries associated with ESL-only sections or mainstreamed sections of First-Year Writing. Matsuda offers an exemplary course that he taught at Purdue University in 1997 and outlines writing projects that focus on cross-cultural experiences as the subject for inquiry in the first-year classroom, such as reflective journal entries on cross-cultural experiences, a profile of a linguistic or cultural group that focuses on dissonance and productive conflict, primary investigation of nonverbal communication within and among groups, a primary survey of a linguistic or cultural group, the translation of insights from writing projects into a forum outside the classroom, and the development of a portfolio that highlights the cross-cultural writing done over the course of the semester. Matsuda's students reported that the cross-cultural course provided an ESL-friendly environment and opportunities for cross-cultural learning. The authors note that writing courses that focus on cross-cultural experiences should be staffed by instructors with experience working with both ESL and native English-speaking (NES) students, that the placement of these students in this course should be an option, and that the class itself should be equally comprised of both ESL and NES students. This course can be especially valuable at institutions where there is little linguistic or cultural diversity.

299   Matsuda, Paul Kei, and Tony Silva, eds. *Second Language Writing Research: Perspectives on the Process of Knowledge Construction.* Mahwah: Erlbaum, 2005. Print.

This volume, consisting of eighteen scholars' self-reflections about their research on writing in English as a second or foreign language, explores the complexities of researchers' thought processes and research decisions, which often are not transparent to readers of their published work. Matsuda and Silva organize the sixteen chapters into four sections that focus on different aspects and issues of second-language writing: research as situated knowledge construction, conceptualizing research programs, collecting and analyzing data, and practical issues of conducting research. Through its inclusion of chapters that bring to bear various aspects of L2 writing research, such as philosophical, historical, and narrative modes of inquiry, multimodal and cross-modal research processes, and discourse analytic methods, this unique, highly informative volume provides both novice and experienced researchers with valuable insights into the decision-making processes behind various research projects; issues in the process of conceptualizing, conducting, and crafting L2 writing research; and how different methodologies might be applied to address specific research questions.

300   McAlexander, Patricia J. "Using Principles of Universal Design in College Composition Courses." *BWe: Basic Writing e-Journal* 5.1 (2004): n. pag. Web. 11 Aug. 2009.

The increasing diversity of college student populations calls for acknowledgment that no single teaching approach will be appropriate for students with wide variations in individual learning strengths and sources of motivation. The Americans with Disabilities Act requires that students with documented disabilities receive accommodations that often include modifying instructional procedures. McAlexander believes that Universal Design for Learning (UDL) theory calls for instructors to do whatever possible to adjust their teaching approaches to meet the diverse learning styles, interests, and abilities of all students. She focuses on three UDL principles: (1) provide material that is personally relevant to students, (2) offer a flexible curriculum with appropriate challenges for each student, and (3) give students individualized feedback. She outlines specific strategies for applying these three principles in the college composition classroom while following a mandated curriculum, maintaining standards, and engaging students in common classroom activities.

301   Mlynarczyk, Rebecca Williams, and Marcia Babbitt. "The Power of Academic Learning Communities." *Journal of Basic Writing* 21.1 (2002): 71–89. Print.

Mlynarczyk and Babbitt describe the Intensive English as a Second Language program developed at Kingsborough Community College to help ESL students complete their English courses before depleting their financial aid. Complementing this objective were three additional goals: helping students to succeed in credit courses during their first semester in college, improving the retention and graduation rates of ESL students, and integrating ESL students into the social and academic life of the college. In the program, students acquired proficiency in "academic English" by taking credit-bearing courses while receiving language support in ESL and speech courses. Mlynarczyk and Babbitt report that the program helped facilitate high pass rates, good grades, and a collegial classroom atmosphere. The authors posit that collaborative, interdisciplinary approaches to learning; student-centered pedagogy emphasizing reading and writing to learn; and enhanced student perceptions of self-efficacy are central to the program's continued success.

302   Murie, Robin, Molly Rojas Collins, and Daniel F. Detzner. "Building Academic Literacy from Student Strength: An Interdisciplinary Life History Project." *Journal of Basic Writing* 23.2 (2004): 70–92. Print.

Recognizing a need for projects structured to encourage the writing of Generation 1.5 students, the authors present a life history project that focuses on a "real" purpose. Generation 1.5 students have experienced a disrupted education transitioning between their native country and an American school. The disruption in education that the misnomer *Generation 1.5* denotes may also include a less developed native language literacy and English learned more through exposure than instruction. Recognizing that the traditional model of ESL courses is not very effective and that many teachers are unprepared to teach a student with these specific issues, the authors developed the Life History Project at the University of Minnesota "to engage multilingual students in extensive writing for real purposes" (71). This project allows students to write to a real audience with a clear purpose; to complete extensive, repetitive data collection contextualized by their understanding of their interviewee's life and culture; to demonstrate a consistent connection between the student's writing and literature with the same themes and situations; to emphasize the creative process of writing; to develop fluency through extensive drafting and reader response; and to demonstrate to students where they fit in the university's curriculum. These personal connections and the positioning of the student writers as bilingual, bicultural experts further strengthen students' development of personal voice and sense of self in their writing. The Life History Project allowed students to build academic literacy by creating a tangible product. Furthermore, the project rejected the "deficit model of 'remediation'"(85), thereby allowing students to see themselves as valuable members of the university community while simultaneously learning "a great deal about writing" (86).

303   Nelson, Marie Wilson. *At the Point of Need: Teaching Basic and ESL Writers*. Portsmouth: Boynton, 1991. Print.

This book describes the findings of a longitudinal qualitative study Nelson conducted as director of a newly established writing center program designed to assist students who had failed the university's English placement exam. In addition to focusing on students, Nelson wanted to explore two apparent characteristics of confident or successful teachers—characteristics lacking in teachers who expressed feelings of frustration, defeat, or ambivalence about teaching. Much of what the research team discovered relates to the process by which the students came to take responsibility for their work. According to Nelson, though, the most significant finding was that the most effective approach to teaching basic writing students centered on one's ability to revise his or her pedagogy in response to the particular needs that students communicated at that moment. This study calls on teachers to recognize a student's intended purpose as a driving force of his or her development as a writer.

304   Ortmeier-Hooper, Christina. "English May Be My Second Language, but I'm Not ESL." *College Composition and Communication* 59.3 (2008): 389–419. Print.

Making a case for what she argues are the "problematic" terms *ESL* and *Generation 1.5*, Ortmeier-Hooper presents three case studies of immigrant first-year composition students. She focuses on the concept of identity—in particular, how students negotiate the multiple identities that evolve out of their cultural, personal, and academic experiences. She argues that as instructors, we often oversimplify our students' performances and forget about the myriad factors that affect their writing and learning. She asserts that our field's current categorizations and labels for second-language learners and writers too fully dictate how we see a student. Ortmeier-Hooper is careful to point out that she is not advocating we abandon our attempts at encouraging openness and diversity in our classrooms. To avoid further essentializing them as we unintentionally do with terms like *ESL*, we need to proceed carefully with the label *Generation 1.5* and instead remember that students do not always want their personal backgrounds and differences becoming their primary attribute. The key to addressing all students' needs is to build stronger rapport with all students. Instructors can also, Ortmeier-Hooper asserts, gain a better understanding of the world circumstances that predate our students' presence in our classrooms. By continuing to support instructor training programs and studies on identity construction, we can move away from a false concept of singular identity and learn to accept that writers' and learners' identities are often multiple and even "messy" (414–15).

305   Pally, Marcia, et al. "What Is Learned in Sustained Content Writing Classes along with Writing?" *Journal of Basic Writing* 21.1 (2002): 90–115. Print.

Sustained content-based instruction, the in-depth studying of one subject over an entire term, was found to foster nonnative speakers' perceptions of "by-products," or aspects of personal growth that resulted from their academic English writing courses. This study, which focused on four courses taught over three semesters in 2000 in both Israeli and New York universities, suggests that sustained content-based instruction provides nonnative speakers with "the kind and extent of the challenge needed for the emergence and recognition of personal growth" (104). The "by-products" of academic and personal development fostered by sustained content-based instruction in English courses may have significant impact on the fulfillment of universities' goals for nonnative speakers.

306   Phillips, Talinn, Candace Stewart, and Robert D. Stewart. "Geography Lessons, Bridge Building, and Second Language Writers." *Writing Program Administration* 30.1/2 (2006): 83–100. Print.

The authors use a bridge metaphor to discuss the divide at their institution, and a number of other institutions, in which native English speakers (NESs) are taught writing in the English department, while second-language writers receive their first-year writing instruction through the TESOL department. Using Paul Kei Matsuda's explanation of a "disciplinary division of labor," the authors illustrate how these disciplinary divisions often persist because those who desire to bridge the disciplines lack institutional power to make that change. The authors describe the university writing center, which at their institution is housed in the university's Writing across the Curriculum program, as a "third site which . . . is *already* cross-disciplinary—for discussions and experimentation in second language writing" (89). In this case, the writing center serves as a resource for L2 writing for the campus community by providing tutoring to L2 writers, workshops for cross-disciplinary faculty, materials for interested instructors, and a space for graduate students from multiple disciplines to develop and experiment with strategies for working with L2 writers. The authors conclude by encouraging readers to view these sites as "places of convergence at which the networks and collaborations we have developed individually can come together to generate larger networks and collaborations" (99).

See: Paul Kei Matsuda, "Composition Studies and ESL Writing" [288].

307 Price, Margaret. "Accessing Disability: A Nondisabled Student Works the Hyphen." *College Composition and Communication* 59.1 (2007): 53–76. Print.

Arguing that the subject of disability is in danger of becoming another "add-and-stir policy" in multiculturalism, Price suggests that teachers of writing move beyond disability to *disability studies* in critical pedagogies. Price describes a student, Tara, who struggled to navigate her nondisabled perspective while she researched and wrote about issues of access for people with disabilities. Based on the texts and interviews gathered in this case study, Price questions the common perception that students' critical thinking can be assessed solely from written texts. She concludes by noting that critical pedagogy at its best calls for change on behalf of the teacher as well as the student, that "no one is excluded, and no one is exempt" (72).

308 Reid, Joy, ed. *Writing Myths: Applying Second Language Research to Classroom Teaching.* Ann Arbor: U of Michigan P, 2008. Print.

This collection of essays addresses common pedagogical "myths" or issues that revolve around ESL education and course instruction, with personal reflections of educators in the field and with research and applications of this research in the classroom, as inspired by Keith Folse's *Vocabulary Myths: Applying Second Language Research to Classroom Teaching.* In her introduction, Reid discusses the need for addressing these common pedagogical assertions, which appear in common misconceptions about fundamental concerns, or "myths," such as regimented teaching of grammar in the classroom. The "myths" in this collection revolve around how to address common beliefs or concerns about ESL education, as Folse addresses in the first essay "Teaching Vocabulary Is Not the Writing Teacher's Job." To develop this argument, Folse uses rubrics and test scores to attend to this issue in the classroom. Other myths addressed are Pat Byrd's "Where Grammar Is Concerned One Size Fits All" and Paul Kei Matsuda's "International and U.S. Resident ESL Writers Cannot Be Taught in the Same Class." Both of these essays utilize personalized teaching strategies and examine how they are implemented, or ignored, in the classroom. The deliberations about each myth are followed by Reid's overview in "Myth(s) 9: Student Myths about Academic Writing and Teaching," which shows how ESL teaching and resources have changed since Reid began teaching in 1966. This last section addresses how students respond to these myths, with an analysis of versions of their own myths, such as "I have to wait until the idea hits me." Reid's approach to these student conceptions offers a more open dialogue with the students, in particular letting them know that writing can be a difficult process, even for educators. In the end, the essays point toward the importance of opening this dialogue between educators and students to address the common "myths" that continually emerge inside and outside the classroom.

309   Rodby, Judith. *Appropriating Literacy: Writing and Reading in English as a Second Language*. Portsmouth: Boynton, 1992. Print.

Rodby problematizes the social and academic rejection of nonstandard written English, examining the social and political gap that divides the English as a second language educators and linguists who contend that ESL literacy can empower those learners. Recognizing the legitimacy of both positions, Rodby explains a series of dialectics that can be explored to bridge this gap. Using narrative examples from some of her students, Rodby illustrates how being "in-between" affects students' attitudes toward standard academic English. However, when many liminars are brought together and form "mutual relationships of neophytes in initiation" (83), they have risen to a state of what Turner calls *communitas*, or a communal consciousness. As a feeling of universality, *communitas* is egalitarian and resists structure; it is not a discourse community because it is a dynamic process that welcomes change. To facilitate *communitas* in the literacy classroom, Rodby advocates beginning with the students' current literacy practices and literacy artifacts, developing collaborative activities, and recognizing and legitimizing students' "otherness" and their appropriation of English.

310   Shuck, Gail. "Combating Monolingualism: A Novice Administrator's Challenge." *WPA: Writing Program Administration* 30.1/2 (2006): 59–82. Print.

Focusing on the pervasive idea of monolingualism in composition instruction, Shuck critiques the ways second-language students are positioned within both composition studies and the pedagogy and administration of her own institution. She critically assesses the ESL sequence at Boise State University, which reaffirms the "myth of transience," an idea that holds that ESL students "simply need a few more courses before they can participate in 'real' academic courses" (62). She shows how this idea and course sequence, inadvertently aided by her positioning within an English department, reaffirms the idea that ESL issues can be considered the sole responsibility of a single person or department, rather than part of the entire university's mission. Describing the steps she has taken within her current university, she offers suggestions to challenge "exclusionary practices based on a fallacious view of the world as essentially monolingual" (68), while considering implications for other writing program administrators and teachers. Shuck concludes with two major suggestions. The first is the development of cross-cultural environments for writing. While not explicitly ESL, these course sections offer greater support for ESL students without labeling them as the "other" within the university. Her second strategy involves educating faculty, finding ways to "help our colleagues understand in more depth the strengths and struggles that multicultural students bring to our classroom" (72), and advocating for programs including faculty liaisons, advisory committees, and public events featuring ESL student voices.

311   Silva, Tony, and Paul Kei Matsuda, eds. *Landmark Essays on ESL Writing*. Mahwah: Erlbaum, 2001.

One in a series of volumes presenting influential essays in various fields, this collection of sixteen previously published articles traces the development of scholarship in English as a second language writing across the last four decades of the twentieth century. The writers represented include some of the most familiar names in second-language writing. In addition, the essays, chosen for their significance in the field, continue to generate numerous further commentaries, rebuttals, and revisions. Perhaps the best example of such a text is Robert B. Kaplan's "Cultural Thought Patterns in Inter-Cultural Education" (the so-called doodles article), in which the author speculated as to the effects of cultural backgrounds on the success or failure of second-language writers. In another example, John Hinds's "Reader-Writer Responsibility: A New Typology" also presented an exploration of the influence of culture on L2 writing, using the difference between Japanese and English writers to explain a distinction between reader-responsible and writer-responsible languages. Possibly indicating the recent explosion of interest in writing skills within ESL research, more than half of the articles included here were originally published in the 1990s. Among the articles from that decade are Joan G. Carson's "Becoming Biliterate: First Language Influences," which added to Kaplan's work by focusing on the effect of culture on L2 acquisition, and Tony Silva's "Toward an Understanding of the Distinct Nature of L2 Writing: The ESL Research and Its Implications," a survey of studies on L2 writers in which he proposed using new methods in the L2 writing classroom that focus on the unique characteristics of students who have to write in a second language. The collection is introduced with a useful historical overview by Silva and Matsuda, cofounders and chairs of the Second Language Symposium, both of whom also contributed to this volume.

312   Silva, Tony, and Paul Kei Matsuda, eds. *On Second-Language Writing*. Mahwah: Erlbaum, 2001. Print.

This collection contains fifteen original articles by the scholars who presented papers at the historic first Symposium on Second Language Writing held at Purdue University in 1998. The symposium has remained an important event in the field, and the contributors and their work have continued to be prominent as well. In the preface, the editors outline a guide both to the volume and to the second-language writing field itself, starting with Barbara Kroll's autobiographical essay and ending with Alister Cumming's study of the problems inherent in applying educational standards to L2 writing. In between, the articles focus on topics that remain a concern to the L2 writing community: the student writers themselves, L2 writing theory, research on L2 writing, assessment, working with university-level ESL students, politics and L2 writing, and the interface between L2 writing and other disciplines, such as second-language acquisition (SLA) and rhetoric. Other contributors include Ilona Leki, Pat Currie, William Grabe, Diane Belcher, Lynn Goldstein, Charlene Polio, Liz Hamp-Lyons, Trudy Smoke, Joy Reid, Sarah Benesch, Terry Santos, Joan Carson, and Carol Severino.

313   Smoke, Trudy. "Mainstreaming Writing: What Does This Mean for ESL Students?" *Mainstreaming Basic Writers: Politics and Pedagogies of Access*. Ed. Gerri McNenny. Mahwah: Erlbaum, 2001. 193–214. Print.

Smoke complicates the notion of mainstreaming as an option for English as a second language students. Smoke questions the new definitions of the ESL student that have emerged as part of recently legislated educational policies limiting college remedial and ESL programs. She then looks closely at the overall sociopolitical context of ESL at the City University of New York and specifically at her own campus, Hunter College. The author also examines a variety of pedagogical approaches developed to meet the needs of ESL students in colleges in Alabama, Arizona, California, Indiana, and other states. After describing stand-alone ESL classes, mainstream classes, and out-of-class workshops, she discusses how teachers perceive the effectiveness of the various models. Smoke advocates offering options to students, and if mainstreaming is chosen, questions the best ratio for native speaker to nonnative speaker students. Smoke recognizes the limitations that today's political environment presents to writing directors and stresses the need to maintain the best program with as many options as are viable while keeping in mind program survivability in an uncertain future.

314   Williams, Jessica. "Undergraduate Second-Language Writers in the Writing Center." *Journal of Basic Writing* 21.2 (2001): 73–91. Print.

Second-language writers are increasingly using writing centers and are often sent there by instructors who are unsure how to deal with L2 problems. Since L2 writers come from diverse social, linguistic, cultural, and educational backgrounds, they are not a monolithic group, but their writing shows many characteristic difficulties. Their limited vocabulary also makes academic reading and hence academic writing challenging for them. Unfortunately, writing center tutors are often unprepared to assist L2 writers. To be effective, tutors should understand English grammar rules, L2 learning processes, and the ways that those processes affect learner production. Two second-language acquisition theories—the interaction hypothesis, which stresses negotiation of meaning in language acquisition, and sociocultural theory, which sees interaction as a social process leading to the creation of new knowledge—can enable tutors to provide guidance at a level appropriate for each learner without editing or appropriating student texts.

315   Zamel, Vivian. "Engaging Students in Writing-to-Learn: Promoting Language and Literacy across the Curriculum." *Journal of Basic Writing* 19.2 (2000): 3–21. Print.

Zamel's article resulted from an invitation by the journal editors to revisit a keynote speech she gave at a faculty development meeting at the City University of New York. Zamel establishes the terrain by using student writing in response to English as a second language classroom activities and also in conjunction with academic work in other disciplines. Analyzing these samples, Zamel demonstrates the efficacy of integrating writing as a learning tool. In her discussion, she indicates how this process—using reading journals, ungraded mini-papers, and in-class summaries of class activities—allows for more open communication between faculty and students. This in turn increases the students' ability to acquire the language and meanings of various disciplines and provides faculty with a better understanding of their students' learning processes. While the article uses examples of ESL student writing, the argument applies to native English-speaking students as well. Zamel concludes that faculty need to attend to meanings and issues in "correcting" student writing. Error correction alone, she notes, leads away from language proficiency and actually may increase student frustrations.

316   Zamel, Vivian, and Ruth Spack, eds. *Enriching ESOL Pedagogy: Readings and Activities for Engagement, Reflection, and Inquiry.* Mahwah: Erlbaum, 2002. Print.

Including the works of such scholars as Mike Rose, Sarah Hudelson, Amy Tan, Stephen Krashen, H. G. Widdowson, Vivian Zamel, Judith Wells Lindfors, and Simon Ortiz, this collection contains twenty-two readings in five sections: "Questioning the Nature of Methods," "Seeing in the Classroom," "Theories into Practice: Promoting Language Acquisition," "Theories into Practice: Keeping Language Meaningful," and "Questioning Assumptions about Language Identity." The readings represent a range of genres, including theoretical explorations, ethnographies, personal essays, and research reports. Each unit begins with open-ended questions about the readings and ends with questions and prompts that help readers make connections between the readings and their own experiences in the academic and personal arenas of life. Each unit also includes a list of recommended readings and possible projects for inquiry.

317   Zamel, Vivian, and Ruth Spack. "Teaching Multilingual Learners: Beyond the ESOL Classroom and Back Again." *Journal of Basic Writing* 25.2 (2006): 126–52. Print.

Zamel and Spack challenge the deficit model of language and learning that views ESOL students as deficient and less competent, a view that permeates the thinking of faculty across the curriculum. They call for all faculty members to facilitate ESOL students' acquisition of language and literacy by assigning meaningful writing tasks, providing supportive feedback, and, most important, acknowledging and valuing ESOL students' unique historical and cultural perspectives.

This article draws on many firsthand experiences of both ESOL students and faculty in undergraduate courses across the curriculum and comes to the conclusion that ESOL students are as fully capable of succeeding in content courses as their English-speaking counterparts are. The ESOL students' successful experience is directly attributable to a variety of pedagogical strategies enacted by some faculty—strategies that benefit English-speaking students as well. The article also provides some pedagogical implications for ESOL composition classes as well as any other ESOL courses, where writing should play a central role because it can provide a chance for students to take risks, generate ideas, engage in intellectual thinking, and promote language and literacy acquisition.

An Administrative Focus

Placement and Assessment

318   Adams, Peter Dow. "Basic Writing Reconsidered." *Journal of Basic Writing* 21.1 (1993): 22–35. Print.

Studying data from students placed into basic writing classes at the community college where he teaches, Adams was curious to learn about the effect of the classes. He found that students who were placed into basic writing courses but enrolled in first-year composition performed better than those who were placed into and took basic writing courses. Adams uses these findings to argue for the mainstreaming of basic writers.

319   Adler-Kassner, Linda, and Susanmarie Harrington. "In the Here and Now: Public Policy and Basic Writing." *Journal of Basic Writing* 25.2 (2006): 27–48. Print.

Adler-Kassner and Harrington discuss how public policy documents, such as those by the American Diploma Project and the Spellings Commission on the Future of Higher Education, offer the public and policy makers conflicting insights and frame education crisis discussions as institutional problems rather than individual learning concerns. As an institutional problem, the education crisis can be seen as requiring reform through national standards and standardized testing. The authors show how a three-part public policy narrative construction can justify the education crisis and the exclusion of educators from reform efforts: secondary schools do not prepare students for college or work, which costs higher education institutions, businesses, and taxpayers; to avoid the consequential extra burden on taxpayers and institutions, agents outside of the secondary school system need to solve the school-based problem of underpreparing or not preparing students and workers. Surfacing this fallacious narrative, the authors remind readers of previous basic writing public policy efforts by Lynn Troyka, Stanford Goto, and Deborah Mutnick, and they review insights offered by basic writing professionals' cultural studies efforts, including the authors' own. The authors also exemplify how to reframe public policy arguments that can meaningfully communicate the knowledge of writing studies professionals to the public and to policy makers. In addition, they call on writing studies professionals to research issues, collect data, and determine useful strategies and program information to share in public policy texts addressed to readers beyond our programs and institutions.

320   Barlow, Aaron. "Leading Writers, Teaching Tests." *BWe: Basic Writing e-Journal* 5.1 (2004): n. pag. Web. 11 Aug. 2009.

Barlow, an adjunct lecturer at the New York City College of Technology, tackles a tough question facing many teachers of composition: that is, how to live up to their own pedagogical standards while also fulfilling the immediate needs of their institutions—in this case, the need to prepare students for success on the CUNY/ACT exam. He discusses his strategies for maintaining a process-centered approach while still addressing the form and style demanded by the exam. Rather than letting his "frustration reign" by falling into current traditional pedagogy that arbitrarily focuses on form, Barlow works on combining the skills that connect both the ACT exam and preparation for Composition I; these skills include the ability to focus on a clear point, to elaborate, and to edit one's own work. Additionally, he makes use of refined prompts for practice (which focus on school and community issues), diagnostic tests, peer review, and portfolio assessment. Anchoring his discussion in work by scholars such as Peter Elbow and Pat Belanoff, Hans-Georg Gadamer, and David Bartholomae and Anthony Petrosky, Barlow also includes practical elements to depict his daily classroom practices. For example, he provides a sample syllabus from his 2002 Developmental Writing II course, which showcases his focus on both pedagogy and exam preparation. Barlow's essay is largely exploratory, offering a kind of snapshot of his current pedagogy and a meta-analysis of his thought process in bridging the gap between teaching to the test and preparing students for success in future, real-world writing.

321   Bedore, Pamela, and Deborah F. Rossen-Knill. "Informed Self-Placement: Is a Choice Offered a Choice Received?" *Writing Program Administration Journal* 28.1/2 (2004): 55–78. Print.

This article draws on communication theories and on assessment research (surveys, focus groups, interviews, and program material review) conducted by the authors in their composition program to discuss whether helping students make informed decisions about their first-year composition course placement (informed self-placement, or ISP) offers students more authentic participation in their own educational choices than does directed self-placement (DSP), to which ISP's origins can be traced. Offering both a review of DSP successes and a nuanced critique, Bedore and Rossen-Knill suggest that communication complications, such as the need for first-year students to learn how to hold critical discussions about their college writing, can hinder students' abilities to engage fully in real and valid placement choices for themselves as they enter college. Thus while the authors embraced ISP, they also engaged in an organic assessment process that added assessment phases based on insights revealed in the process. The authors acknowledge the role of resource reallocation and the value of careful consideration of assessment results in helping to create a dialogic program that educates students about their composition placement and course choices and results in students' enhanced ability to make valid and real choices within the program that the authors facilitate.

322   Bernstein, Susan Naomi. "Teaching and Learning in Texas: Accountability Testing, Language, Race, and Place." *Journal of Basic Writing* 23.1 (2004): 4–24. Print.

Basic writing instructors and students can benefit from tackling the implications of federally mandated standardized testing in public education. Bernstein examines Texas's use of high-stakes accountability testing of public school students—the model for the No Child Left Behind Act—to determine grade promotion and "college readiness" (6). In a basic writing course at an open admissions urban public university, Bernstein focuses on "education as a systemic process" (10) to help her students examine how their subject positions as English language learners are shaped by and through the language education they experienced at secondary public schools that are controlled by state-mandated accountability testing. Focusing on the writing of one student, Noah, Bernstein argues that critical reflection on the chasm between secondary education determined by high-stakes testing and college writing instruction framed by critical thinking can be used to encourage students to occupy a position of advocacy that works toward changing the inequalities of the educational system.

323   Bernstein, Susan Naomi. "Writing and White Privilege: Beyond Basic Skills." *Pedagogy: Critical Approaches to Teaching Literature, Language, Composition, and Culture* 4.1 (2004): 128–31. Print.

Examining the implications of labeling students as "basic writers," Bernstein uses her own experiences of teaching basic writing to argue that standardized tests undermine students' ability to become imaginative thinkers and writers. In her classes, her students explore their personal public school experiences through literacy narratives and analysis, and as a result Bernstein becomes more aware of what she calls the "marker of educated middle class" (130)—being able to write in and recognize standard English. Bernstein argues that the "basic writer" label only widens the education gap between whites and minorities, pointing out that standardized tests are biased toward students from a higher socioeconomic background. The tests are particularly challenging for students whose first language is not

English. Consequently, when students are unable to demonstrate their fluency in "standard" English, they are labeled as "remedial," resulting in minority or nonnative speakers being marked as "other" or "outsider" (130). Using examples of student writing, Bernstein argues that imaginative writing creates a space for students not only to develop analytical skills but to find a forum to speak about and resist the "remedial" label. She issues a call to teachers who occupy the "privilege of educators" (130) to become aware of these issues and challenges.

324   Bruna, Liza, et al. "Assessing Our Assessments: A Collective Questioning of What Students Need — and Get." *Journal of Basic Writing* 17.1 (1998): 73–95. Print.

This is an edited transcript of an online discussion among six City University of New York graduate students who covered theoretical and political issues behind the teaching of basic writing. Much of the discussion centers on students' desire for Standard English as access to power and the political and cultural repercussions of that desire. The graduate students also discuss the insufficiency of assessment, the activist role of the composition class and the composition teacher, the disjuncture between instruction in literature and composition, and the appropriate place of code switching and transculturation in composition pedagogy.

325   Gleason, Barbara. "Evaluating Writing Programs in Real Time: The Politics of Remediation." *College Composition and Communication* 51.4 (2000): 560–88. Print.

Gleason argues that program evaluation is political and requires examination of social context. At the City College of New York, Gleason supervised a pilot program of thirty-seven sections of composition that included basic writing students. To evaluate the program, Gleason examined formative evaluations written by teachers and students, statistical analysis of student success (grades being the main variable), and the expert judgment of an outside observer. Policy at the college dictated that no basic writer could take core curriculum classes until he or she passed basic writing, but the college waived that policy for basic writers in the pilot sections that included first-year and mainstreamed basic writing students. Gleason found that students who first took basic writing and then took the core curriculum classes passed the core courses at higher rates than both pilot students and the general population. After three years of mainstreaming basic writers into standard composition classes, college administrators largely ignored the data that came from the pilot study. Instead, the institutional research office wanted to control distribution of the data and pushed Gleason to use more experimental methodologies. Hostility developed as the faculty council voted to require the passing of both basic writing *and* standard composition before students could enroll in core classes. In the future, various agents should be involved more directly in the execution and evaluation of projects such as this, and researchers should pay closer attention to context.

326   Harley, Kay, and Sally I. Cannon. "Failure: The Student's or the Assessment's?" *Journal of Basic Writing* 15.1 (1996): 70–87. Print.

Harley and Cannon focus on the example of Mica, a nontraditional African American student at Saginaw Valley State University who failed a final portfolio assessment. The authors suggest that the student's failure was the project's failure, demonstrating clearly how the project's monolithic assessment practices could not respond appropriately to the writing strategies of diverse students. They theorize that teachers' criteria for assessing Mica's writing may have been insufficient and that their expectations about academic writing may have blinded them to the strengths in Mica's work. The authors mention a few features of Mica's writing that are insufficiently accounted for in the evaluation criteria: the presence of linguistic markers of Mica's Black English Vernacular dialect, her "strong emotive voice" (75), and her confident use of personal anecdotes. The authors suggest that we need to broaden our understanding of academic discourse to account for features like these, noting that such features are already apparent in the work of some mainstream academic writers.

327   Haswell, Richard H. "Dark Shadows: The Fate of Writers at the Bottom." *College Composition and Communication* 39.3 (1988): 303–14. Print.

Using holistic grading scales of student essays as his database, Haswell discusses the consistency of judgment of bad papers. One criterion he often used was the work done by workplace writers, who presumably had been chosen to write material for their companies because they were considered competent writers in their workplaces. Because such writers have a lean style both in classrooms and in the workplace, their abilities and disabilities are much easier to diagnose. Among the disabilities are causes that teachers often regard as behavioral (lack of confidence or motivation, confusion of context), but Haswell suggests that simplicity and wit can often be the better framework for building up a student's writing rather than tearing it down.

328   Hilgers, Thomas. "Basic Writing Curricula and Good Assessment Practices." *Journal of Basic Writing* 14.2 (1995): 68–74. Print.

Hilgers argues that students become basic writers through assessment, most often through their scores on inappropriate tests like the SAT, ACT, or Nelson-Denny. Furthermore, these bad assessments drive the curriculum and the evaluation procedures in many basic writing classes. Viable assessment methods, such as those employed by Mina Shaughnessy, can be used to discover students' needs, but these are not as cheap and easy as standardized, multiple-choice instruments. The Conference on College Composition and Communication Position Statement on Assessment can ensure that better assessments are used to identify basic writers at the college level and to certify them as ready for "regular" composition. The reauthorization of Chapter I funds of the Elementary and Secondary Education Act, which supports educational remediation, offers additional hope that assessment will focus more on helping identify students' needs so that all students can achieve high standards.

329   Miraglia, Eric. "A Self-Diagnostic Assessment in the Basic Writing Course." *Journal of Basic Writing* 14.2 (1995): 48–67. Print.

Miraglia puts the traditional basic writing diagnostic essay into context, suggesting that the genre helps to situate writers in their own lived experience and to evaluate the student's writing characteristics. However, the prompts on which the diagnostic essay usually depends may elicit misleading data and results because they make three questionable assumptions: masked intentions, in which the prompt's question is poorly designed; magical thinking, in which (after Janet Emig) it is assumed that the teacher can both diagnose and address the range of writing problems in a writing class; and assumptions of expertise, in which rhetorical expertise is assumed to rest with the teacher, not the student. Miraglia describes a new diagnostic essay model that emphasizes students' assessment of their own needs, which results in a rubric of attributes, concerns, and desired skills, as articulated by the incoming basic writing student. Because the model is based on attention to rhetorical levels of content and form, with less emphasis on intimate personal revelation, the result is a more reliable map of discourse characteristics to help guide a student throughout the course.

330   Shor, Ira. "Illegal Literacy." *Journal of Basic Writing* 19.1 (2000): 100–12. Print.

Shor argues that the City University of New York burdens students with excessive assessments of their reading and writing proficiencies. Basic writers must pass the remedial composition course and a timed impromptu writing test before they are permitted to register for regular composition. In some cases, students who fail the timed writing test violate policy and register for regular composition anyway. Such students, Shor writes, are "guilty of illegal literacy and unauthorized progress" (102) and are examples of resistance to the bureaucratic and oppressive nature of testing and remediation. This process is part of a conservative attempt to discourage success among the minority and working-class populations that are heavily represented in basic writing classes. A more democratic alternative, Shor writes, would involve mainstreaming basic writers and transforming first-year writing into Critical Literacy across the Community. This new curriculum would consist of community service, field research, and ethnographic writing instead of drills in usage and mechanics and allegiance to academic discourse.

331 Singer, Marti. "Moving the Margins." *Mainstreaming Basic Writers: Politics and Pedagogies of Access*. Ed. Gerri McNenny. Mahwah: Erlbaum, 2001. 101–18. Print.

Stories shared among basic writing professionals seem to carry common themes: student access and success in the academic community, teachers' experiences, and the training of writing instructors. Singer argues that we need to revisit and to listen to our stories, whether they exhibit successes or generate questions or propose new programs, if we are to understand the political and cultural impact of decisions made about basic writing. The article focuses on the story of one faculty member's reflections on marginalization. It describes a course created to bridge the isolated remedial courses to the freshman composition program without entirely mainstreaming the students. Singer explores multiple perceptions of language use, audience, collaboration, and belonging in the academic community; her twenty years' experience of teaching, research, and service in a basic writing program at a large urban university; and the constant moving of the margins during that time.

332 Sweigart, William. "Assessing Achievement in a Developmental Writing Sequence." *Research and Teaching in Developmental Education* 12 (1996): 5–15. Print.

Emphasizing that writing program administrators should respond to both local needs and increasing demands from administrators (and legislatures) for sensible assessment procedures, Sweigart reports on an evaluation of the developmental writing program at a midsize public university. A two-year study within the writing program generated an assessment model whereby essays written for placement were compared to essays the same students wrote at the end of the semester. Using the model, the author demonstrates that statistically significant gain scores (p < .01) are achieved for the writing program based on the writing scores at these two times. The study provides one method for establishing a baseline measure in a writing program, and it supports a systematic assessment of writing that can be used to link developmental writing courses to the regular, first-year English classes. The author notes that "while campuses obviously differ, the model may prove useful for assessment in a variety of settings" (6).

333   White, Edward M. "The Importance of Placement and Basic Studies: Helping Students Succeed under the New Elitism." *Journal of Basic Writing* 14.2 (1995): 75–84. Print.

White argues that the movement in the 1990s to abolish the first-year composition requirement masks a dangerous elitism that is trying to prevent opportunities for the poor, for racial minorities, and for students who come to the university underprepared for its writing requirements. This elitism stems from budget cuts that have led to raised tuition and restricted enrollments, turning writing into a gatekeeping "wing of the admissions office" (76). To counter what he sees as an elitist abolitionist movement, White uses data from two sets of studies—one of "1978 First-Time Freshmen" in the California State University system and one from New Jersey postsecondary institutions conducted in 1988, 1991, and 1992—to suggest that effective placement programs and supportive basic writing programs will help to retain minority and underprepared students who might otherwise leave the university. While there are various reasons for students to leave school at various points in their studies, White argues that well-supported placement and basic writing programs will keep basic writers in school. At the very least, he hopes such studies will shed some light on the social biases he sees behind the abolitionist movement of the last decade.

See: Sharon Crowley, "Response to Edward M. White's 'The Importance of Placement and Basic Studies'" [349].

See: Edward M. White, "Revisiting the Importance of Placement and Basic Studies" [335].

334   White, Edward M. "Process vs. Product: Assessing Skills in Writing." *AAHE Bulletin* (October 1988): 10–13. Print.

White examines fundamental issues behind different methods of writing assessment, dividing his discussion into two parts. In the first part, White explores the two paradigms of writing instruction, product and process, by teasing out the pedagogical and political implications behind each. He concludes that the product approach and its concomitant means of assessment disrupt the development of writers' attitudes toward writing as discovery and as a valuable exercise. The second, much briefer section lists the advantages and disadvantages of the three basic writing assessment methods—multiple-choice usage tests, essay tests, and portfolios—concluding that portfolios best measure writing as process. The discussion of portfolio assessment is admittedly limited, given the date of the article. Nonetheless, White provides a lucid summary of the principles that underlie writing assessment methodology.

335 White, Edward M. "Revisiting the Importance of Placement and Basic Studies: Evidence of Success." *Mainstreaming Basic Writers: Politics and Pedagogies of Access.* Ed. Gerri McNenny. Mahwah: Erlbaum, 2001. 19–28. Print.

A new elitism and its (however unintended) theorists, the new abolitionists, seek to abandon the required freshman composition course and the placement tests that help students succeed in the course and in college. This essay is a follow-up to White's "The Importance of Placement and Basic Studies" [333]. As the data show, a placement program, followed by a careful instructional program, allows many students who would otherwise leave school to continue successfully in the university.

336 White, Edward M. *Teaching and Assessing Writing: Recent Advances in Understanding, Evaluating, and Improving Student Performance.* 2nd ed. San Francisco: Jossey-Bass, 1994. Print.

White offers advice on assessment both inside and outside the classroom in this 1994 update to his 1985 book. Working from the theory that assessment is part of learning, White argues that it should also be part of the teaching and administration of writing and writing programs. White's discussion of assessment begins by looking at the design of writing assignments and test questions. The book includes a detailed discussion of three popular methods of writing assessment: multiple-choice tests, essay tests, and writing portfolios, which White clearly prefers. A new addition to the original text is a chapter on how theories of reading affect teachers' responses to writing. White argues that because poststructural theories of reading incorporate ideas associated with interpretive communities, they can help teachers write more constructive responses to student papers. Discussing more summative assessment, White describes some of the different ways that groups within the university envision writing assessment. He cites examples of the practical difficulties that result when such visions collide, revealing the importance of the writing faculty's active involvement in the large-scale assessment of students' learning and of programs. White concludes with a new chapter that reviews the historical and political issues in writing assessment since the 1970s.

337   Wiener, Harvey S. "Evaluating Assessment Programs in Basic Skills." *Journal of Developmental Education* 13.2 (1989): 24–26. Print.

In 1983, three professors at the City University of New York conducted a national survey in which they discovered that 97 percent of the 1,269 responding institutions assess entering students. The assessments were often used to determine admission, program acceptance, and placement, and students' persistence often was affected by the assessments. Wiener wondered how educators know if assessment tests measure what they are supposed to measure and if basic writing assessment programs are working. Thus Wiener and two colleagues, in association with the National Testing Program in Writing, followed up on this study with another designed to find out what types of instruments were being employed. Their study revealed resistance by many postsecondary institutions to using nationally developed standardized tests; instead, many institutions employ instruments that are not evaluated for reliability, validity, or even relationship to current curricula. Furthermore, those institutions that do employ nationally developed tests are using the SAT or ACT incorrectly since these tests are designed to measure potential college success and create a stratification among students; they are not intended to evaluate skill levels. In response to the ongoing institutional desire for assessment, Wiener and his colleagues developed the College Assessment Program Evaluation (CAPE), a self-assessment program, and trained facilitators to use it. CAPE allows institutions to engage in self-evaluation and to design instruments that relate to their particular curricula.

338   Wolcott, Wilma. "Evaluating a Basic Writing Program." *Journal of Basic Writing* 15.1 (1996): 57–69. Print.

Instructors do not like writing assessment because it is often not an indicator of student writing ability. Based on a program she developed with a colleague, Wolcott advocates a more accurate picture of student assessment that includes before and after impromptu essays, a multiple-choice editing test, and portfolio assessment. After evaluating this program, Wolcott found that "multiple sources of data [are] preferable to a single data source" (67). Balancing writing assessments with portfolio assessment gave a more comprehensive picture of student writing ability. Through multifaceted program evaluation, instructors are more accountable to themselves, the program, and basic writers.

339 Yancey, Kathleen Blake. "Outcomes Assessment and Basic Writing: What, Why, and How?" *BWe: Basic Writing e-Journal* 1.1 (1999): n. pag. Web. 11 Aug. 2009.

Yancey briefly outlines possibilities for what program assessment might look like within a basic writing program and discusses what needs to be addressed before assessment begins. The practical considerations outlined include considering the purpose of the assessment, identifying stakeholders, identifying materials already in place and available, and determining the time frame during which the assessment must take place. A variety of scenarios for assessment are outlined, with links included to either Web sites or e-mail addresses so that readers can contact others who have used these methods (portfolio assessment, faculty surveys, and follow-up studies done with graduating seniors).

340 Young, Sandra. "Academic Legerdemain: When Literacy Standards Become a Sleight of Hand." *Open Words: Access and English Studies* 1.1 (2006): 37–53. Print.

Young describes the impact of a FIPSE grant designed to help Native Alaskan students at a university acclimate themselves to academic life through the creation of a living situation similar to their home communities and through recruitment of local Native Alaskans to serve as mentors. Examining what happens when "assessment, standards, and culture collide" (38), Young responds to factors that curtail the project's effectiveness: difficulties involved in locating mentors and approximating students' home lives within such a short amount of time and increased pressure to retain students through relaxed standards and assessment. Ultimately, Young argues, the grant isolates students from their peers and generates an environment where maintenance of the grant outweighs its educational aims. Taking these contextual elements into account, she reflects on her own struggles as the students' writing instructor and on their inconsistent attendance, underpreparedness, and resistance to western culture. Borrowing from Kathleen Cotton, Young recommends a restructured grant that would involve culturally heterogeneous cooperative learning teams rather than exclusionary enclaves.

Writing Program Administration

341 Adler-Kassner, Linda. "Digging a Groundwork for Writing: Community Service Courses and Underprepared Students." *College Composition and Communication* 46.4 (1995): 552–55. Print.

For underprepared students, community-service courses emphasizing academic writing may serve students better than traditional writing classes, because of the service-learning aspect. When students combine community service with their writing assignments, the "sum" of what they get out of the classes is often greater than its component parts. Adler-Kassner shows how a service-learning model got students to consider how to write most effectively for their college courses.

342 Adler-Kassner, Linda. "Service Learning in the Basic Writing Classroom: Mapping the Conceptual Landscape." *BWe: Basic Writing e-Journal* 1.1 (1999): n. pag. Web. 11 Aug. 2009.

This article, based on a presentation at an all-day workshop at the Conference on College Composition and Communication in Atlanta, discusses how service-learning activities can be included in the basic writing classroom without interfering with the intended goals of the composition course. With careful planning, Adler-Kassner suggests, teachers can facilitate an integration of service-learning goals and writing goals. The article includes a detailed matrix that describes the goals, sites, literacies, relationships, and means of assessment for socially and academically motivated writing. It also includes brief summaries of comments, suggestions from participants in the workshop, and several definitions of service learning.

343 Baker, Tracy, and Peggy Jolly. "The 'Hard Evidence': Documenting the Effectiveness of a Basic Writing Program." *Journal of Basic Writing* 18.1 (1999): 27–39. Print.

Baker and Jolly provide conclusive proof that the basic writing program administered at their university has had a positive impact on student retention and persistence. Through the use of statistics gathered on 685 basic writing students over a period of two years, Baker and Jolly document the influence of basic writing instruction through the use of four variables: retention rate, current classification, grade point average, and writing course sequence completed. The data collected enabled the authors to demonstrate that retention rates for basic writing students were 17 percent higher than for regularly admitted students. Furthermore, fourth-year retention rates were higher for students admitted as basic writing students than for regularly admitted students. This applies for both full-time students (16 percent higher) and part-time students (38 percent higher). While basic writing students progressed through their courses at a slower rate, they still survived the first- and second-year attrition at a higher rate than others.

344 Berger, Mary Jo. "Funding and Support for Basic Writing: Why Is There So Little?" *Journal of Basic Writing* 12.1 (1993): 81–89. Print.

Acknowledging the history of limited support for basic writing in higher education, Berger analyzes the positive role basic writing teachers can play in gaining budgetary support for their programs. She discusses characteristics of higher education that have budgetary implications and that stress the importance of individual participation. She recommends becoming a member of decision-making committees, attending meetings, seeking political allies across the disciplines, staying in touch with former students and their parents, organizing for action in favor of basic writing programs, and informing administrators and other teachers about "how much more challenging and how much more fulfilling it is to teach the underprepared than the already prepared" (88).

345   Boylan, Hunter R., and Barbara S. Bonham. "The Impact of Developmental Education Programs." *Research in Developmental Education* 9.5 (1992): 1–3. Print.

Boylan, director of the National Center for Developmental Education (NCDE), and Bonham, a senior researcher at NCDE, report some of the results of a comprehensive national study of the effectiveness of developmental education, specifically focusing on the effects of developmental programs on cumulative grade point average (GPA), long-term retention, and subsequent performance in regular college courses. These programs appear to succeed since developmental students have cumulative GPAs above the minimum 2.00, pass initial courses, and are likely to graduate. This study could serve as a model for collecting empirical data at any college or university.

346   Collins, Terence, and Melissa Blum. "Meanness and Failure: Sanctioning Basic Writers." *Journal of Basic Writing* 19.1 (2000): 13–21. Print.

Collins and Blum focus on the state of meaningful access to higher education among disenfranchised students, particularly low-income single-parent women, in the wake of national and state welfare reform and the 1998 election. They describe the previously successful Higher Education for Low-Income People program in the General College at the University of Minnesota; the potential of the Minnesota Family Investment Program (MFIP), the pilot program that followed it; and the change in the political climate that caused the sanctioning of basic writers. Using the writing of two women enrolled in the MFIP, the authors attempt to put a face on the issue to illustrate the real economic and social possibilities traditional baccalaureate education once offered to disenfranchised students and their children.

347   Collins, Terence, and Kim Lynch. "Mainstreaming? Eddy, Rivulet, Backwater, Site Specificity." *Mainstreaming Basic Writers: Politics and Pedagogies of Access*. Ed. Gerri McNenny. Mahwah: Erlbaum, 2001: 73–84. Print.

Collins and Lynch argue for restraint in the conversation about mainstreaming because dialogues about it often ignore the fact that basic writing programs operate in specific institutional settings under local constraints. Collins and Lynch note that the case for mainstreaming often has been built on theoretical narratives that posit an overly—sometimes conveniently—homogenized basic writing status quo against which mainstreaming is placed as a universally desirable fix. They also illustrate that competing research bases are relevant to the discussion of mainstreaming and that these databases need to play a more significant role in the discussion than they have to date. They note that basic writing, specifically, and developmental education at large are varied as a function of the local situation.

348   Crouch, Mary Kay, and Gerri McNenny. "Looking Back, Looking Forward: California Grapples with Remediation." *Journal of Basic Writing* 19.2 (2000): 44–71. Print.

This study examines documents issued by legislative bodies and public responses from the press and writing programs as they grapple with the changing scenario of remediation in California's higher education system. More conflicts seem to arise about the needs of nontraditional students as defined by legislators, scholars, and program administrators at times when the social and academic profiles of students entering the college system undergo rapid changes. Crouch and McNenny argue that these conflicts can best be addressed if needs assessment relies on collaboration between community leaders, college and high school instructors, and writing professionals. They also argue for collaborative outreach programs at the high school level that can address the needs of basic writers.

349   Crowley, Sharon. "Response to Edward M. White's 'The Importance of Placement and Basic Studies.'" *Journal of Basic Writing* 15.1 (1996): 88–91. Print.

Crowley agrees with Edward White that elitist forces are threatening open admissions and other initiatives to increase campus diversity. However, she refutes White's suggestion that abolishing composition as a requirement might further the same elitist ends. The abolition argument, made most vocally by Crowley herself, is a response to composition's historic role as an "instrument of exclusion" (89). White's attempt to situate the abolition argument as complicit with exclusion is misguided, Crowley writes, since conservative groups like the National Association of Scholars are threatening diversity initiatives and are also calling for higher standards and more requirements in subjects like composition. Further, when

White paints abolitionists as "conservative," he appeals to the "liberal" nature of compositionists. A more viable position, Crowley writes, is "radical" ideology that critiques elitist movements and makes progressive suggestions (like abolishing required composition) for more ethical and diverse institutions.

See: Edward M. White, "The Importance of Placement and Basic Studies" [333].

350 Fitzgerald, Sallyanne. "Basic Writing in One California Community College." *BWe: Basic Writing e-Journal* 1.2 (1999): n. pag. Web. 11 Aug. 2009.

Since basic writers are unique to each community and situation, programs need to develop comprehensive approaches that enable students to meet the goal of successful college-level writing. Fitzgerald details the evolution of Throughline, a comprehensive program philosophy at Chabot College. This philosophy does not approach basic writing as a separate entity. It allows basic writing courses to flow smoothly into other courses by integrating reading, writing, thinking, speaking, and listening at all levels. The program at Chabot serves as a model for those who advocate mainstreaming basic writers, especially since it addresses the needs of students to establish college-level writing skills within a specific context.

351 Fitzgerald, Sallyanne H. "Serving Basic Writers: One Community College's Mission Statements." *Journal of Basic Writing* 22.1 (2003): 5–12. Print.

Fitzgerald chronicles her experience at Chabot College to illustrate how revising a community college's mission statement can be a legitimizing force in re-envisioning the role that basic writing plays in that mission. Previously, basic writing courses were taught with a concentration on a "hierarchal model of English where skills proceed from words to sentences to paragraphs to essays" (10). The new, refashioned mission statement and "throughline"—a semester-by-semester sequence of courses and expected outcomes for those courses—replaced this "skills" model with "a basic writing curriculum that mirrors the demands of the transferable freshman composition courses" (11). These guidelines better articulated the assumptions that would form the basis for basic writing pedagogy at Chabot, including a clear statement of what students who completed these basic writing courses should be able to do. By fashioning a "throughline" for all English courses, this particular community college was able to include a strong commitment to basic writing as more than just "a legal mandate" (5).

352   Glau, Gregory R. "Hard Work and Hard Data: Getting Our Message Out." *The Writing Program Administrator's Resource: A Guide to Reflective Institutional Practice*. Ed. Stuart C. Brown and Theresa Enos. Mahwah: Erlbaum, 2002. 291–302. Print.

The bane of most newly minted writing program administrators is the level of hard data that university administrators require. Early in their careers, most writing program administrators do not have the training or expertise to undertake high-level quantitative program-assessment projects. Glau believes that even the busiest, most inexperienced administrator can mine for "nuggets" of statistical data. He suggests looking at the percentage of students who pass first-semester composition and move directly into second semester and how that number has changed, how enrollments have varied with funding changes over the past few years, and what the grade distribution in first-year writing is. Glau states that thinking about the situation rhetorically is key: ask who wants the data and for what purpose, find out if the data are already being collected, and— if they are not—design surveys or other data-gathering tools to do so. Glau suggests designing invention heuristics for determining what data to track, what information is already available, and how to process it.

353   Glau, Gregory R. "*Stretch* at 10: A Progress Report on Arizona State University's *Stretch Program*." *Journal of Basic Writing* 26.2 (Fall 2007): 30–48. Print.

Glau chronicles the inception of the Stretch Program at Arizona State University (ASU), the changes that have marked the program, and its successes and struggles. In 1992, Director of Composition David Schwalm and John Ramage (then director of the Writing across the Curriculum Program at ASU) designed two pilot programs to better aid students recognized as "high risk" in terms of university success. The first program, named Jumbo, was a six-semester-hour basic writing class. The second program, called Stretch, was "a two-semester sequence designed to stretch ENG 101 over two semesters" (31). The Stretch Program was markedly more successful and is still in use at ASU today. Glau describes the Stretch Program in detail, focusing on results as seen through long-term statistics. The Stretch Program utilizes the same texts, the same assignments, and the same teachers as the more traditional first-year composition curriculum at ASU. This "stretching" of the content to a two-semester sequence allows a more guided writing experience and ideally allows students to build a stronger writing community. Statistics from the last ten years show this two-semester sequence not only increased students' pass rates for their entire first-year composition sequence (English 101 and 102) but also increased overall college retention. Taking into account the profile of a Stretch student, Glau contends that the long-term benefit to the student is worthwhile. He acknowledges that this program may not be the perfect model for every institution but notes that as students' needs change, the Stretch Program can be adapted accordingly.

354   Goen-Salter, Sugie. "Critiquing the Need to Eliminate Remediation: Lessons from San Francisco State." *Journal of Basic Writing* 27.2 (2008): 81–105. Print.

For more than two decades, the California State University (CSU) system has been trying unsuccessfully to "reduce the need for remediation" on its campuses, primarily through initiatives aimed at high schools. This article examines a basic writing reform project, San Francisco State's Integrated Reading/Writing Program, in the context of CSU's history of remediation. The success of this project, in light of CSU's remedial past, provides the grounds to advocate for higher education as the appropriate location for basic writing and reading and to advocate, in turn, for the resources necessary to theorize, develop, and sustain a rich variety of approaches to basic writing instruction. Goen-Salter's analysis also suggests the need for more graduate programs and faculty development initiatives to help prepare a new generation of basic writing teachers and scholars to meet the needs of the next generation of basic writing students.

355   Goggin, Peter, et al. "The Universal Requirement in First-Year Composition: A Forum." *BWe: Basic Writing e-Journal* 1.2 (1999): n. pag. Web. 11 Aug. 2009.

In a special event at the Western States Composition Conference in October 1999, Sharon Crowley and John Ramage debated the politically charged first-year writing requirement. This article provides a transcript of the debate as well as a succinct introduction written by Peter Goggin and a transcript of the discussion following the debate compiled by Kohl Glau. During her opening remarks, Crowley provides an overview of her well-known arguments for the abolishment of the first-year writing requirement. Ramage responds by noting that, while he usually argues against the "status quo," doing away with the requirement entirely is not the answer. As Goggin notes in the introduction, there was no clear "winner" of the debate, but the presentations of Crowley and Ramage and the discussion that followed provide a helpful overview of this complex issue, which is of the utmost importance to writing instructors. In fact, Goggin suggests that the lack of a clear winner of the debate simply underscores the fact that the field is "far from resolving the pedagogical and political conflicts that mark the requirement" (par. 5).

356 Grego, Rhonda, and Nancy Thompson. "Repositioning Remediation: Renegotiating Composition's Work in the Academy." *College Composition and Communication* 47.1 (1996): 62–84. Print.

At the University of South Carolina, writing histories and portfolios are examined to identify students who would benefit from participation in the Writing Studio. In the Writing Studio, students from different sections of English 101 discuss assignments, drafts, and other texts, including teacher comments, related to their instruction in writing. These components have been overlooked in institutionally sanctioned ways of talking about student writing and writing instruction that are based on a nostalgic and idealized literary view of authors and good writing. The Writing Studio thus puts the relationship between words, institutions, and people, not textbooks and mass writing assessments, at the center of the professional work of writing instruction. Finally, it encourages the view of basic writing as intellectual and academic work, not just as a "slot" in the remedial curriculum.

357 Gunner, Jeanne. "The Status of Basic Writing Teachers: Do We Need a 'Maryland Resolution'?" *Journal of Basic Writing* 12.1 (1993): 57–63. Print.

Gunner discusses major examples of the rhetoric of professional statements, including the Wyoming Resolution, the Statement of Principles and Standards of the Conference on College Composition and Communication (CCCC), and the Portland Resolution of the Writing Program Administrators (WPA). Of the three, the Wyoming Resolution most usefully addresses the issues that concern basic writing instructors, providing for professional self-definition and solidarity as well as recognition of teaching as a central and viable intellectual activity. However, while the CCCC and WPA documents succeed in a political sense by focusing on the status of individual professional groups, Gunner suggests that the Wyoming Resolution ultimately fails, primarily because its rhetoric tends to separate its constituents from institutional power structures. She argues that members of the Conference on Basic Writing should compose a professional statement that combines ideology with rhetorical efficacy. This Maryland Resolution would help to construct basic writing teachers "as a presence and force in the profession at large" (61).

358 Kraemer, Don J. "The Economy of Explicit Instruction." *Journal of Basic Writing* 26.2 (2007): 93–112. Print.

Kraemer highlights the economic metaphors guiding some discussions about explicit instruction and suggests that explicit instruction does not have to position students as passive consumers of knowledge. Rather, explicit instruction that takes account of both the practical and human elements of writing instruction can position students as apprentices to the academic community. Kraemer discusses a curriculum he developed that emphasizes economics. It is based on the explicit teaching of Steven Levitt and Stephen Dubner's *Freakonomics*, a book that challenges conventional wisdom through a rhetorically savvy presentation of data and facts. He found that asking students to read and challenge the ideas and rhetoric in the book in their writing gave them an opportunity to practice the knowledge-making rituals and intellectual practices of the academic community they hoped to enter.

359   Kraemer, Don J. "Servant Class: Basic Writers and Service Learning." *Journal of Basic Writing* 24.2 (2005): 92–109. Print.

Kraemer describes three rhetorical situations for writing in service-learning projects: writing *with* the community, writing *about* the community, and writing *for* the community. But Kraemer notes that because of the lack of university funding for oversight of their work with service-learning projects, students often are left writing *for* the community. Even though service learning is supposed to blur the lines of hierarchy inside and outside the classroom by empowering students through the collaborative production of a document, students often have little to say regarding the content or design of the final written text, and thus are relegated to the "servant class." Kraemer points out that John Dewey's aim for "perplexity, confusion, and doubt" in the classroom was reduced to easy work within clearly prescribed or heavily guided parameters in service-learning projects; academic writing, on the other hand, challenged students and allowed them room for interpretation and agency. With some service-learning projects, time constraints denied the students an opportunity to do reflective writing about the implications of a document's complexity, their claim on it, or their roles in persuading an audience with it. However, academic writing allowed students to have a thoughtful "role in public deliberations." Thus the realities of service-learning projects should be measured against the pedagogical claims suggested that service-learning provides.

360   Lalicker, William B. "A Basic Introduction to Basic Writing Program Structures: A Baseline and Five Alternatives." *BWe: Basic Writing e-Journal* 1.2 (1999): n. pag. Web. 11 Aug. 2009.

Lalicker describes a brief survey that was conducted via the Writing Program Administrators e-mail list. The survey asked respondents to identify their basic writing program as approximating one of five models: the prerequisite model, in which basic writing students take a course before the standard first-year composition course; the stretch model, in which basic writers take the standard first-year course over two semesters rather than one; the studio model, in which the standard course is augmented by additional hours of small-group work; the directed self-placement model, in which students are guided in making their own choice about which writing course in a sequence they would like to take; and the intensive model, in which the basic writing course mirrors the standard course but with "additional instructional time or writing activities tailored for basic writers" (par. 8). Respondents also provided insight into the advantages and disadvantages of each model. No pattern was discovered between type of program and institution size, demographics, or mission. Specific institutional needs and the "theoretical or epistemological assumptions driving the writing program" (par. 2) seemed to exert greater influence on program design.

361 Lamos, Steve. "Basic Writing, CUNY, and 'Mainstreaming': (De)Racialization Reconsidered." *Journal of Basic Writing* 19.2 (2000): 22–43. Print.

Lamos argues that the current movement toward eliminating open admissions, mainstreaming basic writers, and ending first-year composition programs exists in the context of an institutionalized racism that continues to reinforce racialized thinking in both students and institutions. Lamos describes the overt racism with which open admissions was greeted in New York in the early 1970s.

362 Laurence, Patricia. "The Vanishing Site of Mina Shaughnessy's *Errors and Expectations*." *Journal of Basic Writing* 12.2 (1993): 18–28. Print.

In this article, first presented as a talk at the Fourth National Basic Writing Conference in 1992, Laurence asks all practitioners in the field of basic writing to consider the factors that influence basic writing at particular times and institutions. Min-Zhan Lu's "Redefining the Legacy of Mina Shaughnessy: A Critique of the Politics of Linguistic Innocence" [98] and Stephen North's *The Making of Composition: Portrait of an Emerging Field*, both reassessments of Shaughnessy's 1977 landmark *Errors and Expectations* [117], are critiqued for what they fail to consider—the complexities, multiplicities, histories, and differences present in any educational movement. Laurence's defense of Shaughnessy and her colleagues' work at the City College of New York (CCNY) points to the lack of historical understanding in Lu's and North's critiques. Each situation has its political needs, and the 1970s was a time that called for subtlety in expression regarding open admissions students at CCNY. These students' abilities were questioned, as was their credibility and potential as students. Laurence contends that Shaughnessy should be praised for her understanding of the political situation.

363   Lewiecki-Wilson, Cynthia, and Jeff Sommers. "Professing at the Fault Lines: Composition at Open-Admissions Institutions." *College Composition and Communication* 50.3 (1999): 438–62. Print.

Open admissions work largely remains invisible to the general public and even to the profession of rhetoric and composition. Intellectual work can and does take place in open admissions settings, such as the basic writing classroom and various domains within two-year colleges. Through qualitative interviews and thick description, Lewiecki-Wilson and Sommers outline what constitutes this particular academic lifestyle. Critical pedagogy, process-based teaching, and teacher research all thrive in open admissions environments, so the field should stop devaluing knowledge construction there. Also, practitioners at open admissions institutions get the chance to be agents of institutional, curricular, and social change because teaching various sections over a longitudinal period of time is conducive to reflective, developmental teaching and sustained research. Therefore professionals in the field should work on placing open admissions practice at the center of our disciplinary identity.

364   McAlexander, Patricia J. "Mina Shaughnessy and K. Patricia Cross: The Forgotten Debate over Postsecondary Remediation." *Rhetoric Review* 19 (2000): 28–41. Print.

McAlexander reconstructs the dialogue between Mina Shaughnessy and K. Patricia Cross on open admissions and remediation for "new college students" in the 1960s and 1970s. Both educators favored doing away with elitist admissions policies and replacing them with open admissions to accept the low-achieving students. Shaughnessy saw the problems in racial terms; students at the City College of New York were minorities who had previously attended racially prejudiced schools. Cross believed her students at the University of California at Berkeley were different; because of California's three-tiered system, only the top 12 percent of high school graduates appeared at Berkeley; the others were enrolled at either state colleges or in two-year programs. Cross's "new college students" were different from Shaughnessy's in that they were "mostly [not] socially disadvantaged minorities" (33). They were not motivated and lacked the proper effort for success. Cross recommended alternative curriculum routes (vocational and business training) for the "new college students."

Shaughnessy favored strengthening the remedial methods. Today, most agree that Cross's conclusions were correct: that remedial classes do not help the students and may, in fact, harm them.

365 Miller, Susan. "A Future for the Vanishing Present: New Work for Basic Writing." *Journal of Basic Writing* 19.1 (2000): 53–68. Print.

Miller maps the external and internal contests over the function and value of basic writing, illustrating how society and higher education together have established it as a credible academic enterprise. As a professionalized field, basic writing is a site where leaders question the motives, theories, and material realities of its curricula. One critique arising from this questioning involves a paradox of intention: the goal of basic writing is to mainstream basic writing students and professionalize its practitioners so that all may improve their status and work, but only a few students achieve this goal, and many departments hire part-time instructors to teach. To address this paradox and strengthen composition studies' commitment to teach and research writing, Miller draws on James Gee's notion of recognition work to create a new root metaphor on which basic writing should ground its work. In her view, this term offers composition studies a way both to recognize underprepared students in terms that would benefit their academic progress and to foster conditions that would enlarge the scope and function of basic writing curricula.

366 Pine, Nancy. "Service Learning in a Basic Writing Class: A Best Case Scenario." *Journal of Basic Writing* 27.2 (2008): 29–55. Print.

Pine explores the particular challenges and possibilities of service-learning pedagogy for basic writers. Because a number of scholars of service learning and basic writing (such as Linda Adler-Kassner and Don Kraemer) are concerned primarily with developing underprepared students' academic literacies, Pine investigated how the students in a service-learning basic writing class situated their service experience—represented that "text" rhetorically—in their major academic research essay for the course. The article draws on one student's experience of making connections among the "rich mix" of course texts, including personal experience, as a best case. From this example, Pine argues for strategies of service-learning pedagogy that could better help basic writers achieve their goals for academic writing.

See: Linda Adler-Kassner, "Service Learning in the Basic Writing Classroom" [342].

See: Don J. Kraemer, "Servant Class" [359].

367 Preto-Bay, Ana Maria, and Kristine Hansen. "Preparing for the Tipping Point: Designing Writing Programs to Meet the Needs of the

Changing Population." *WPA: Writing Program Administration* 30.1/2 (2006): 37–58. Print.

The "tipping point" that lies ahead for writing programs is the demographic shift that brings increasing numbers of immigrants and refugees into college composition classrooms. The needs of these "crossover" or "Generation 1.5" populations are different from those of other international and multicultural students and must be equally considered and represented in curriculum design. Training programs for graduate students and adjunct faculty, as well as books and materials for preparing teachers of composition, still largely assume a homogeneous, English-speaking, American-acculturated student population. A rhetorical or socioliterate approach to composition curriculum design will better serve the needs of crossover groups than formalist, critical-cultural, or expressivist approaches. Greater collaboration between mainstream and second-language fields, including the hiring of L2 professionals in writing programs, is also a vital part of the adjustment.

368 Reynolds, Thomas. "Training Basic Writing Teachers: Institutional Considerations." *Journal of Basic Writing* 20.2 (2001): 38–52. Print.

Reynolds notes that the training of basic writing teachers has not received sufficient attention by researchers. This problem can and should be addressed within the sponsorship and care of institutional structures. Teacher training can also be seen as a space to study and make critical decisions about whether and how to perpetuate institutional histories. Linking teacher training to the interests and concerns of an administration produces an effective situation, he argues, because the training can serve as an instrument for connecting basic writing programs to an influential administrative structure. In addition, practitioners should be willing to meet across institutions to establish ties and examine common issues concerning training. Reynolds concludes with a set of useful questions for discussion regarding the training of basic writing teachers.

369 Reynolds, Tom, and Patty Fillipi. "Refocus through Involvement: (Re)Writing the Curricular Documents of the University of Minnesota–General College Basic Writing Program." *Journal of Basic Writing* 22.1 (2003): 13–21. Print.

Reynolds and Fillipi briefly describe the challenges and rewards that they and their colleagues experienced while collaboratively rewriting the curricular documents for the basic writing program at their school. The process of collaborative revision was sometimes challenging because not everyone's vision prevailed. The authors point to several positive outcomes: considering connections between the writing program and the university's mission, creating space for the needs of a diverse writing faculty, and including faculty in the curriculum's design. All of these reduced the sense of faculty isolation and created a greater sense of mission and purpose within the program. Reynolds and Fillipi include the opening statement of the resultant document, "Toward a Deepened Notion of Access: The Writing Program at the University of Minnesota General College."

370   Rigolino, Rachel, and Penny Freel. "Re-Modeling Basic Writing." *Journal of Basic Writing* 26.2 (2007): 49–72. Print.

Rigolino and Freel describe the SUNY–New Paltz basic writing program as a model of supplemental writing workshops (SWWs) and seamless support, where basic writing students attend a for-credit Composition I class, meet with their instructors in workshop one hour per week, and meet with a Writing Center tutor one hour per week. This model places students directly into the first-year composition sequence without a semester's detour in a noncredit writing course. The idea of seamlessness is central to providing three spaces of instruction that are separate yet holistically bound to one another. Assessment measures after ten years suggest that SWW students approach the levels of achievement and retention of non-SWW students.

371   Rodby, Judith. "What's It Worth and What's It For? Revisions to Basic Writing Revisited." *College Composition and Communication* 47.1 (1996): 107–11. Print.

Rodby focuses on the efforts and complications involved in the reconfiguration of instruction of basic writers at California State University, Chico. Because of the stigmas and limitations attached to the "basic writing" category, administrators and teachers decided to mainstream basic writing students. Rodby discusses two predominant issues that arose against this effort that suggest that the slotting of basic writers is largely political in nature. First, she describes the administration's circular arguments against giving credit for the course: that the noncredit course was necessary for the students to take the work seriously and that it was also important for the retention of minority students. Foundational to the resistance to change, Rodby argues next, is the issue of nostalgia as an ideological state that shapes everything from attitudes toward basic writing students to curricular and institutional choices. Rodby concludes by suggesting steps to break nostalgia's grasp and urges increased and constant communication and learning among others in the field as a shield against the assault by those who would eliminate these programs altogether.

372   Rodby, Judith, and Tom Fox. "Basic Work and Material Acts: The Ironies, Discrepancies, and Disjunctures of Basic Writing and Mainstreaming." *Journal of Basic Writing* 19.1 (2000): 84–99. Print.

Rodby and Fox outline how and why they dismantled the noncredit basic writing curriculum at California State University, Chico. Working from the belief that designating students entering their institution as "basic" did not describe students' writing abilities but merely created a population for basic writing courses, they mainstreamed all students into first-semester composition courses and provided additional adjunct workshops for students with low test scores. Consequently, first-year writing has come to be seen as more meaningful by students. Additionally, instructors of first-year writing and adjunct workshops have a more complex context for discussions of student writing.

373   Rogers, Laura. "Finding Our Way from Within: Critical Pedagogy in a Prison Writing Class." *Open Words: Access and English Studies* 2.1 (2008): 22–48. Print.

Rogers presents a narrative analysis of her attempt to implement Freirean pedagogy as a teacher of college writing in a correctional facility. She discusses ways this institutional context complicates principles of trust, ethics, and power. Even though the pedagogy helps generate interesting student papers and class discussions, issues of surveillance and facility control compromise the degree to which her students can critique larger institutional forces that shape their lives. These factors restrict the extent to which they can share knowledge of this institutional life with their teacher, let alone make public their compositions or realize desired changes in their circumstances. In the end, Rogers uses her example to point to ways all teachers and students work within some institutional limitations, and she suggests acknowledging that these conditions of living "can help both students and teachers, as they listen to each other, become more fully human" (44).

374   Rose, Mike. "Remedial Writing Courses: A Critique and a Proposal." *College English* 45.2 (1983): 109–28. Print.

Rose argues that basic writing classes need to offer students challenging, engaging work that will enable them to participate more fully in the discourse of the university. In particular, five common practices tend to limit students' experience of writing and need to be examined and changed. First, basic writing courses need to move from being self-contained to fitting into the intellectual context of the university. Second, topics for writing need to be substantial rather than simplistic. Third, students need opportunities to experience the composing process as complex and expansive rather than as narrow and rule-bound. Fourth, the writing course needs to integrate reading and thinking into the composing process rather than focusing exclusively on skills. Finally, teachers should re-imagine ways of using academic discursive strategies to enable, rather than restrict, students' writing.

375   Royer, Dan, and Roger Gilles. "Basic Writing and Directed Self-Placement." *BWe: Basic Writing e-Journal* 2.2 (2000): n. pag. Web. 11 Aug. 2009.

Directed self-placement "fosters student agency, particularly for basic writers who have historically been given very little control over the shape and focus of their early college careers." Royer and Gilles cite scholars specializing in education, learning, thinking, and psychology as providing the philosophical and pedagogical justification for directed self-placement. Readers are referred to an earlier article titled "Directed Self-Placement: An Attitude of Orientation" for a detailed explanation of the system. Royer and Gilles also believe this system creates an important initial educative moment for college students through a re-articulation of the following elements involved in placement decisions: agency (both student knowledge and faculty expertise matter), articulation (students clarify their experiences and skills through thought and discussion with parents, teachers, and counselors), and assessment (students are assessed when they have completed a course instead of at the beginning with an unreliable one-shot instrument).

376   Segall, Mary. "The Triple Helix: Program, Faculty, and Text." *BWe: Basic Writing e-Journal* 2.1 (2000): n. pag. Web. 11 Aug. 2009.

At Segall's college, basic writers enroll in a jumbo composition course in which they meet with instructors for five hours per week. Developmental reading, basic English, and first-year composition are rolled into one for this program. Arguing that most developmental textbooks are simplistic and "convey a powerful message to developmental students about their place in the academy" (par. 7), Segall and her colleagues decided that they needed a textbook that provided readings with a range of levels of difficulty and that offered interrelated reading and writing activities. They used the same text for the regular and jumbo sections of composition, a decision that allowed them to justify granting the same credit in the end to students enrolled in the jumbo sections. Citing a plethora of compositionists who argue that the teaching of basic writing is still essentially conservative, Segall claims that writing program administrators can effect gradual change in their programs by bringing attention to textbook selection for basic writing classes.

377   Severino, Carol. "An Urban University and Its Academic Support Program: Teaching Basic Writing in the Context of an 'Urban Mission.'" *Journal of Basic Writing* 15.1 (1996): 39–56. Print.

Urban universities and academic support programs are unified through the trope of the "urban mission," a university's responsibility to serve the citizens of its city. Severino describes how the University of Illinois at Chicago's changing perception of its own urban mission affected the way basic writing has been taught there. Throughout its early history, the university had an ambivalent attitude toward its own urban mission, but the social revolutions of the 1960s saw the birth of the Educational Assistance Program, an "urban mission" initiative that targeted inner-city minority recruitment and administered a full complement of basic writing courses. Unfortunately, in its effort to attain the image of a first-rate research institution during the 1980s, the university abandoned its urban mission by raising admission standards above those achieved by many inner-city minorities and by firing two-thirds of the Educational Assistance Program's basic writing teachers. At this and other urban universities, therefore, the strength and purpose of basic writing programs can often be gauged by the strength of the school's commitment to an urban mission.

378   Soliday, Mary. "From the Margins to the Mainstream: Reconceiving Remediation." *College Composition and Communication* 47.1 (1996): 85–100. Print.

Soliday describes the development of a basic writing student, Derek, who participated in a pilot project designed to promote a progressive version of mainstreaming while supporting the goals of open admissions. Derek was enrolled in a writing course at the City College of New York. The Enrichment Approach project, sponsored by the Fund for the Improvement of Postsecondary Education, bypasses test scores that place students in remedial courses and instead places college students in a six-credit, two-semester writing course. The course's curriculum is responsive to the experiences and histories of nontraditional students with diverse language and cultural backgrounds and encourages students to describe, interpret, and analyze aspects of everyday language use and familiar cultural experience in the unfamiliar language of the academy. The mainstreamed curriculum enabled Derek to use the forms of academic discourse to more deeply explore complex, personal topics, such as Black English and rap music, in ways that helped him negotiate two "codes," his own and academic discourse, positioning himself as both an insider and a cultural critic. A mainstreamed curriculum that emphasizes such linguistic and cultural self-consciousness offers a progressive alternative to traditional remediation.

379   Soliday, Mary, and Barbara Gleason. "From Remediation to Enrichment: Evaluating a Mainstreaming Project." *Journal of Basic Writing* 16.1 (1997): 64–78.

Soliday and Gleason describe the pilot of a three-year enrichment project that substituted a two-semester writing course in place of the traditional sequence of two remedial courses and one college-level course. The two-semester course, in contrast to the traditional sequence, carried full college credit, mainstreamed students who placed into remedial writing with students who placed into college-level writing, and allowed teachers rather than exit tests to decide whether students should pass their courses. The two-semester course was designed to build a stronger community of peers, class tutors, and teachers and to utilize students' cultural diversity. Assessments of student writing indicated that most students in the two-semester course improved their ability to produce good essays, evaluate their own writing, and conduct research. The writing assessments also indicated that students who would have been placed into remedial courses were competitive with students who would have been placed into college-level courses. Student self-assessments and teacher assessments of the same students generally indicated that students in the two-semester course were satisfied with their learning and could concretely describe what they had learned. Soliday and Gleason recommend giving students the option of taking either the traditional or the mainstreamed course sequence.

380   Strickland, Donna. "Errors and Interpretations: Toward an Archaeology of Basic Writing." *Composition Studies* 26.1 (1998): 21–35. Print.

Strickland addresses basic writing scholarship that claims composition studies should abolish basic writing programs because such programs often fail to mainstream basic writers and position basic writing students as "other." Strickland contends that the decision to terminate or sustain basic writing programs will not be made by scholars but rather by deans and legislators. What scholars can do, however, is interrogate the discourse of basic writing, which works to convince teachers and university administrators to conceive of basic writers as educable and to understand the ways in which this discourse competes for the power to interpret and thereby construct basic writing. To view discourse in this way, Strickland suggests that scholars examine the history of basic writing scholarship, reflect on their positions as "knowers" in relation to students' positions as "known," and listen to students' words, reading students' texts as "living acts of communication from other human beings" (33).

381   Tabachnikov, Ann. "The Mommification of Writing Instruction: A Tale of Two Students." *Journal of Basic Writing* 20.1 (2001): 27–36. Print.

Tabachnikov examines the dynamic of "teacherhood as motherhood" that is at work in composition classrooms, especially when student writing becomes intensely personal. Tabachnikov uses two of her own students to illustrate opposite ends of the motherhood spectrum. The first student, Cindy, was repeatedly ill and expected to be treated as a sick child might be. Tabachnikov responded to Cindy as a guilt-inducing mother might. Unable to endure this treatment, Cindy quit coming to class, and Tabachnikov dropped her from the class roster. This behavior led Tabachnikov to question and then embrace her "mommyness"—her parental role in teaching. The second student, Pete, was a middle-aged man who was eager to learn. His openness, candor, and eagerness to succeed led Tabachnikov to respond to him with a friendship that had an appropriate amount of distance but was reminiscent of the adult-child relationship where power and role differences are omnipresent. Despite being protective of Pete, a behavior she identifies as maternal, Tabachnikov maintained that her dynamic regarding him was parental rather than simply motherly. This parental role is one that Tabachnikov believes needs further consideration.

382   Tassoni, John Paul. "(Re)membering Basic Writing at a Public Ivy: History for Institutional Redesign." *Journal of Basic Writing* 25.1 (2006): 96–124. Print.

Tassoni recalls the evolution of the Miami University basic writing program and its studio counterpart. For Tassoni, the supplemental writing studio workshop is concerned with "reinforc[ing] for us the importance of students' understanding the rhetorical contexts within which they write, as well as the ways these contexts affect how and what students write" (102). Additionally, he demonstrates how many basic writing programs are implemented as reactionary retrofits as opposed to curricular redesigns that accommodate the changing literacy patterns of at-risk students. Thus, Tassoni perceives the basic writing course, along with a studio workshop, as a way of making the university more accessible to students who have been traditionally excluded from the Public Ivy university.

383   Tassoni, John, and Cynthia Lewiecki-Wilson. "Not Just Anywhere, Anywhen: Mapping Change through Studio Work." *Journal of Basic Writing* 24.1 (2005): 68–92. Print.

In this "autoethnographic, institutional narrative," the authors draw on cultural geography and postcolonial theory to think through their efforts to reform basic writing at their university. Through Tassoni and Lewiecki-Wilson's account of their struggle to implement a version of Rhonda Grego and Nancy Thompson's "Studio" alternative to remedial coursework, they illustrate how curricular transformation necessarily takes place in spaces already "densely populated by overlapping and knotted social, cultural, and institutional contexts and constraints" (81). Yet the authors find this transformation worthwhile, for "colonizing" sites of composition instruction for students from multiple classrooms creates opportunities both to provide a broader context to specific pedagogies "tucked away within individual writing classrooms" as well as to incrementally "intervene in our campus's writing culture" through strategic outreach to instructors about the work going on in their students' writing studios (83–84).

See: Rhonda Grego and Nancy Thompson, "Repositioning Remediation" [356].

384   Uehling, Karen S. "Creating a Statement of Guidelines and Goals for Boise State University's Basic Writing Course: Content and Development." *Journal of Basic Writing* 22.1 (2003): 22–34. Print.
Uehling describes the development of the statement of goals and guidelines for Boise State University's basic writing course. She also considers the statement's effects, emphasizing that its goal was to transform attitudes and that it structured the required first-year writing sequence. She also analyzes the conditions that produced the document—the urban, commuter nature of the institution; its fulfillment of various community college functions; the placement of the course in the English department; and the noncredit, one-semester status of the course. In addition, she shares her thoughts about the student competencies that the document supports, including building confidence; viewing writing as a multifaceted process; using multiple strategies for viewing written texts over time; producing coherent drafts with introductions, body paragraphs, and conclusions; employing format in appropriate ways; reading actively and critically; and editing assignments so that surface features do not interfere with communication.

385   Wiley, Mark. "Mainstreaming and Other Experiments in a Learning Community." *Mainstreaming Basic Writing: Politics and Pedagogies of Access.* Ed. Gerri McNenny. Mahwah: Erlbaum, 2001. 173–91. Print.
Debates over mainstreaming basic writers often settle into either-or positions and fail to consider local institutional factors. Before deciding whether to mainstream basic writing students, writing program administrators need to examine the basic writing courses

offered at their respective institutions, the type of literacy promoted, and any extracurricular factors that might affect the long-term success of these students. Knowing that the merits of mainstreaming basic writing students are open to debate, Wiley reports on the generally successful results of several experiments that he and his colleagues conducted with their institution's learning community, the Learning Alliance. The experiments include trying to mainstream a contingent of basic writing students and combining two semesters of basic writing into one. The results of these experiments have been instructive for all parties involved, and several program changes followed. The lower-level basic writing course was dropped; the upper-level course was increased from three to four instructional hours per week; the English placement test cut-off score for eligibility for the university-level writing course was lowered three points; and more mainstreaming experiments were planned. Most important is the change in thinking about how the campus perceives and works with basic writers as students in transition.

386   Ybarra, Raul. "Cultural Dissonance in Basic Writing Courses." *Journal of Basic Writing* 20.1 (2001): 37–52. Print.

Ybarra seeks to understand the cultural implications of basic writing as a mainstream educational framework imposed on Latino students through placement procedures, retention methods, and pedagogical assumptions. This qualitative study of one Latino student and a basic writing instructor argues that theories of resistance alone do not address the specific problems presented by Latino dropout rates within the university system. Ybarra suggests that placement in basic writing courses sends Latino students the message that they are not good enough to communicate within the mainstream culture. This misunderstanding is then compounded when writing instructors do not understand patterns of Latino discourse, resulting in a general dismissal of students. Ybarra suggests that instructors might actively seek out and motivate those students who do not participate in class discussions, who are regularly absent, or who might otherwise disappear from the class.

Electronic Writing Technologies

387   Crank, Virginia. "Asynchronous Electronic Peer Response in a Hybrid Basic Writing Classroom." *Teaching English in the Two-Year College* 32.2 (2002): 145–55. Print.

Crank reports on a peer-response experiment that began when she converted her traditional composition classes to a hybrid of online and traditional models. She discovered that asynchronous electronic peer response helped students become better responders to each other's texts and created a "new kind of composing community" in her classes (147). Asynchronous peer response offered certain strengths lacking in synchronous electronic or traditional peer response. Students engaged with the texts as genuine readers, took more time and care in composing responses, responded with more specificity, wrote to one another rather than the instructor, and valued the flexibility they had when they responded in the asynchronous environment.

388   Cummings, Martha C. "'Because We Are Shy and Fear 'Mistaking': Computer Mediated Communication with EFL Writers." *Journal of Basic Writing* 23.2 (2004): 23–48. Print.

Cummings reports on an online writing course she taught at a Japanese university. She used Nicenet.org to set up the classroom. Her study analyzes the extent to which computer-mediated communication alleviates the stress students in Japan feel when using English as an interactive tool with native speakers of English and its impact on the quantity and quality of student output. Results suggest that although students in the computer-mediated course did not produce texts of a higher quality than those of traditional students, they did develop a more positive attitude "toward writing, learning English, accuracy, and communicating with each other, their instructor, and native speakers of English in general" (36). Students valued three aspects of the computer-mediated classroom: learning from one another, the possibility of communicating with real native speakers, and communicating with the instructor. At the same time, some missed the benefits of face-to-face instruction. The computer-mediated classroom also had a positive effect on the author, who found out things about her students she would not have learned in the face-to-face classroom, causing her attitude toward them to change for the better.

389   Grabill, Jeffrey T. "Technology, Basic Writing, and Change." *Journal of Basic Writing* 17.2 (1998): 91–105. Print.

Grabill asserts that writing teachers commonly think of adapting curricula to meet the needs of students to effect change but that true change in curriculum, institutions, and students will not result until the institutional view of basic writing is altered radically. He demonstrates that the level of technology available for basic writers reveals the lowly position of basic writing in the institution. However, for basic writing to gain a more important position in academia, developmental writing students need meaningful access to technology, and their courses must be credit-bearing. Grabill used his institution's emphasis on access to technology for all students as an "institutional wedge" to attempt to improve the position of basic writing. The introduction of advanced technology into the basic writing courses changed the attitude of the instructors and the students: Both saw the class as an intellectually stimulating course that "counts." The university has yet to make the class credit-bearing, but some movement toward change has been possible because of technology.

390 Grobman, Laurie. "'I Found It on the Web, So Why Can't I Use It in My Paper?': Authorizing Basic Writers." *Journal of Basic Writing* 18.1 (1999): 76–90. Print.

Because Internet sources are easily accessible to students, basic writing instructors should consider the influence of the Web in the context of their pedagogical practices. The Internet enables basic writers to join the "conversation of ideas," thereby authorizing them as members of an academic community. Part of this authorization is based on writers' abilities to evaluate and question the credibility of Internet sources and on their use of critical reading and thinking skills, even though the Internet "necessitates" a reexamination "of the relationship between authority, academic discourse, and basic writers" (77).

391 Kish, Judith Mara. "Breaking the Block: Basic Writers in the Electronic Classroom." *Journal of Basic Writing* 19.2 (2000): 141–59. Print.

Kish uses her 1997–1998 computer-assisted "stretch" class at Arizona State University as a case study to explore connections between the difficulties of basic writers and the difficulty of writer's block. Connections between the two — problems with genre and problems with the linearity of texts — are identified. To help to alleviate the students' problems, hypertext and basic hypertext theory were introduced to the class, a method that proved to be useful in helping students with their writing difficulties.

392 Otte, George. "Computer-Adjusted *Errors and Expectations*." *Journal of Basic Writing* 10.2 (1991): 71–86. Print.

Otte examines papers written by his basic writing students, who have failed the City University of New York Writing Assessment Test, for patterns of error and the students' ability to correct them. As a reader of the test, Otte knows that a high incidence of error causes students to fail. Using a computer program called Error Extractor, he developed a list of eighteen categories of errors he found in his students' papers. With the program, which coded errors in their papers, Otte had students go through their essays, editing errors they found. Their successes and failures to edit were then recorded by the program and could be tabulated both synchronically and diachronically throughout the term. Otte found that using handbooks or covering in class the general types of errors he saw in the students' papers did little to help students edit. Instead, individual conferences, during which he discussed a particular student's particular errors, aided his students in editing their papers. Statistics gathered over the term indicate that students did become better editors of their own writing through the conferencing method: When retested, 79 percent of his students passed the Writing Assessment Test.

393   Otte, George, and Terence Collins. "Basic Writing and New Technologies." *BWe: Basic Writing e-Journal* 1.1 (1999): n. pag. Web. 11 Aug. 2009.

In a two-part essay, Otte and Collins describe Web resources available for teachers of basic writing and English as a second language. Otte offers a link and directions for using the Currtran Database, a collection of innovative teaching-with-technology practices and ideas for use in basic writing and other courses. Collins provides a collection of links to Web sites that offer grammar resources, e-journals, and reference works for ESL teachers.

394   Pavia, Catherine Matthews. "Issues of Attitude and Access: A Case Study of Basic Writers in a Computer Classroom." *Journal of Basic Writing* 23.2 (2004): 4–22. Print.

Most research that considers the use of computers in basic writing classrooms emphasizes technology's positive pedagogical value for students and teachers. Pavia urges teachers to consider student attitudes and access to computers before they "jump on the technology bandwagon" (20). She asks, "What happens when basic writers, who by definition lack experience in writing, also lack experience with computers?" (14) Through case studies of two basic writing students with limited access to technology, Pavia concludes that computers both "create opportunities" and "accentuate differences in opportunity" (15). Students who have had few chances to work on computers at home or in previous schools may appreciate the exposure to technology, but they will not necessarily transfer that positive attitude about computers to their writing (12). In addition, Pavia notes that students will need much more than equipment to truly access computer literacy; some students will struggle to write effectively on computers if they lack typing skills or a familiarity with word processing (18). Therefore, basic writing instructors who use computers should assume neither that their students are computer literate nor that presenting students with computers will ensure that they become computer literate. Rather, Pavia suggests that teachers take steps to understand and address the disadvantages some students may face when using computers in a basic writing classroom. First, she recommends assigning a technology narrative at the beginning of the semester that asks students to reflect on their relationships to and histories with technology. Then, she suggests teachers make use of the information they gather about student backgrounds from the technology narratives to build flexibility and balance into the curriculum. Computers should neither overshadow writing instruction nor hinder student learning. Rather, technology should be understood as a tool that teachers and students can choose to access when it will help them best meet their goals in the writing classroom.

395   Stan, Susan, and Terence G. Collins. "Basic Writing: Curricular Interactions with New Technology." *Journal of Basic Writing* 17.1 (1998): 18–41. Print.

According to a survey of basic writing teachers across the country, a disparity exists in the use of technology in developmental programs. Reinforcing the claims of earlier empirical studies, Stan and Collins find that using computer technologies in developmental classrooms positively influences students' attitudes toward writing and improves both the appearance and quantity of student writing. However, numerous institutional issues affect successful computer use, such as differences in the levels of technology currently available, resistance among faculty and students, lack of infrastructure, uneven access to professional development among staff, and lack of visibility for successful efforts.

396   Stine, Linda. "The Best of Both Worlds: Teaching Basic Writers in Class and Online." *Journal of Basic Writing* 23.2 (2004): 49–69. Print.

In her discussion of the incorporation of computer technology and online resources into the composition classroom, Stine begins with an overview of both the potential problems instructors could encounter and the benefits this transition could bring to the classroom. Rather than favoring online instruction over classroom instruction, Stine argues for a "hybrid" environment, one in which students can benefit from both forms of learning, while avoiding their negative aspects. Using her experience in classroom curricula as an example, Stine establishes seven principles for teaching effectively in a curriculum that is heavily reliant on online spaces and resources. As the teacher of a first-year composition course comprised primarily of nontraditional students, most of whom commute to campus, Stine offers a unique perspective into the benefits of online resources such as e-learning and chat rooms.

Cross-Institutional Connections

397   English, Hugh, and Lydia Nagle. "Ways of Taking Meaning from Texts: Reading in High School and College." *Journal of Basic Writing* 21.1 (2002): 37–51. Print.

English and Nagle describe a collaborative, qualitative study of reading practices that grew out of their participation in a seminar on "Looking Both Ways," a project that brings together faculty from City University of New York universities and colleges and New York public school teachers to share and reflect on their literacy education practices. As part of their work, the authors visited each other's classrooms at Queens College—CUNY (English) and Flushing High School (Nagle). Borrowing from Shirley Brice Heath's "What No Bedtime Story Means: Narrative Skills at Home and School," English and Nagle were interested in learning about students' expectations about reading practices in each other's classrooms. They found fewer differences between students' reading practices in high school and college than they expected. In both places, they found similarities between students' reasons and purposes for reading when compared to the motivations ascribed to reading by high school and college instructors.

398   McNenny, Gerri. "Collaborations between Basic Writing Professionals and High School Instructors: The Shape of Things to Come." *BWe: Basic Writing e-Journal* 4.1 (2002): n. pag. Web. 11 Aug. 2009.

For successful collaborations between high school instructors and basic writing professionals, McNenny argues, power relations must be acknowledged, and roles reconsidered. In response to mandated state standards and in an effort to cut costs, the California State University system issued a call for proposals for aligning students' writing competence at high school graduation with college entry-level requirements. This alignment would preempt the need for remediation in college. The CSU initiative tied the success of the collaboration directly to the English Placement Test, a timed exam that includes writing. Under these conditions, McNenny's university team and high school partners designed and proposed a partnership that reflected Freirean principles of learning. The resulting project emphasized high school teachers' roles in identifying site-specific issues and solutions, stressed the role of basic writing professionals as facilitators to help bridge the gap between experience and scholarship, and used teacher-researcher projects and reflective writing to help high school writing instructors create real-world rhetorical situations that engage students.

399 Otte, George. "High Schools as Crucibles of College Prep: What More Do We Need to Know?" *Journal of Basic Writing* 21.2 (2002): 106–20. Print.

Otte outlines the growing pressure on high schools to prepare an increasing number of college-bound students, noting that some 50 percent of beginning college students require remedial classes. While high schools are blamed for these students' need for remedial attention, Otte notes that about one-third of underprepared students did not take requisite classes and that nearly 50 percent of them are at least twenty-two years old—long out of high school. These pressures—often in the form of state-mandated tests—are turning high schools into "crucibles of college prep," rendering high schools and colleges the "most essential learning communities we have" (112–13). Otte suggests that creating high school and college collaborative partnerships is a better solution than state mandates and quick fixes. (He is involved with Looking Both Ways, a collaborative effort to resolve mutual problematic issues.)

See: Hugh English and Lydia Nagle, "Ways of Taking Meaning from Texts" [397].

Developmental Books
from Bedford/St. Martin's

Below, you'll find a list of Bedford/St. Martin's titles that are of interest to developmental and basic writing instructors. We publish a complete line of handbooks, rhetorics, readers, research guides, and professional resources. Please visit our Web site <bedfordstmartins.com> for full descriptions and ordering information, or contact your local sales representative.

Developmental Writing Texts

Susan Anker, *Real Essays: Writing Projects for College, Work, and Everyday Life*, 3rd ed., 2009.
———, *Real Writing: Paragraphs and Essays for College, Work, and Everyday Life*, 5th ed., 2010.
Larry Beason and Mark Lester, *A Commonsense Guide to Grammar and Usage*, 5th ed., 2009.
Chris Juzwiak, *Stepping Stones: A Guided Approach to Writing Sentences and Paragraphs*, 2009.
Laurie G. Kirszner and Stephen R. Mandell, *Focus on Writing*, 2008.
———, *Foundations First: Sentences and Paragraphs*, 3rd ed., 2008.
———, *Writing First: Practice in Context*, 4th ed., 2009.
Kate Mangelsdorf and Evelyn Posey, *Choices: A Basic Writing Guide with Readings*, 4th ed., 2008.
Barbara D. Sussman, Maria C. Villar-Smith, and Carolyn Lengel, *From Practice to Mastery*, 2005.

Developmental Writing Media

Diana Hacker and Wanda Van Goor, *Bedford Basics: A Workbook for Writers*, 3rd ed., 1998.
Make-a-Paragraph Kit <bedfordstmartins.com>, 2007.
Richard Nordquist, *Passages: A Writer's Guide*, 3rd ed., 1995.
Elliott L. Smith, *Contemporary Vocabulary*, 4th ed., 1995.
Writing Class, online course space <http://yourwritingclass.com>

Developmental Reading Texts

Robert DiYanni, *Making It Work: College Reading in Context*, 2003.
———, *Putting It Together: Basic College Reading in Context*, 2002.

Handbooks

Diana Hacker, *The Bedford Handbook*, 8th ed., 2010.
————, *A Pocket Style Manual with 2009 MLA Update*, 5th ed., 2009/ 2008.
————, *Rules for Writers with 2009 MLA Update*, 6th ed., 2009/2008.
————, *A Writer's Reference with 2009 MLA Update*, 6th ed., 2009/2007.
Andrea A. Lunsford, *EasyWriter: A Pocket Reference*, 4th ed., 2010.
————, *The Everyday Writer with 2009 MLA Update*, 4th ed., 2009.
————, *The St. Martin's Handbook with 2009 MLA Update*, 6th ed., 2009/ 2008.

Readers

Jane E. Aaron, *The Compact Reader: Short Essays by Method and Theme*, 8th ed., 2008.
Robert Atwan, *America Now: Short Readings from Recent Periodicals*, 8th ed., 2009.
Paul Eschholz and Alfred Rosa, *Models for Writers: Short Essays for Composition*, 10th ed., 2010.
Joan T. Mims and Elizabeth M. Nollen, *Mirror on America: Short Essays and Images from Popular Culture*, 4th ed., 2009.

Instructors' Resources

Susan Naomi Bernstein, *Teaching Developmental Writing: Background Readings*, 3rd ed., 2007.
Ellen Cushman, Eugene R. Kintgen, Barry M. Kroll, and Mike Rose, *Literacy: A Critical Sourcebook*, 2001.
Lisa Ede and Andrea A. Lunsford, *Selected Essays of Robert J. Connors*, 2003.
Katherine Gottschalk and Keith Hjortshoj, *The Elements of Teaching Writing: A Resource for Instructors in All Disciplines*, 2004.
Beth Finch Hedengren, *A TA's Guide to Teaching Writing in All Disciplines*, 2004.
Russ Hodges, Michelle S. Simpson, and Norm A. Stahl, *Teaching Study Strategies in Developmental Education*, 2011
Nedra Reynolds, Patricia Bizzell, and Bruce Herzberg, *The Bedford Bibliography for Teachers of Writing*, 6th ed., 2004.
Nedra Reynolds, Rich Rice, *Portfolio Keeping*, 2nd ed., 2006
————, *Portfolio Teaching: A Guide for Instructors*, 2nd ed., 2006.

Leigh Ryan, Lisa Zimmerelli, *The Bedford Guide for Writing Tutors*, 5th ed., 2010.

Edward M. White, *Assigning, Responding, Evaluating: A Writing Teacher's Guide*, 4th ed., 2007.

Index of Authors Cited

Numbers refer to entries within the bibliography.